Praise for *How NASA Builds Teams*

"Ever wondered how you and your team stack up against the very best at NASA? Through this book, you can dare to find out. But more important, if you (like me) didn't like the answer to this question, what would you do about it? I have felt the power of Charlie's technology. It offers not only candid feedback, but also the tools to make real and measurable improvement. That it's presented using colorful examples and an easy reading style makes it all the more compelling."

—Tim Barnett
Founder, Caledonia Wealth Management, Ltd.

"Charlie Pellerin and the 4-D approach to teambuilding are indeed revolutionary and effective. Charlie is well experienced in NASA's way of operating as well as the industrial element that supports NASA. His workshops were instrumental in raising the leadership level of my NASA teams to exceptionally high levels. Charlie's thought provoking ideas are clear and easy to implement. For those interested in raising their team's performance, his 4-D System is a must."

—Michael Rudolphi
Former Director of Engineering,
NASA Marshall Space Flight Center

"I strongly endorse this book that has become such an integral part of my life. The material provides a course of action for dealing with some of the complex problems that we have to face on a daily basis— it is priceless. I am a witness and a firm believer in the 4-D concept."

—John Morton
Vice President, Arctic Slope Regional Corporation

"Charlie Pellerin is a NASA legend. As Director of NASA's Astrophysics Division, he initiated one of the agency's most complex missions—the repair of the faulty optics with which the Hubble Space Telescope had been launched into space. The phenomenal success of that repair has made Hubble the most productive astronomical telescope ever constructed. *How NASA Builds Teams*, is full of practical advice based on this and a wealth of other examples. Anyone setting out on a project requiring the teamwork of a talented group of professionals will find Pellerin's eloquent book an indispensable guide."

—Martin Harwit
Former Director, National Air and Space Museum,
Washington, DC

"During my 45-year career, I found it crucial to have a high performing team in order to be successful in the unforgiving business of space. I was frequently astounded at the effectiveness of Charlie's process for building better teams. This book will be invaluable to anyone who is faced with the not-uncommon challenge of trying to get dissimilar people to work well together."

—Bill Townsend
Vice President and General Manager,
Ball Aerospace, 2004–2008

"The 4-D assessment methodology, honed through 15 years of team-building with NASA project, engineering, and management teams, has the potential to improve team performance in almost any enterprise. This book emphasizes the importance of understanding cultural norms and social behaviors which are often overlooked in technical projects, and yet can play a critical role in their success."

—Dr. Anthony J. Calio
Former VP & GM, Raytheon Corporation

"Charlie does a masterful job in *How NASA Builds Teams* bringing his vast experience in NASA to troubled projects with developed 4-D tools for building teams. He aids people in identifying their innate personality types, thus bridging gaps in communication. His stories are engaging and relevant to today's issues in multidicipline, technical organizations. He lays out the tools for teams to shift their mindsets toward a successful completion of their goals. NASA is fortunate to have this resource and the guidelines laid out in *How NASA Builds Teams*."

—Helen Hall
Science Operations Manager, Stratospheric
Observatory for Infrared Astronomy (SOFIA),
University Space Research Association

HOW
NASA
BUILDS
TEAMS

HOW NASA BUILDS TEAMS

Mission Critical Soft Skills
for Scientists, Engineers, and Project Teams

CHARLES J. PELLERIN

WILEY

John Wiley & Sons, Inc.

Published by John Wiley & Sons, Inc., Hoboken, New Jersey.
Published simultaneously in Canada.

Disclaimer: The National Aeronautics and Space Administration (NASA) has neither endorsed, sponsored, nor authorized this publication. The views expressed herein are solely those of the Author and do not necessarily represent the views of NASA.

For general information on our other products and services or for technical support, please contact our Customer Care Department within the United States at (800) 762-2974, outside the United States at (317) 572-3993 or fax (317) 572-4002.

Wiley also publishes its books in a variety of electronic formats. Some content that appears in print may not be available in electronic books. For more information about Wiley products, visit our web site at www.wiley.com.

ISBN: 978-0470-45648-4

Printed in the United States of America

10 9 8 7 6 5 4 3 2

*I dedicate this book to brave astronauts Tom Akers,
Jeff Hoffman, Story Musgrave, and Kathy Thornton
who risked their lives to fix the Hubble mirror flaw.
Without their magnificent achievement,
I could not have written this book.*

CONTENTS

PART III

4-D DIAGNOSTICS: HOW TO COLOR CODE YOUR TEAM'S CONTEXT   57

PART IV

SHIFTING THE CONTEXT   117

ACKNOWLEDGMENTS

Skip Borst, my business partner from the start, provides encouragement and essential contributions every day. He left a good job at GE and joined this quest in 1995 when we had no business income. Ed Hoffman of NASA provides the unwavering support and encouragement that makes all this possible. Ed has been our "patron" as surely as the Medici family was for the Renaissance. JoMarie Dancik funded the workshop that birthed our company, now called "4-D Systems." Doris Michaels, of DSM Agency, has been a perfect agent, with more than enough expertise and enthusiasm to overcome my limitations as a writer. Richard Narramore, my editor from Wiley, has been an ideal advisor shaping this book into an important contribution. I cannot say Doris and Richard are the only people who could bring *How NASA Builds Teams* to the market. However, I can say nobody else could have made this process so enjoyable.

The Vision—Moving Your Team's Performance into the Top 20 Percent

You now have access to what I believe is the most effective teambuilding system in existence. No, it is not this book, *How NASA Builds Teams*. It is this book combined with (free) assets available at www.4-DSystems.com. I know this because we have developed nearly 200 NASA project, engineering, and management teams over the past five years.

I urge you and your teammates to begin improving your team's performance by reading, and perhaps discussing, *How NASA Builds Teams*. Equally important, go to www.4-DSystems.com and initiate your 15-minute online *Team Development Assessment* to benchmark your team's current performance relative to high-performing teams. After you and your teammates digest your *Team Development Report*, conduct analogous *Individual Development Assessments* to see how each of you contributes to your team's behavioral norms. If you then decide that you want to work in a productive and rewarding environment, repeat these assessments every three to six months. Our experience with NASA teams suggests that your team will reach, and sustain, the performance of the top quintile (top 20 percent) of the teams (300) in our database. Even if you start in the bottom quintile, you can improve performance by one quintile per assessment cycle.

Your team will increasingly attract and retain top talent. You will efficiently solve technical problems, meeting your milestones in an atmosphere of mutual respect. Team members will have a sense of belonging and willingly contribute to team-level creativity and problem solving. Moreover, for many of you, your spouse will say something like, "I do not know what you are doing, but you are surely a better person to live with and a better parent." What is the cost of all this to you? All you need is commitment to high team performance, this book, regular use of online assessments, and of other assets at www.4-DSystems.com.

How This All Began

Twenty years ago, John Mather, NASA's Nobel Laureate in physics, said to me, "Charlie, I'm convinced that half of the cost of a project is socially determined." I began thinking deeply about the role of social forces in project performance because I had so much respect for John, as a scientist and human being. At the time, I was NASA's director of astrophysics overseeing a budget for contracts of about $750 million per year and one for support services, like Space Shuttle launches, for my projects in the billions. As you will read, I learned the cost of ignoring social contexts the hard way—launching Hubble Space Telescope in 1990 with a flawed mirror.

In the horrible aftermath of the discovery of the flawed mirror, I used many of the methods in *How NASA Builds Teams* to mount a space repair mission for Hubble. For this, NASA awarded me a second Outstanding Leadership Medal (only 50 people in NASA's history had such recognition, including astronauts). The NASA administrator then promoted me into the "front office" and charged me with developing NASA's post–Cold War strategy. NASA then awarded me the Distinguished Service Medal, which is bestowed when the "contribution is so extraordinary that other forms of recognition would be inadequate."

Despite this extraordinary job and recognition, my life changed when the Hubble Failure Review Board named the cause of the flawed mirror a "leadership failure." I left my top-management position at NASA and joined the University of Colorado's business school as a professor of leadership. This began 15 years of experimentation with *human physics*. I used my background in physics and success in leading technical teams to develop the teambuilding processes described in this book.

Dr. Ed Hoffman, director of the NASA "APPEL" (Academy for Program/Project and Engineering Leadership) followed our progress closely. NASA formed APPEL after the Challenger disaster to prevent future space mishaps. In 2001, Ed tasked us to apply our "4-D System" to NASA's most important project teams to improve their performance and prevent future space disasters. As of this writing, more than 500 NASA project and engineering teams and more than 2,700 scientists, engineers, and managers have voluntarily used these "4-D" processes. Here is a quick preview of some results.

NASA's Bottom-Quintile Teams Improve

Human error causes technical disasters of all kinds. *How NASA Builds Teams* describes both the behavioral norms that foster such errors and the behavioral norms that prevent them. The behaviors of teams that measure in the bottom quintile (bottom 20 percent) are spawning grounds for disasters like Challenger's explosion or Hubble's flawed mirror. Figure I.1 below shows NASA teams that began with behaviors in the bottom quintile. Each of the rectangular blocks represents a quintile (20 percent) of the 300 team's first assessment scores. The grey diamond is the average beginning score of the 41 bottom-quintile NASA teams who elected to do reassessments. Note that it is off-center because 19 teams that began here did not have a second assessment. Management disbanded many of these troubled teams before they could reassess.

The teams in the figure used the processes described in this book to improve. You can see that by the second assessment they have moved (on average) to near the middle of the below-average (< average) quintile. After their third assessment, their performance is above the lower boundary of the average quintile. The forth assessment has moved these teams above the lower boundary of the above-average (> average) quintile. The results for teams starting in the other four quintiles are equally remarkable, as you will see in Chapter 5, "NASA's 4-D Teambuilding Results."

**FIGURE I.1   NASA Bottom-Quintile Teams' Progress
with Successive Assessments**

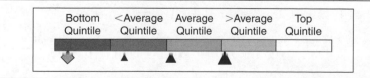

Moreover, teams at the grey diamond on the left are only about 50 percent productive. Teams at the triangle on the right-hand side of the diagram are about 80 percent productive. (The benchmarking scale is nonlinear.)

Teambuilding for Technical Teams

Unfortunately, many technical people do not see teambuilding as essential to their success. Moreover, they frequently associate team-building with "touchy-feely," a notion they despise. For example, a client recently asked us to help with a troubled relationship between NASA scientists and engineers. We sent physicist Dr. Frank Martin to facilitate discussions using the tools in this book. He began with, "I need to tell you that I am not a trainer or facilitator . . ." Before he could continue, the touchy-feely-phobic room exploded with spontaneous applause. My point is that while there are many excellent teambuilding trainers and facilitators, they have special challenges in dealing with scientists and engineers.

How NASA Builds Teams speaks to technical audiences because technical thinking developed the processes it describes. This book is not teambuilding for dummies. It describes teambuilding for smart, logical people. However, you do not need a PhD to understand it. Einstein's "Everything should be made as simple as possible, but not more so" guided every step in the 15-year development of *How NASA Builds Teams*. With my PhD in astrophysics, simplicity is as naturally appealing to me as it is for all physicists.

One simplifying method comes from my undergraduate physics classes, when we used to joke with each other, "The right coordinate system can turn an impossible problem into two really hard ones." We use the 4-D System to analyze team and individual performance into four simpler components that you and your team can develop.

Here is a chapter-by-chapter overview of the book.

Part I: Understanding and Analyzing Context

1. Chapter 1 describes my personal experience of the dire consequences of failing to manage team social contexts: Hubble Space Telescope's flawed mirror.

2. Chapter 2 explores the profound power of context to drive behavior.

3. Chapter 3 validates our central analyzing tool, the 4-D System, with research and project data.

Part II: Using 4-D Assessments and Representative Results from NASA

1. Chapter 4 explains how to use this book as a team development system in conjunction with online assessments. I describe our most effective long-term team context management tools—our 15-minute online assessments and reassessments.

   Knowing that reassessments are coming motivates people to pay attention to their behaviors. The fact that our 4-D team members reassess me every four to six months is my most powerful motivation for keeping my behaviors in the top quintile. Your team can realize excellent results by combining periodic 4-D reassessments with the information in *How NASA Builds Teams*.

2. Chapter 5 provides an overview of NASA's broad teambuilding results showing what is possible for your team.

Part III: 4-D Diagnostics: How to Color Code Your Team's Context

Each of these three chapters contains a simple and powerful diagnostic. Our web site, www.4-DSystems.com, provides all the resources you need (without cost) to perform these three diagnostics using animated PowerPoint slides. Each diagnostic generates color-coded data products displaying team performance parameters. Download the slides, do the exercises, and post your data products in your conference rooms.

1. In Chapter 6, you chart the *innate* (present at birth) personality foundation of your teammates. Action here mitigates the risk of failure to perform.

2. In Chapter 7, you chart your team/organization's culture's field (like a magnetic field) direction. Managing your field's direction mitigates, for example, the risk of losing tough competitions (without ever knowing why you lost).

3. In Chapter 8, you identify the color of your project's mind-set (paradigm) and examine its coherency across stakeholders. Incoherency results in your customer firing you.

Part IV: Shifting the Context

1. Chapter 9 integrates the context shifting processes of the entire 4-D System into a tool called the Context Shifting Worksheet (CSW). The CSW launches you into the wonderful world of context management. Einstein inspired my development of the tool with this famous quote: "You cannot solve a problem with the level of thinking that created it." I say, "You cannot solve a problem in the context that created it."

The remainder of *How NASA Builds Teams* prepares you to use the CSW to manage ad-hoc contexts. The CSW is our most powerful situational context-shifting tool. Figure I.2 maps each chapter of the book onto the CSW.

FIGURE I.2 The Context Shifting Worksheet

Context Shifting Worksheet ("CSW")

1: SET THE STAGE:
- The Situation: _____
- The desired Outcome: _____
- My/our *story-lines* in play: **Chapter 10: Red Story-Lines Limit Team Performance**
- Their *story-lines* in play: **Ditto**
- My/our feelings about this Situation: **Chapter 11: Manage Your Emotions to Manage Your Team's Energy**

2: CULTIVATING DIMENSION–Being Grateful
☑ What can I/we appreciate about the people/situation?
Chapter 12: People Need to Feel Appreciated by You
☑ What do they want that I can want for them also?
Chapter 13: Mine the Gold in Your Shared Interests

4: VISIONING DIMENSION–Being Creative
☑ Any truths that need to be stated to move from optimism to hope?
Chapter 16: Creating the Future You Want (Both Visioning Behaviors)
☑ Outcomes we are 100% committed to?
See Above:

3: INCLUDING DIMENSION–Being Authentic
☑ Who do we need to include in working this?
Chapter 14: People Need to Feel Included by You
☑ Agreements I/we are committed to keeping? Broken agreements that need processing?
Chapter 15: Building Trustworthy Contexts

5: DIRECTING DIMENSION–Response-able
☑ Any drama states we need to avoid/exit?
Chapter 17: Your Team Can't Afford Drama
☑ Any individual/team-level RAA issues we need to address?
Chapter 18: Don't Put Good People in Bad Places

Specific actions/Requests I will take/make: **Also, Chapter 17.**

©4-D® Systems, 2009

Using the CSW is as simple as sequentially filling it out. This usually takes about an hour. You can get help from a 4-D certified coach or consultant at www.4-DSystems.com.

A Broader Perspective on Teambuilding

Most of the emphasis in the book is about improving performance within teams by changing the internal context. These processes also potently enhance team performance across institutions by changing the context of the relationship. We consider this activity teambuilding as well. Indeed, much of our most important work has been in enhancing teamwork between NASA projects and their contractors. I close the introduction with the following example from a commercial aerospace team.

Jack Moves His Profit from 67 Percent to 96 Percent

Frustration filled Jack as he looked out his office window. I have tried everything, he thought. Nothing except simply saying "Yes, sir" seems to appease my customer, Harry. However, I cannot do that. I wonder if the 4-D people can help.

Jack called me and gloomed, "My most important customer relationship is broken. Can you help me?" I answered, "This is right down the fairway for us. Let's get going." Jack replied, "I don't see how we can fix this relationship without my customer's participation." I answered, "You will understand once you use the 4-D System to change the context. Context is everything, shaping the customer's perceptions of what you say and what you do."

Jack replied, "I still don't understand." I said, "Let's try a technical metaphor. Imagine that you and your customer are both electrons. What happens?" He answered, "There is strong repulsion." "Right, now what happens if you become a neutron?" Jack answered, "The repulsion goes away. I understand—changing me changes the relationship." I answered, "The metaphor is not exact, but that's the idea."

We began our team development process as we always do, with an eight behavior *Team Development Assessment*. It is simple, fast, and revealing. The data revealed that his team's internal working context was okay.

We conducted a three-day workshop six weeks later. As usual, we provided *Individual Development Assessments* to all workshop participants to prepare for the event. We call the basic workshop process "AMBR": changing *Attention*, *Mindsets* and then *Behaviors* to change your *Results*. We spent the final workshop hours using the Context Shifting Worksheet (CSW) to prepare the entire team for interactions with their counterparts the following Monday.

The team had a major customer meeting the Monday following the workshop. Jack called me after the customer meeting, "I did a lot of soul searching over the weekend. I knew the mindsets that I needed to hold. However, could I be authentic? Could I keep my attention on the new mindsets? Frankly, I was not sure. However, when the meeting started, I found this was much easier than I had thought. The workshop and CSW process had actually shifted my mind. The mood in our meeting shifted, too. Our communications were clear, crisp, and open for perhaps the first time."

Jack then e-mailed the following to his boss with a copy to me: "Just to let you know, the meetings this week with Harry et al., went extremely well. Taking the learning from last week's 4-D offsite, and changing our attitude to one of 'thanks for what you've done, you can count on us' worked. We told our customer, 'If we express concern it's because we want to deliver on our commitments, not because we are trying to resist you.' The shift paid off. We had lots of good discussions on tasks, priorities, budgets, areas for focusing effort, etc. . . ." WOW!

Then about a month later Harry wrote to us, "The Performance Evaluation Board met and recommended an award fee for the last period of 96 percent of the available profit pool. This is a stunning turnaround from 67 percent last period. Our 4-D Systems activity is getting a lot of the credit. Even grouchy Bob said, 'Don't quote me on this, but that darned 4-D thing really worked.'"

An Application Summary for this Introduction

You have everything you need to improve the performance of your team. Use the tools described in *How NASA Builds Teams* with these assets on www.4-DSystems.com:

- Free (simplified) *Team Development Assessments* to benchmark your team's behavioral norms (and, hence social context) against high-performing teams;
- Free (simplified) *Individual Development Assessments* to benchmark your behaviors against highly effective leaders;
- Free animated PowerPoint slides for the three additional context diagnostics (innate personalities, culture field, and project paradigm);
- Free introductory briefings in PowerPoint that overview the 4-D System laying the groundwork for initiating a *Team Development Assessment*;
- Free PDF color "leader badges;"
- Free animated PowerPoint slides for our most powerful, experiential workshop segment, "Expressing Authentic Appreciation";
- Free 8.5 × 11 copies of the Context Shifting Worksheet for processing ad-hoc situations;
- Sample assessment reports in color; and
- Access to 4-D Network Member certified coaches, consultants, workshop presenters, and more sophisticated assessments (for fees).

All these options may seem daunting. You will know what to do as you read along. Start your teambuilding, as we do, with a *Team Development Assessment*. First, take data.

Finally, I should note that many do this development work as individuals with good results. Success is easier, however, if you develop yourself along with your team.

HOW
NASA
BUILDS
TEAMS

PART I

UNDERSTANDING AND ANALYZING CONTEXT

The next three chapters explore the primary driver of team performance, the context.

- Chapter 1 describes my experience of launching Hubble Space Telescope with a flawed mirror and learning that a flawed social context was the root cause.

- Chapter 2 validates the power of context with research and empirical data.

- Chapter 3 introduces the 4-D System, our primary organizing tool for analyzing context into simpler, manageable components.

Think You Can Ignore Context? Hubble's Flawed Mirror Might Wake You Up

Hubble Space Telescope—April 23, 1990

It was late in the evening at the Kennedy Space Center. A TV camera technician was taping a large cable onto my leg. I had just returned from a final look at the Hubble Space Telescope in the Space Shuttle's cargo bay. It was an awesome sight—the gleaming telescope surrounded by the shiny cargo bay doors of the Space Shuttle. After 15 years, $1.7 billion, and the hard work of thousands of people, the time had come. Tomorrow morning, Hubble would launch into space.

I was the featured guest on "Nightline," the nationally televised news show with Ted Koppel. Not being much of a TV watcher, I had never seen the program. The local producer had me stare into glaring lights for more than 30 minutes before the show. I suppose that tired, unnerved (and scared) people made good late-night television guests. They promised that questions would be polite and easy. They were neither. After all the usual stuff about whether NASA money would be better spent on social programs, I was asked the big one, "Will it work?" I expressed strong confidence in our team, talked about the thoroughness of the test program. and said squarely, "It will!"

Actually, I had my doubts, but that was the only rational response. If difficult times were to come, I needed my Hubble team to see me as confident and fully behind them. They deserved this kind of support. Moreover, there was no alternative except to launch the telescope and see what happened. Either it worked or it did not. It was time.

After a few hours sleep, I returned to Kennedy for the final countdown in the launch control blockhouse. Gazing at the Space Shuttle five miles away, I listened to the launch director's voice in my headset. As NASA's director for astrophysics, my role was to provide quick recommendations if major problems occurred during the launch and deployment. After a textbook launch, the telescope deployed, powered up, and communicated with the ground just as we had planned. Everything was, in NASA parlance, "nominal."

However, Would the Telescope Work?

In order to achieve the benefits of being above the atmosphere, the telescope's body must point to a given location in the sky with a stability of .007 arc-seconds. This is equivalent to aiming a laser in Washington, DC and hitting a target in New York City the size of a quarter.

In the late 1980s, the White House decided to open space science cooperation with the Soviet Union. I cochaired the first working group with my Soviet counterparts. When I put up the chart describing the Hubble pointing specification, there was a murmur on the Soviet side. I asked my counterpart what was happening. He said, "It's nothing, just a translation problem." I said, "Please explain." He answered, "Your chart says 0.007 arc-seconds as the pointing stability. We are sure that you really mean seven arc-seconds." It took some time to convince them that we were actually building a system to achieve seven *thousandths* of an arc-second. These highly accomplished space experimenters could not fathom achieving that kind of performance.

What would happen if Hubble's performance was a technically respectable 0.07 arc-seconds? Hubble would be a total loss because the resulting images would scarcely be better that what the best ground-based telescopes would do. We would have squandered $1.7 billion of taxpayer money! There was no way to be certain we would reach this level of performance before our public debut.

Hubble Looks Good, So Off to Japan

With the world watching, we opened the aperture door and let starlight in. I heaved a sigh of relief as a fuzzy spot of light appeared on our monitors. "It works," we shouted. My engineers told me not to worry about fuzziness. We had intentionally launched the telescope slightly out of focus.

With Hubble looking good, I decided to visit my colleagues in Japan. I met with my boss, Len Fisk, just before my departure.

He asked if he should do anything for me while I was gone. I said, "Len, we've just succeeded with what is perhaps the grandest science project in history. Surely, there will be medals in the Rose Garden for all of us." I continued, "Your job is to get George Bush and not Dan Quayle to pin my medal on." He laughed and said that he would do what he could. Looking back, this was pure hubris. I would soon learn that the gods do not like hubris.

My Japanese counterparts knew that I liked to meet in Ryokans (Japanese Inns) where no foreigner had ever been. I had no contact with my headquarters office for a week. As I flew from Narita to St. Louis, I wondered how things had been going in my absence.

"Conscious Expectation of the Unexpected"—An Early Hubble Motto

I entered the St. Louis airport lounge to await my flight back to Washington. I was in good spirits, although feeling like I was on "sake time." I called my secretary to check in. She immediately said, "Have you talked to Dr. Fisk lately?" "No," I answered. She said, "I'll put you right through." I wondered what was so important. Ah, this must be about the medals in the Rose Garden. A surprising few seconds later, I heard Len Fisk saying, "Charlie, where are you?" After I told him that I would be back in DC that evening, he said, "I'm glad to hear that."

He continued, "Charlie, what do you know about spherical aberration?" As I wondered why he might be asking, I replied, "I know that it is a common mistake by amateurs. They sometimes make mirrors with a 'down-edge.' A telescope with a spherically aberrated mirror is useless."

Len then said, "What would you say if I told we launched Hubble with a spherically aberrated mirror?" I answered, "I would say that you are annoyed that I had a good time in Japan, while you had to tend to the Washington bureaucracy. This is a really bad joke."

He persisted, but I remained unconvinced. He finally said, "Okay, put the phone down, but don't hang up. Just find the front page of any major newspaper and bring it back." I returned with the *St. Louis Post-Dispatch* in hand. He then asked me to read the headline to him over the phone. It said, "NATIONAL DISASTER, HUBBLE LAUNCHED WITH FLAWED MIRROR." "Now what do you say," Len asked? I replied, "You guys are really something.

How did you plant a fake newspaper in here?" Later, I named this moment "denial is not a river in Egypt."

Back in Washington, reality sank in. A trivial and obvious error overshadowed the accomplishments of thousands of dedicated people! The following months were to be a kind of living hell for my Hubble team.

The Congressional testimony was brutal. At that time, news of the Savings and Loan scandal was just emerging. Congressional representatives preferred to appear on TV beating up on NASA executives than explaining that crisis. During one session, a member asked me, "Dr. Pellerin, you've told us that the greatest advance of Hubble over prior missions is in the ultraviolet?" "Yes, that's true," I said. I thought he was getting ready to ask me how I knew the mirror was not contaminated. One molecular thickness of oil would have made the mirror black in the ultraviolet. We worried constantly about contamination of the optics.

Instead, the representative looked at me accusingly and said, "Mr. Chairman, the witness is lying. Everyone knows that ultraviolet radiation is invisible." My first thought was to explain that we had detectors that converted ultraviolet radiation into electrical signals. Then I had a better idea. I said, "Sir, x-rays are also invisible to the human eye, yet you can see x-ray images on film." The chairman said, "You are out of order. Let the record end with the member's remarks!"

After the first week of testimony, a friend invited me to a concert at Wolf Trap Park, an outdoor park just outside Washington. The world seemed an okay place after a bottle of wine, a nice dinner, and a beautiful sky. Judy Collins walked over to the microphone and began to sing. No sound came out. She went to another microphone and said, "Aren't you glad that the idiots that built Hubble Space Telescope didn't build this sound system. At least, we have a backup." I felt terrible. Our failure had permeated popular culture.

While I avoided late night television, there was more to come. The movie *Naked Gun 2½* had a bar scene with several paintings in the background. The camera panned over the paintings: the Hindenburg on fire; the Titanic sinking; and the artist's concept of the Hubble Space Telescope on orbit that I had on the wall in my office.

NASA people are proud, and the humiliation of all this began to take a toll. Doug Broome, my brilliant manager of the Hubble flight systems, took the failure very personally. He suddenly contracted cancer and was dead a few months later. He was a great person; he also had the unusual honor of two NASA Outstanding Leadership Medals. He received one for his work on Apollo and the second for Hubble (before we knew of the mirror flaw).

One of the lessons Len learned from the *Challenger* disaster was to create our own Failure Review Board before someone picked one for us. Len quickly charged the highly respected General Lew Allen, director of NASA's Jet Propulsion Laboratory, to assemble experts and find out what had happened. Len named me as the NASA liaison to the board because I was at that optimal intersection of political visibility and technical understanding of the telescope's systems. Besides, I joined the division in 1982 and the contractor manufactured the mirror in 1977, so I had nothing to do with the flaw. Or did I?

The Failure Review Board Found the Problem

The board met time after time with little progress. Then a member calculated that an unimaginably huge error (centimeters) in adjusting the null corrector used to figure the mirror could cause the flaw. The device was still in bonded storage at the contractor's plant. They measured it and verified the calculation. Great, I thought, I can go back full time to my regular job, leading my division.

However, Lew continued his investigation. He found that there were hints of the mirror flaw in numerous tests. He wondered why smart technical people had not rigorously pursued these hints. He found that the schedule and budget pressures caused them to move relentlessly forward.

Next, he wondered why the NASA scientists and engineers had not addressed these inconsistencies. The board then made a disturbing discovery. The contractor never forwarded these troubling results to NASA. Now, the board's question was, "Why not?"

A Leadership Failure Caused the Flaw

The board finally told Congress that a leadership failure caused the flawed mirror in our $1.7 billion telescope. Lew reported that NASA's management of its contractor had been so hostile that they would not report technical problems if they could rationalize them. They were simply tired of the beatings. This finding astounded me.

During this period, no one in NASA, Congress, or the Administration wanted to talk about Hubble, or a mission to repair it. They just wanted it to go away. Fate placed me in the unique position of being the only person with sufficient motivation and power to mount a Hubble servicing mission.

The studies I had funded when the flaw surfaced were paying off. The error in spacing the null corrector meant we had a near-perfect mirror with the wrong prescription. Scientists from around the world rapidly designed ways to correct the aberrated beam. It only took a few hours with my budget analyst to delay or cancel Division activities yielding the $60 million we needed immediately. I asked the best and brightest at NASA to join me in fixing Hubble, and they all said yes. The mission to repair Hubble in space was underway.

Most of you will never experience a failure as publicly traumatic as the one I just described. The point is that unnoticed social shortfalls destroyed this high-visibility, tightly managed program. This is unfortunately a common problem for teams of technical people. Social shortfalls are the root cause of disasters ranging from Challenger's explosion and Columbia's disintegration to airplane crashes.

Here, however, is very good news. You can use *How NASA Builds Teams* to reduce or remove social context risk from your team. It does not matter whether your team is large or small or whether you are developing new software or drugs, these processes are effective—if you are committed to this work.

An Application Summary for Hubble Trouble

I hope you found my Hubble story interesting. I first related it around a campfire on a White Rim bicycling trip at Moab, Utah. I did not think much of it until a few nights later when my fellow cyclists asked me to tell it again. We all tell an abbreviated version at the start of each workshop. I believe it helps set the stage for everything that follows.

We now explore the dominant driver of team performance, the *context*.

CHAPTER 2

Managing Social Context Manages Technical Performance

The Power of Context

Have you every thought about the power of the social context to influence your team's performance? Technical workers often focus so intently on their task that they fail to notice, much less manage, their team's social context. As I stated previously, combining the intellectual foundation of *How NASA Builds Teams* with 4-D online assets makes your team's social context not just visible, but directly manageable.

In fact, management of contexts to influence our behaviors is common in ordinary life. For example, cafeterias display expensive high-protein items last and in difficult-to-reach locations to modify our behavior. For most of us, ploys like these are transparent. We look the entire offering over before putting anything on our plate.

Wilson and Kelling (1982) made a more sophisticated argument about the power of context to influence behavior. They argued that crime increases in tenements when no one repairs broken windows. Unrepaired windows create a context in which people assume there is no authority and crime increases. This led to a massive and successful experiment to lower crime in the New York City subway by enhancing the context. Strategies included cleaning the subway cars and arresting fare jumpers.

Politicians understand the power of context to alter behaviors. Campaigns are all about framing so we will vote the way they want us to.

The core idea in this book is that social contexts drive our behaviors, and hence drive a technical team's ability to perform or not. We now examine a context/behavior management tool, the "AMBR" process.

The "AMBR" Process—How the Brain Works

The "AMBR" process:

- Is what you pay _attention_ to.
- Combines with your _mindsets_.
- Influences your _behaviors_.
- Produces _results_ you realize.

I use the AMBR process repeatedly in _How NASA Builds Teams_ as a simplifying device. We now look at attention and how it influences our perceptions.

An Example of Attention's Influence on Perception

If you are interested in this phenomenon, I recommend you buy this DVD by D. J. Simons, _Surprising Studies of Visual Awareness_, of students playing basketball in a hallway. Show it to your colleagues and instruct them to count the number of times the students wearing white shirts pass the ball (focusing their attention). Tell them that this count is important so please get it right (further focusing attention and creating a competitive mindset).

When the video finishes, your participants will enthusiastically offer their count, usually 17 passes. Inquire whether they noticed anything unusual in the video. Most will say "nothing." Tell them that a person in a black gorilla suit walked into the scene, drummed his chest, and exited five seconds later. Many will not believe you. Show the same video again. Now, _everyone_ will see the gorilla. Some people will be so incredulous that they insist that you showed a different video the second time.

This illustrates a challenge for technical team members. Like our participants watching the video, technically trained people can focus their attention so intently on their work ("counting the passes") that they never see the "social gorillas." Thus, they have no capacity to manage the unseen social context. Just as everybody saw the gorilla in the film after we brought their attention to its presence, you will notice dangerous social gorillas after reading this book.

Was our failure to pay attention to Hubble's social gorillas the cause of the telescope's flaw? Was it possible that a gorilla that we never saw condemned us? Apparently, this was the case. Are unmanaged social contexts the most frequent cause of underperformance and failures? We now look at dramatic space mishaps.

Unseen and Unmanaged Social Contexts

Investigations into space mishaps provide deep understanding of the risks of ignored social contexts. When accidents kill astronauts and teachers, the inquiry is very thorough. NASA's Stephen Johnson (2008) wrote, "Frequently, we find that the failure effects and proximate cause are technical, but the root causes and contributing factors are social or psychological. . . . Although the statistics have not been studied fully, my sense, from experience in the field and discussions with other experienced engineers, is that 80 to 95 percent of failures are ultimately due to human error or miscommunication."

Here are a few sample findings from NASA failures.

- Diane Vaughan wrote the following about the Challenger explosion (*The Challenger Launch Decision*, 1996). "I present evidence that refutes the traditional explanation that blames managerial wrongdoing . . . an incremental descent into poor judgment. . . . The revisionist history and sociological explanation presented here is more frightening than the historically accepted interpretation, for the <u>invisible</u> and <u>unacknowledged</u> tend to remain undiagnosed and elude remedy." (Note the underlined words. We will return to them shortly.)

- Recall that a context management failure was the root cause of the Hubble mirror failure. Hubble attracted first-rate technical minds. We, the management, created a social context that put these good people in bad places. NASA managers at headquarters and Marshall Space Flight Center, the managing field center for Hubble, including me, relentlessly criticized and pressured our contractors. The contractors, operating from a place of relative powerlessness, engaged in guerilla tactics by withholding troubling information.

- A crew of technicians destroyed a nearly finished $200 million satellite, "NOAA-N-prime." They turned a cradle holding the satellite on its side not realizing that another crew had removed the fastening bolts beneath. They ignored a procedure that required verifying that the bolts were in place. The Lockheed-Martin failure review board asked me to join them in the failure investigation because they thought an institutional culture of sloppiness might be the root cause. I passed because I did not have the available time. They asked me to meet with them after they drafted their report. They said, "We wanted to talk to you because we are reporting that the culture was root cause."

I later read the government review team's report (2004): "The operations team's lack of discipline in following procedures evolved from <u>complacent attitudes</u> toward routine spacecraft handling, <u>poor communication</u> and coordination." (Underlined for emphasis.)

- The context that typically causes plane crashes is rushing tired pilots in poor weather leading to communications breakdowns (Gladwell, 2008). A typical accident involves seven consecutive human errors. These errors are rarely errors of knowledge or flying skill. They are errors of teamwork and communication.

- During the period 1988 to 1998, Korean Air was crashing at a rate 17 times greater than the industry average. Investigators found that the root cause was transference of the Korean social context into the cockpit. The captain's social status was so high that the junior officers in the cockpit could only communicate obliquely and deferentially. The captain was flying the plane by himself. Modern jets require a team of two or three for safe flight. No amount of individual training in flying skills would help. Today, Korean Air's record is as good as the overall industry's because experts from Aleton (a subsidiary of Boeing) changed the social context to a team of equals.

We now examine a simple analysis of the power of context.

Harry's Diner

Stolovitch and Keeps (2004) argue persuasively that lack of performance in the workplace is far more frequently caused by environmental than individual factors. (I prefer the word "context" instead of "environment.") The authors report that researchers associate team performance with environment (context) about 80 percent of the time and with individuals' abilities about 20 percent of the time. Moreover, they claim that training is often necessary, but rarely sufficient to produce long-term performance. Based on these findings, I suggest that once individuals' have the essential skills, training them in anything but context management is a waste of money. Therefore, the effective action is to analyze, then manage the context. *Training Ain't Performance* illustrates this with a story about Harry's Diner.

Excellent toast was central to Harry's competitive position. Yet, the waiters had difficulty producing consistent, high-quality toast. When fast-food chains appeared nearby, Harry hired *Training Ain't Performance* consultants to create a training program to train waiters to produce toast more consistently. They analyzed the situation using these six items:

1. Did the waiters have good performance incentives? Yes, tips were important to the waiters.

2. Did the waiters have the skills and knowledge to make toast? Yes, they all knew how.

3. Did they have the physical/emotional capacity to handle making toast? Yes, waiting is a tough job, and Harry was a very demanding boss.

4. Were they motivated? Yes, the waiters, like most of us, wanted to do the job right.

5. Did the waiters have clear, doable RAAs? (This is our terminology for Roles, Accountability, and Authority. In short, does everybody know their expectations of team members and do they have the resources to succeed?) No, they had many competing tasks including taking orders, cleaning the bathrooms, keeping the salt and pepper shakers full, and delivering the food and toast.

6. Did the waiters have sufficient resources, for example, toasters? No, there was only one toaster and the preparation area was inadequate.

Items 5 and 6, context shortfalls, were the root causes of poor performance, not poorly trained people.

The way to improve toast quality was to address Items 5 and 6:

1) Hire busboys and cleaners to allow the waiters to focus on customer service and toast, and

2) Expand the number of toast preparation stations.

Training the waiters would have been a waste of money.

How about your team—any parallels with Harry's Diner? Next, we explore the relationships between context and behavior.

Context Examples from Everyday Life

Here is a very simple example of how context drives behavior. Would not we all behave differently in these contexts?

- We first realize we are dating the person you want to marry;
- Have dinner with his or her minister's family;
- Attend our bachelor/bachelorette stag party; or
- Have been married 25 years.

If you behaved in ways that were incongruent with each context, would others sanction you? Of course they would. Could you measure a person's behaviors and identify which of these four contexts they were experiencing? Yes, you certainly could.

This is exactly what we do with teams and individuals. Individual and 4-D team assessments benchmark the behaviors of your team and its members against those of high-performing teams and individuals. Thus, you measure the context your team is creating and experiencing.

Context Trumps Character

Malcolm Gladwell (2000) argues that our character has more to do with environment/context than who we are innately. He says, ". . . the reason that most of us seem to have a consistent character is that most of us are really good at controlling our environment." This claim is astounding. Does it bother you? The notion that character is primarily a function of social context troubled me greatly when I first read it. I believed, for example, that my consistently good and ethical behaviors were from my upbringing. Similarly, I believed that my children's good character flowed primarily from their upbringing. I had pretty well bought into "inside-out" advocates.

I am now convinced that Gladwell is correct in his claim that context trumps character. My test of a theory is that of any physicist: Does it explain observed reality? Gladwell's premise explains many behaviors, for example, Enron, the White House, the U.S. Congress, and the movie "War of the Roses."

Is my own character actually more about what's inside or the environment outside? I like to believe that I am inherently a good and ethical person independent of context. However, I (jokingly) say, "If I had a gun in my hand at the peak of my divorce stress, I would be in prison now."

A Brief Detour into the Concept of *Story-Lines*

Occasionally the notion that context trumps character troubles a workshop participant. *Blue* Visioning intellectuals (more about this characterization is coming later) like to aggressively challenge anything they disagree with. They strongly assert some version of "That's not the truth."

Rather than engage in argument about the matter, I take this opportunity to introduce them to another notion we explore deeply later in this book, and respond, "Of course, it is not *the* truth because it is arguable. It is, however, true for me because it is consistent with my experience and observations. Thus, it is what we call a *story-line*." The vast majority of our statements to each other are *story-lines*, as is much of this book.

The key question is whether running a particular *story-line* is useful. I continue, "Since I am not claiming this is truth, I have no need to engage you in a dispute about it. All that really matters to me is the effect that any *story-line* has on behaviors. Running this *story-line* motivates me to take care about the environments I create around me. This *story-line*, perhaps more than anything else, creates a context that supports a productive business environment and a delightfully happy marriage."

Take the opportunity to reflect on the statement and decide if this *story-line* might be true for you. If it is, you will begin to manage the contexts you create around you. In any case, Gladwell's argument is very good news for our work. It is more productive to enhance team context than replace team leaders, a far more common management practice when difficulties arise.

An Attribution Error

Many of the very best project managers in NASA and the aerospace industry—the people running the $1 billion-plus projects—tell me that they expect top management to fire them from their jobs within the next two years or less. The reason for this is that overruns are inevitable in major programs. When project managers present the overruns, management tends to blame them for what they are reporting.

We are moving NASA away from firing their project managers, and instead conducting context inquiries like that for Harry's Diner using the diagnostics in this book. Building and sustaining high-performance team contexts is the only way to ensure ultimate success. I hope that *How NASA Builds Teams* will motivate you to take similar action.

An Application Summary for Context

By now, I hope that I have persuaded you that social (that is, relating to the interactions of people) context drives behavior and perception. Flawed social contexts cause space disasters, airplanes to crash, and dysfunctional families. You can manage your contribution to your work and family contexts by managing your behaviors.

Refer back to the end of the introduction for the extensive context management assets at www.4-DSystems.com.

We next look at how we can simplify contexts so you can measure and manage them.

CHAPTER 3

The 4-D System

A Simple Tool to Analyze Team and Individual Performance

I began my time at the University of Colorado ravenously reading the business book genre. Most contained anecdotes about well-known industry personalities such as Jack Welch, Bill Gates, and Andy Grove. Then, there are lists of the four things, six things, seven things, and so on that great leaders do to succeed. I even have a card deck of the 67 things great leaders do.

Although these books are entertaining to read, my technical mind wants fundamental principles, as physics has. Logical constructs are simple and easy for me to apply. A reporter asked Einstein if he knew what the speed of sound was. He answered, "No, why would I clutter my mind with something I can find in a book?" I agree. I prefer thinking to memorization. Further, the various lists built on peoples' taste are difficult to apply because they are inconsistent. Which list is the right one?

Moreover, people demand leadership during chaos and confusion. When I was in chaotic situations and was asked to lead, I could never remember the six (or whatever) things great leaders did and then do them.

Think back to Harry's Diner. How did the consultants choose the six questions they used? I have no idea, and this is not okay. We need a systematic process to understand the underpinnings of high-performance teams and effective leaders.

Coordinate Systems Simplify

In my office at CU, I pondered how I might use my physics background to simplify teams and leaders. As I related in the introduction, my undergraduate physics colleagues and I used to say to each other "The right coordinate system can turn an impossible problem into two really hard ones." Therefore, I began to play with coordinate systems. I spent an entire summer trying to find coordinate systems that logically organized the lists in popular business books. I had no success. Then, I saw a Dilbert cartoon that said, "Every consultant makes a living with a two-by-two matrix." Bingo! I focused all future energy on X–Y coordinate systems.

The great physicist Richard Feynman invented simple diagrams for illustrating scattering (for example, electron-positron annihilation) in quantum field theory. The 4-D coordinate system does something similar—it simplifies the key components of high-performance teams and effective leaders. Carl Jung's theory of personality development published in 1905 inspired my approach. Some terms I use may look familiar since they are similar to the terms used in the well-known Myers-Briggs Type Indicator, a psychological test developed during World War II that categorizes personalities into 16 types. There is, however, no connection between my work and theirs except that both spring from interpreting Jung's papers.

Organizing Teams and Leaders

A reporter asked Richard Feynman to define physics. He answered, "Physics is what physicists do late at night." Actually, physicists work to understand nature with mathematical models called "laws." These generalizations simplify nature and allow us to make reliable predictions about the future. These laws are only as valid as the results of experiments that test them. Physicists begin by guessing the law. Therefore, I will guess what kind of X–Y system might simplify our understanding of teams and leaders. It is reasonable to begin with the most fundamental actions of leaders—using information to make important decisions.

Therefore, I guess that "deciding" would work for our X-axis in Figure 3.1. Now, what are the ways we decide? Fortunately, there are two, so we can label the two ends of our X-axis. Some of us prefer to use emotions for decisions, and some prefer logic.

FIGURE 3.1   The 4-D Organizing System

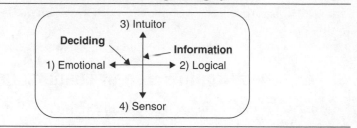

A workshop participant once said, "I cannot believe anyone would make an important decision using emotions." So, playing a little, I asked, "So how did you pick your wife, with a questionnaire?" He responded, "As a matter of fact, I did." Ah, engineers.

As you will see, great leaders like Gandhi and Eisenhower are emotional deciders. They use their connection to their emotions to give passion to their values and to care authentically about other people. They inspire people to follow them and create intense loyalty.

Great scientists and engineers are usually logical deciders. Later we will look at Howard Hughes and the coach in the movie Hoosiers as examples of logical deciders. In addition, Einstein was likely a logical decider. It turns out that people's *innate* deciding preference is about 50 percent emotional and 50 percent logical.

What shall we choose for our Y-axis? We need to gather information in order to make decisions. Therefore, we choose "information" for the vertical or Y-axis. Fortunately, there are two basic kinds of information: what we sense empirically and what we intuit. Seventy percent of us innately prefer to rely on our senses for observation. There are five classic senses: seeing, hearing, tasting, smelling, and touching. About 30 percent of us innately prefer intuited information.

How we sense information is straightforward. Mostly, this is about seeing and hearing. How imagination/intuition works is not so clear. Gary Klein (1999) studied firefighters and intensive care providers. He concludes intuition is "the way we translate our experience into action." Intuition seems to be a very rapid, unconscious integration of our experiences.

Daniel Gilbert (2005) notes that, "The human animal is the only animal that thinks about the future." On average, we spend 12 percent of our time thinking about what could be that has not yet happened. Gilbert also asserts that we use imagined futures (based on imperfect memories) to make decisions. These decisions include choosing to go to war or to marry a particular person. Thus, I also use the term "imagined information" for decision making when it makes sense to do so.

4-D Organization of Leadership

Now, proceeding as a physicist, I inquire into the implications of my guesses. I try using our 4-D organizing system to analyze (separate into simpler parts) a leader's attributes into four core elements that I call "dimensions." (I chose the term dimensions because the usual term "quadrant" sounds so lifeless.) The result is Figure 3.2. You can see the four dimensions named and color coded.

How did I derive these names? The Emotional and Intuiting (Cultivating) Dimension suggests deep feelings and what could be, wanting a better world, and caring deeply about other people. Thus, actions in this dimension address people's needs for feeling appreciated and their needs for others to address the interests they share with us. I color the Cultivating Dimension *Green*.

The Emotional and Sensing (Including) Dimension suggests emotional experiences in the present, the deepest of which come from relationships with other people—harmony, inclusion, and relationships. Thus, actions here address people's deep needs for inclusion in relationships. People also bring integrity to relationships by rigorously keeping all their agreements. We color the Including Dimension

FIGURE 3.2   The 4-D System Analyzes Leadership

Cultivating *Green* Feeling and intuiting, they *Intuited* appreciate others, share interests for a better world, caring for others.	Visioning *Blue* Thinking and intuiting, they constantly create needing to be best, smartest.
Emotional ←————→ *Logical*	
Feeling and sensing, they include others, bring integrity to relationships and *Sensed* build teams.	Thinking and sensing, they take organized action and direct others toward results.
Yellow Including	*Orange* Directing

Yellow because we exhausted the purest colors on the other three (Although the connation is needlessly negative, you could color this dimension *Yellow* because it is so conflict averse.)

During workshops, I demonstrate this dimension by approaching a participant and shaking his or her hand. We both smile broadly. I then point out that this act of including involves an emotional and sensed experience.

In a high-performing team context, members go out of their way to include other's opinions, addressing the deep need we all have to feel heard.

The Logical and Intuiting (Visioning) Dimension suggests thinking about possible futures. Leaders' actions here include visioning the impossible while acknowledging difficult realities, so they can create what they want. We color the Visioning Dimension *Blue*, as in blue-sky thinking.

Finally, the Logical and Sensing (Directing) Dimension suggests taking action—organizing and directing others. Leaders' actions are management—planning, organizing, directing, and controlling. We color the Directing Dimension *Orange*, symbolic of how the sun organizes our days and seasons.

Notice that the first word characterizing each dimension was from the deciding axis, emotional or logical. The *deciding* characteristic is more important than whether the information comes from intuition or sensing. We find the difference so striking that we often refer to "emotional-side" or "logical-side" leaders. With practice, you can usually make this diagnosis of a person a few minutes after meeting them. The difference is palpable.

In our work with teams, we find people prefer to name the four personality types by their colors. These same color codes ultimately organize everything, including personalities, cultures, and project paradigms as in Figure 3.3.

FIGURE 3.3 The 4-D System's Color Codes

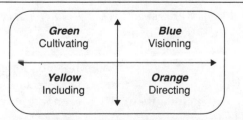

Green	*Blue*
Cultivating	Visioning
Yellow	*Orange*
Including	Directing

Let's Pause and Review

Before we continue to explore teams and leaders with the 4-D System, let us pause and see where we are. These are my assertions so far:

- Hubble's "leadership failure" was, in fact, a social context management failure.
- Social context is a more powerful determinant of team performance than individuals' skills or abilities.
- Collective behaviors, or team behavioral norms, define team social contexts.
- The 4-D (coordinate) System simplifies leadership into four dimensions you must address to be an effective leader.

We now compare the predictions of the 4-D System with data to confirm that we can use it like a law of physics—as a broad social context analysis tool.

Validation—The 4-D System with Research

My work with the 4-D System began when I was at the University of Colorado in 1994. Kouzes and Posner's book, *The Leadership Challenge* (2008), was popular. I opened my copy looking for empirical data on leadership effectiveness and found a summary combining:

1) A 1,500-person survey by the American Management Association;
2) A follow-up study of 80 senior executives in the federal government; and
3) Finally, a study of 2,600 top-level managers who completed a checklist of superior leadership characteristics.

When individuals were asked, *"What do you most admire in leaders?"* these studies reported the following:

- First, 80 percent of the respondents said honesty. We demonstrate our honesty by how truthfully we relate with others and how openly we include them. This is a good match to the *Yellow*, Including leadership;

- Second, 67 percent said competence (productive, efficient). This is a good match to the *Orange*, Directing leadership;
- Third, 62 percent said forward looking. This is a perfect match to the *Blue*, Visioning leadership; and
- Fourth, 58 percent said inspirational. Caring about other people and appreciating them is a most effective way to inspire people, a good match to the *Green*, Cultivating leadership.

The correlation of the 4-D System with research data was encouraging. I began applying the system to teams in workshops with great success. Then I came across a paper too interesting to ignore.

Gallup's High-Performance Teams' Leading Indicators

Curt Coffman and Jim Harter (1999) reported the following: "Organizations traditionally have relied heavily upon financial measures or 'hard' numbers to evaluate their performance. . . . Proactive leaders have come to rely more and more upon the 'soft' numbers to best predict direction and action planning."

We continue our validation with research from this extensive Gallup study. Incredibly, they analyzed a million employee responses from 450 companies in 12 industries using 12 key indicators that consistently correlated with productivity, profitability, employee retention, and customer loyalty. Every team, anywhere, wants these things.

The 4-D analysis in Figure 3.4 of Gallup's "Leading Indicators" reveals the following. (Note: I have shortened and rewritten Gallup's terms as Gallup claims these results are proprietary as they match their questionnaire.)

1. First, Gallup's results address all four dimensions. Addressing all four dimensions is, I believe, necessary and sufficient for high team performance and leadership effectiveness.
2. Next, while there are many ways one could word the specific behaviors in each dimension, each dimension's core themes are present in our Gallup example. For example, in the Including Dimension we see inclusion as a best friend, and inclusion of other's opinions.

FIGURE 3.4   4-D Analysis of Gallup's "Key Indicators"

Green Cultivating Dimension	***Blue*** Visioning Dimension
Often praised; Commitment to quality; Supervisor cares; Opportunities to grow.	Do what I do best every day; The vision/mission/ purpose makes my job important.
Spoken with me about my progress; Been my best friend; Encouraged my development; My opinions matter.	I know what is expected; I have the resources to do my job right.
Yellow Including Dimension	***Orange*** Directing Dimension

Once more, the 4-D System made a prediction that empirical data supported. It is standing as a law. You may be wondering whether Gallup's work context just described occurs in the real world. Let us see.

The Compton Gamma Ray Observatory (CGRO)

Some years ago, I spoke at a colloquium celebrating the 10th anniversary of the Compton Gamma Ray Observatory (CGRO) launch. The experience was incredible—person after person described CGRO as a wonderful working experience. This 44,000-pound system of gamma ray telescopes mapped nature's scarcest photons—emanating from black holes and quasars.

Their CGRO experience was not just about feeling good. The team completed the complex observatory on budget and schedule. (Although, to be frank, the launch delays after the Challenger explosion gave us much needed extra time and money.) The CGRO team won the National Space Club Award. The contractor (TRW) won NASA Goddard Space Flight Center's "Contractor of the Year" award. Moreover, the CGRO performed as intended on orbit.

Terry Watson, TRW's operations manager, presented a slide at the colloquium describing his experience of the CGRO context. I took his slide exactly as he presented it and used the 4-D System to analyze his observations as seen in Figure 3.5. Notice the moving statement spanning both of the emotional-side dimensions: "An atmosphere of honesty, mutual trust & understanding prevailed."

FIGURE 3.5 4-D Analysis of CGRO's Context (Environment)

Cultivating	Visioning
Lots of little things like patches, stickers, mugs, etc. to say "Thanks" to the team members.	Team members were given freedom to depart from "business as usual." Talented and creative people were drawn to the program.
An atmosphere of honesty, mutual trust & understanding prevailed.	A "Can Do" attitude was inspired.
Program focused on teamwork and people in addition to ...	
Frequent face-to-face meetings ... time for "after work" social events.	Program management stayed "in touch" with the realities of the program ... was kept up to date and well informed.
Including	Directing

Notice the now recurrent pattern:

1. First, all four dimensions are addressed, and
2. The specific words are consistent with the sense of each dimension.

This analysis of CGRO's high-performance context bolsters our core assumption that addressing the 4-D System's four dimensions is both necessary and sufficient for high performance. The powerful testimonials at the colloquium suggested that the CGRO team leaders and members behaved four dimensionally.

Moreover, the 4-D System's broad applicability allows us to organize all our processes, assessments, workshops, coaching, and context shifting into a coherent whole. We now examine the inadequacy of developmental processes that lack this coherency.

A Limitation of Conventional Methods

Unfortunately, many teambuilding and leader development interventions lack this coherency between measurements and development processes. Years ago, a prominent training company conducted my "360" assessment. (The term "360" refers to "up" for bosses' opinions, "sideways" for peers, and "down" for subordinates.) Ten people filled out questionnaires with about 50 questions. They then mailed the forms back to the company for analysis. The company prepared my report and mailed it to me about a month later. I opened it and saw the first finding: "You can be difficult to work with." I immediately discussed this with my boss. He said, "It's true. And, you are my best manager." I then asked, "What should I do about this?" He said, "I have no idea, why don't you call the training company and ask them." I did and they said that they did not know. What a waste of everyone's time! (My next performance evaluation included the words, "Charlie would do better if he could learn to suffer fools gladly.")

In contrast, the 4-D System aligns team and individual measurements with development processes. Every 4-D process measures or develops the same four dimensions and associated eight behaviors.

An Application Summary for 4-D Analysis

This chapter has been about replacing the lists of "what matters" for team and leadership excellence with a system akin to a law of physics. Here is an interesting aspect of how physics works. We can never *prove* a law of physics. All we can do is apply laws and fail to disprove them in enough applications that we have faith in their predictive powers. The 4-D System analyzes leaders and teams with sufficient repeatability that I have faith in continuing its use. We next examine the online 4-D assessment system.

PART II

USING 4-D ASSESSMENTS AND REPRESENTATIVE RESULTS FROM NASA

T he two upcoming chapters are about the team and individual assessments and the NASA results they largely caused. Chapter 4 describes our online *Team Development Assessments* and the analogous *Individual Development Assessments*. Together, they are our most effective long-term team context management tools. (The Context Shifting Worksheet, or CSW, is our most effective ad-hoc, situational tool.) The description includes why we believe they are so effective, the logic that they are built on, and sample data products.

Chapter 5 summarizes NASA participation and results. I show the progress for NASA teams starting in each of five quintiles. Next, I present evidence for systemic performance improvement across NASA. Teams' first assessment scores systematically rise each year. These are teams with no prior encounter with 4-D Systems. I estimate a return on investment for these NASA teams comparing annual costs with 4-D with first assessment score improvements.

CHAPTER 4

The 4-D Assessment Process

You can conduct the 4-D assessments described in this chapter at no charge at www.4-DSystems.com. The web site also has other resources that are free or purchasable. We name them *Team Development Assessments* and *Individual Development Assessments* to emphasize their role as aids to development, not evaluations. I do not even like the word "assessment" in their title, but that is what they are—measurements against standards. I liken them to doctors' physical examinations. Whether you are feeling good or not, it is useful to have a health check-up. Moreover, just as doctors assess your blood indicators by comparing them with norms of others, our assessments compare your scores with peer teams and individuals to assess your performance.

I organized this chapter as follows. I begin with my first realization of the power of 4-D assessments to modify behaviors. Next, I describe the assessment process. Finally, I show you samples of the free assessments' data products.

Potency of Team Assessments to Drive Behavioral Change

Some years ago, my financial investment firm reviewed our team-building company's (4-D Systems) business strategy. They were so impressed with our 4-D processes that they engaged us to address their ongoing problems, including employee retention. I began, as always, with *Team Development Assessments* for the two sides of the company. Both sides of the company had behavioral norms in the bottom quintile, the bottom 20 percent of the 300 teams in our database.

These low scores triggered an examination into the "Seven Deadly Sins" described in Chapter 18, "Don't Put Good People in Bad Places."

I suspected that the team leaders' behaviors were limiting their team's performance. We verified this with follow-up *Individual Development Assessments*. One team leader took this very seriously and worked with a 4-D coach to improve his behaviors. The other did not.

The *Team Development Assessment* data (you will see this graphic later in this chapter) indicated that the highest leverage improvement was in their roles, responsibility, and accountability. This small company was struggling to move from *Blue* entrepreneurial practices to *Orange* institutionalized systems.

As I read the team assessment reports, I noticed something interesting. Although the behavioral scores were low, the explanations indicated a deep intellectual grasp of the material. I then learned that the two teams had many years of coaching and annual workshops from another development company. It became apparent that intellectual knowledge is insufficient to create behavioral change. Consistent with our usual process, I reported the results to the team leaders, who in turn briefed their teams. As I suggested, they announced that they would reassess their team's behavioral norms, with the same *Team Development Assessment*, in about four months. I also conducted the personality diagnostics in Chapter 6, "Using the 4-D System to Color Your Personalities," to see "Who's on the bus?" (Collins, 2001). I wanted to defuse some of the personality conflicts, particularly with the very *Blue* founder. Naming these differences as innate personality might make them less annoying.

I reassessed the teams and leaders about five months later. The reassessment of the first team showed the team moved from the bottom quintile to near the top quintile. (Usually this kind of dramatic improvement requires several rounds of reassessment.) These team members confirmed that their behaviors, both with each other and with their clients, improved in concert with their new scores. Their leader also improved significantly.

The other team and its leader improved marginally. It is our consistent experience that 4-D processes are highly effective if, and only if, the team leader is committed to improvement.

How do these 4-D assessments improve performance? I believe there are several effects. Consider the expression, "Where attention goes, power flows." First, the assessments require so little participant time that you can repeat them quite often—bringing people's attention to their behaviors repeatedly. In addition, the repetition of the reason for measuring particular behaviors creates a small, but important, mindset shift. Together, the attention and mindset shifts support behavioral change. This is an important difference between our assessments and the more typical 60 to 70-question opinion assessments. NASA people have participated in nearly 50,000 4-D assessment events during the past five years, with dramatic, organization-wide results. I display the systemic change this participation produced in Chapter 5, "NASA's 4-D Teambuilding Results."

Second, the educational components of 4-D assessments support creation of a common vocabulary to discuss the team's social context and ways to improve it. Technical people are accustomed to tight, efficient communications. The technical world even has a common, international vocabulary. For example, I can travel anywhere in the world and talk about first derivative, enthalpy, or coefficient of expansion and be totally understood. This is not the case in the social world. For example, what exactly does "expressing authentic appreciation" conjure up for you? I suspect its exact meaning is different for each of us. NASA teams report that it is very beneficial to have this common social vocabulary. They are able to have conversations that were previously impossible.

Finally, *Team* and *Individual Development Assessments* benchmark people's behaviors against peers in our database—few of us want to be below average in anything important. For example, how many people do you know who consider themselves below-average drivers? The assessment data engage our natural competitiveness.

Launching and Managing Your Team Development Assessment

Your first step in developing your team is using 4-D *Team Development Assessments* to measure the current behavioral norms within your team. This provides a baseline for tracking all future progress. (If you are not the team's leader, I recommend you obtain your leader's support before proceeding, lest they misunderstand your intentions.) You can use the introductory PowerPoint briefing from www.4-DSystems. com to explain 4-D team assessments to your teammates. Alternately, here are five talking points. (I describe the assessment data products in detail later, including examples.)

1. With only eight behavioral measurements, you can complete an assessment in an average of 15 minutes each.

2. You see our team's behavioral norms (performance) bench-marked against about 300 peer teams. This is very interesting information.

3. Actionable color graphics indicate high-leverage behaviors for improvement.

4. *How NASA Builds Teams* provides comprehensive guidance for improving each behavior.

5. Surely, anybody doing something important would want to benchmark his or her team.

We recommend inviting from 12 to 25 people to participate in your team assessment. This generally corresponds to the number of people reporting directly to a single supervisor (team leader). Inviting too few participants risks individual's anonymity. In fact, we only report assessments results with five or more respondents. Alternatively, inviting too many people blurs the results. It is a little like mixing so many colors that your result is grey.

Once you have your colleagues' agreement to proceed, all you need is their e-mail addresses. You, the sponsor, then enter these e-mail addresses and your desired start date on your assessment management dashboard. You start the assessment by forwarding a predrafted e-mail from you to your participants. This also authenticates the e-mails that will immediately follow from our system.

The system sends out automatic reminders to people who have not completed the assessment. You, as sponsor, receive participation reports showing who has completed and who has not. However, in no case will we associate responses with who provided them; all responses are confidential. The system sets a default close date of two weeks. If participation reaches a sufficient level before the close date, you can manually close the assessment. The system electronically sends the assessment report to you including guidance about debriefing your team. If the participation is inadequate, you can extend the close date. Note: We frequently perform assessments for both project and functional (for example, engineering) teams in the same institution.

An Assessment Participant's Experience

The next several paragraphs describe an assessor's experience and the logic behind the assessment design. After I complete this explanation, I show you sample assessment data products.

As discussed previously, each person you chose as an assessor will see an e-mail from you verifying that you authorized the assessment and encouraging him or her to participate. Your e-mail also informs him or her that an e-mail from Assessments@4-DSystems. com soon follows. If they do not see that e-mail, they need to check their junk e-mail folder or spam filters. They then click on a link in our e-mail to open the assessment. An information page explains the rationale for the assessment. Clicking on the "Next" button brings them to the first of eight behaviors, "Expressing Appreciation."

Next, Assessors See Explanations for the Behaviors

Here is the team assessment language for the first behavior, "Expresses Authentic Appreciation."

People name "feeling appreciated" as what they most want at work and in life. Expressing appreciation for others and their contributions meets this need and sustains an atmosphere of mutual respect. Appreciation is as simple as habitually noticing and then acknowledging the valuable contributions of others.

I (Charlie Pellerin) see the power of appreciation not just in teams we work with, but also in our own team. For example, our 4-D Systems team members habitually and authentically appreciate the contributions of others every day and in every way. Our people work harder and have more fun than any team I know.

Next, They Assess Behaviors Against Standards

Why do we need to measure behaviors against standards? We turn again to the deep analysis of NASA failure review boards. Diane Vaughan, author of *The Challenger Launch Decision* and member of the Columbia Accident Investigation Board, named "normalization of deviance" as a root cause of both the Challenger and Columbia accidents.

Normalization of deviance occurs when deviant behaviors become normal in the local context. For example, at the time of the

Challenger mishap, managers required much stronger technical arguments to delay a Shuttle launch than to proceed. Discrimination because of gender, race, or religion is another example of localized normalization of deviance. The 4-D assessments mitigate normalization of deviance by assessing behaviors against defined standards.

This is the assessment standard for "expresses authentic appreciation."

Teams meet the standard when members appreciate others:

- Habitually
- Authentically
- Promptly
- Proportionally
- Specifically

We call this "HAPPS" appreciation.

Finally, participants assess behaviors by clicking on a radio button, a graphical user interface that allows people to choose options. The name comes from older car radios used to select preset stations. When you push one button, other buttons pop out. You choose one of the following for your team's behavioral norms:

- Fully meet the above standard.
- Usually meet the above standard.
- Seldom meet the above standard.
- Never meet the above standard.

(Note: In-between choices are also available in the actual assessments.)

Participants continue through the eight behaviors with the same pattern on each assessment page:

1. Explanation of the behavior's importance;
2. The measurement standard; and
3. Assessment of the behavior by clicking on a radio button.

An Overview of the Eight Assessed Behaviors

Figure 4.1 shows the eight behaviors (two behaviors in each of the four Dimensions) that assessors measure during team or individual assessments. I numbered them in the sequence that they appear in the assessment. (There is a reason for this sequence that I discuss later in some detail. The 4-D pattern addresses the emotional side first, "lubricating" stuck situations.)

Here is more detail about each of the eight behaviors:

- We chose "1) Express Authentic Appreciation" and "3) Appropriately Include Others" because they address very fundamental human needs. I believe that we technical people tend to err in assuming that we are more independent and self-contained than we really are. Actually, we all require quality relationships with others to meet our needs for feeling appreciated and included. Abraham Maslow, for example, places our need to belong just above physiological and safety needs in his well-known hierarchy of needs.

- "2) Address Shared Interests" reduces cross-organizational conflict, a major source of team breakdown. I began playing with shared interests when I was in the Harvard Business School's Program for Management Development (an executive program). As with nearly everything, I tested the shared interests inquiry repeatedly in our workshops. I found that addressing shared interests

FIGURE 4.1   4-D Organizing the Eight Behaviors

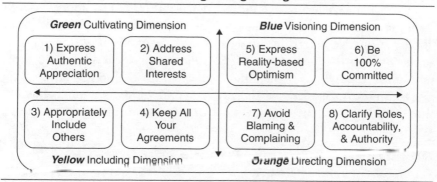

was especially useful across multiorganizational (for example, government, contractor, and sub-contractor) project teams.

- "4) Keep All Your Agreements" sustains trustworthiness. This is the simplest, and for some the most challenging, behavior. Once teams adopt this habit, everything is easier. Would you like to work with people who consistently do exactly what they said, when they said?

- "5) Reality-Based Optimism" provides a foundation for creativity. For years, I read books looking for ways to stimulate creativity—nothing was very effective. I then began experimenting with acknowledging unpleasant reality as a foundation for creativity, and it is only human to avoid unpleasant realities. However, if you can face unpleasant truths optimistically and proactively, creativity surges.

- "6) 100 Percent Commitment" alters perception and reveals solutions. This is the most magical behavior in the set as it alters our most complex and imperfect process: how we perceive reality.

- "7) Resist Blaming & Complaining" directs your energy to effective action. As you will read later, there are four "drama-states"—victim, rescuer, rationalizer, and blamer—corresponding to the four dimensions. This melodrama directs your energy away from solutions and destroys productivity.

- "8) Clarify RAAs" (Roles, Accountability, and Authority) defines what others can expect of you. If RAAs are not clear for every team member, you will have chaos.

Chapters 12 through 18 in *How NASA Builds Teams* address developing each of the eight behaviors in detail. Note: Although we have good reasons for selecting these behaviors, *working in all four dimensions is more important than these specific behaviors*. Said another way, developing these eight behaviors is sufficient for high productivity. I do not claim they are necessary because there could be similar behaviors that would work to the extent they address the four dimensions.

Do Just Eight Behaviors Provide a Sufficiently Accurate Measurement?

There are many firms offering team and individual assessments. Those that I am aware of survey 60 to 70 opinions. Is it possible that measuring eight behaviors is more accurate than measuring 60 opinions? When we began, we measured 12 behaviors (three per dimension). Malcolm Gladwell (2005) convinced us to reduce this to eight to improve the accuracy and simplicity of our measurement. Here is the story he told.

When Brendan Reilly became chairman of the Department of Medicine at Cook County Hospital, he engaged physicists skilled in statistical analysis to improve the diagnosis process. Their analysis found that a four-parameter algorithm (EKG + Angina + Lung fluid + systolic < 100) provided the most accurate diagnosis.

The staff doctors resisted the simple, four-part algorithm. They wanted to ask additional questions like the following: "How long have you been experiencing chest pain and what is your cholesterol level?" Frustrated, the chairman forced a runoff between the two methods. The runoff showed the simple algorithm to be more precise than conventional, more expansive inquiries. The resisting physicians had wanted more data to feel more confident (an emotional need) about their diagnosis. Surprisingly, their desire for increased confidence diminished the accuracy of their decisions. *The extra information was more than useless—it was harmful!*

This story launched us into an inquiry of whether measuring fewer behaviors would improve accuracy. We concluded that carefully consolidating from three to two questions per dimension would improve assessment accuracy. The reduction would also reduce the assessment respondent's time by one-third. Our assessments, measuring only eight behaviors (plus two open-ended questions in full assessments), now require only 15 minutes on average to complete. I know of no other assessment, so rich in valuable information, which requires so little time from participants.

Assessment Reports—What They Look Like

We now look at a sample assessment report. You can view samples in color at www.4-DSystems.com. You will receive your *Team Assessment Report* in a PDF file set up for projection in slide format. I recommend you present your assessment results to your team with a projector. *Individual Assessment Reports* arrive in letter format PDF files. The assessed individuals read these and only share their results as they choose.

Assessment Product 1—Who Participated?

Assessment reports begin with pie charts showing the response level. We also display the e-mail addresses of those who completed the assessment and those who did not so you can see whose perceptions the report contains. People can also opt-out of the assessment with their reason displayed on the same page. (Note: We only produce reports when the number of participants is five or greater to protect respondents' anonymity.)

Calculating Assessment Scores

We make the assessments quantitative by assigning numerical values to the assessor's choices shown here. We assign zero percent to a "Never meets" choice and 100 percent to "Fully meets." We assign 25 percent to "Seldom meets" and 75 percent to "Usually meets."

We compute an average score for each assessment using all the assessment choices. For a typical team assessment, we are averaging about 24 participants *times* 8 behaviors per participant, or about 192 behavior measurements.

Assessment Product 2—Where You Benchmark

Assume, for example, that a team's average assessment score is 74 percent. Is this a good score? To answer that question we use benchmarking, comparing that score to other teams in the database.

Figure 4.2 shows the distribution of the first assessments of the recent 300 teams in our database at this time. (We made modest changes in assessment language a few years ago and reset the benchmarking database. Otherwise, there would be 500-plus teams in the benchmark.) The five equal-area zones are quintiles, each containing about 20 percent of the assessed teams.

FIGURE 4.2   Team Development Assessment Benchmarking Curve

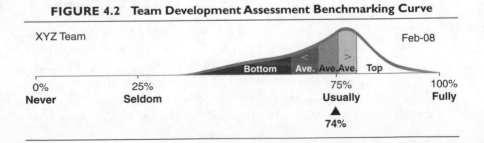

The percent scale along the bottom ties the team average to its quintile. You can see the black triangle at 74 percent showing this team near the top of the "average" quintile. Whether that performance is good enough is up to the team leader.

The benchmarking process also reduces the effect of errors in our intermediate scoring choices. If, for example, those choices should have been 33 percent and 66 percent, instead of 25 percent and 75 percent, the score would be slightly different. However, the benchmarking curve would shift as well so the effect on quintile ranking would be negligible.

The teams in our database are mostly aerospace project teams. Do they serve well as peers for other teams? We think so. We have cut these data by institution, project complexity, and government versus industry. We see no statistically significant differences with two exceptions. Project teams in the earliest phases tend to score somewhat higher. These teams have yet to encounter the daunting difficulties of project implementation. Proposal teams tend to score a bit lower. Stress is usually high in these enormously ambiguous contexts.

Assessment Product 3—Distribution of Perceptions

The next assessment product, Figure 4.3, shows the distribution of individuals' perceptions.

The example shows a typical skewed "normal" distribution. Therefore, the term "average" has its usual meaning.

Bimodal distributions appear occasionally indicating an in-group and out-group. For example, we saw a bimodal distribution when we measured a NASA center director's leadership team. He quickly realized that the half of the team inside the glass doors

FIGURE 4.3   Distribution of Individuals' Perceptions

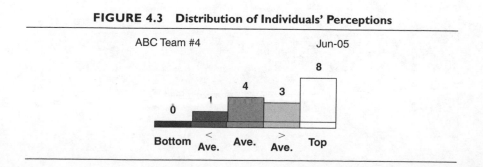

felt much better about being team members than the half outside the glass doors that separated his office. This average is a bit like having one foot in a bucket of cold water and the other in hot water and naming your average experience as warm.

Assessment Product 4—Relative Behaviors Display

Figure 4.4 shows the eight behaviors relative to each other. It is very useful for targeting the high-leverage behavioral improvements. The eight behaviors are sufficiently interrelated that improving the lowest behavior tends to lift the rest. For example, teams prone to blaming and complaining have difficulty in expressing appreciation or addressing shared interests. If the result in the display was from your team, you should make a concerted effort to improve "Resisting Blaming or Complaining" using the materials in Chapter 17.

Debriefing Your Team

It is important to present your assessment results to your team promptly. Encourage dialogue throughout the presentation. When issues arise, assign action items that include task, responsible

FIGURE 4.4   Relative Behaviors

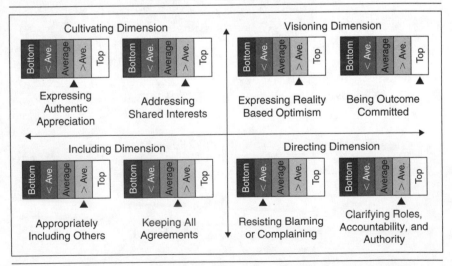

individual, and due date. An action item is not an action item without all three elements. Your assessment report package will contain additional suggestions about conducting your team's debriefing. Above all, secure members' agreement for a reassessment at an appropriate future date. Multi-year project teams reassess every four to six months. Four-month proposal teams reassess every three weeks.

What Progress Do Teams Experience?

Figure 4.5 shows the progress of a typical flight project team with a committed leader. The first assessment is on the bottom with more recent assessments as you move up the display. Each of the small bars is an individual's perception of the team's behavioral norms. Changing habitual behaviors is not easy for any of us, and this team took two

FIGURE 4.5   Representative Team Progress

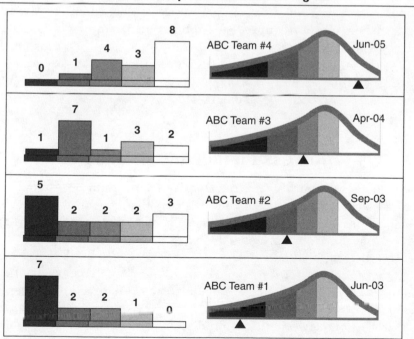

years to move from a bottom-quintile to a top-quintile performing team. Note the sustained progress in the face of constantly increasing stress of later project phases.

Individual Development Assessments

After you debrief the team report to your teammates, urge each member to initiate their *Individual Development Assessment*. These are essentially similar to the team assessment except that the inquiry is about each person's behaviors rather than the team's behavioral norms. Thus, any individual's improvement simultaneously improves the team context. The assessment software inserts the individual's name into the questions. As in the team assessments, individuals receive participation reports and can close or extend their assessment. Each team member sees their contribution to the team's behavioral norms and hence performance.

If all team members undertake individual assessments, and the team is 20 people or so, each person will be assessing someone else about 10 times. This at first might appear to be a burden. We estimate that a person requires an average of 15 minutes to complete an assessment the first time. We also estimate one can complete 10 assessments in about two hours. Repetition has great positive influence on adult learning. Participating in reassessments powerfully cements essential behavioral changes.

What Progress Do Individuals Experience?

Individuals with burning desire can advance much faster than teams. It is easier to change one person's behavior than an entire group. This person's progress (Figure 4.6) was a bit slower than most, perhaps because he started from such a deep *Red* benchmark.

Notice the first assessment in the lowest panel. All eight assessors saw John Smith's (a fictional name) behaviors in the bottom (left) quintile in November 2003. He made steady progress; most assessed his behaviors in the top quintile in June 2005. Note: John attended a 4-D workshop between his first and second assessments and engaged in intermittent 4-D coaching.

FIGURE 4.6 Representative Individual Progress

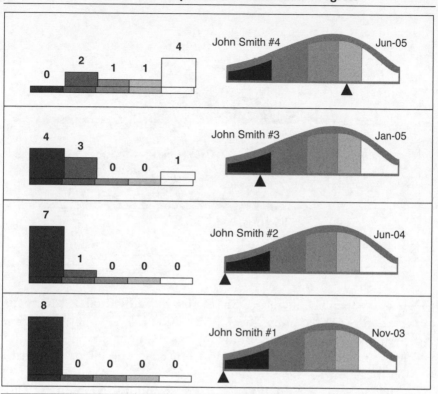

Differences in Team and Individual Benchmarking Scales

Figure 4.7 on page 44 displays the benchmarking scales for team assessments and individual assessments. The difference is striking. Note the vertical arrow at a score of "usually meet the standard" (75 percent). A team's assessment benchmarks usually meet at the boundary between "average" and "above average." In contrast, an individual's assessment benchmarks usually meet in the middle of the bottom quintile.

I have two explanations for this dramatic difference. First, group behavior tends toward the lowest individual's behavior. Therefore, for the sake of the team, low-scoring individuals should take action

FIGURE 4.7   Contrasting Team and Individual Benchmarking Scales

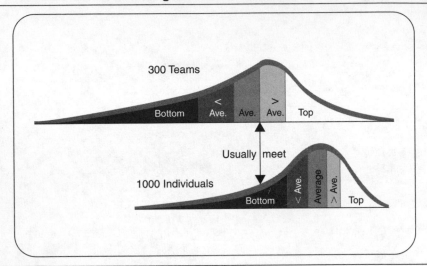

to enhance their behaviors with recurrent individual assessments and perhaps 4-D coaching. The 4-D coaching (also available at www.4-DSystems.com) enhances individual assessment scores about 1.5 percentile points per session. Most of our coaching clients have two sessions per month.

The second explanation is from Reinhold Niebuhr (2006): "As individuals, men believe that they ought to love and serve each other and establish justice between each other. As racial, economic and national groups they take for themselves, whatever their power can command." We just behave differently in groups than in one-on-one interactions. Would you prefer your anniversary dinner in a restaurant with tables for two or to dine between two groups of 20 people?

An Application Summary for Social Context

I believe I made the case for the power of social context with my story about Hubble's flawed mirror, other space missions, and even airplane crashes in Chapters 1 and 2. Chapter 3 validated the 4-D System, which identified four dimensions that you must address.

This chapter provided an overview of the 4-D online assessments available at www.4-DSystems.com. All you have to do is go to that web site and launch your *Team Development Assessment* (or, persuade your team leader to do so). After your team is debriefed, encourage the members to initiate their *Individual Development Assessments*, which can run while you finish reading *How NASA Builds Teams*.

If you are doing this work by yourself, go to www.4-DSystems .com and launch your *Individual Development Assessment* immediately. This will provide your starting point, from which you track future progress.

Next, we examine some results from these processes.

CHAPTER 5

NASA's 4-D
Teambuilding Results

The weather was miserable on what we now refer to as "that rainy day at Wallops." (Wallops Flight Facility is a small NASA facility on Virginia's Eastern Shore.) I was talking with Dr. Ed Hoffman, director of the NASA APPEL (Academy for Program/Project and Engineering Leadership). NASA formed APPEL after the Challenger disaster to prevent future space accidents. Ed asked me to undertake a pilot project—to see if I could get NASA's busy project managers to use the 4-D System's process of assessments, workshops, coaching, and reassessments.

Would NASA project managers trust me enough to undertake this work? At the time, the data were sparse, and I had left NASA eight years ago. It helped that I had a distinguished career at NASA. Most important, perhaps, I had a reputation for being competent, tough, and fair—people generally liked me.

With Ed's support, I began work. I met with NASA top management at two centers that had managed many of my programs. One was the Goddard Space Flight Center in Greenbelt, Maryland, and the other was the Jet Propulsion Laboratory in Pasadena, California. I described our 4-D processes and explained how they would enhance the performance of project teams. We insisted that management put no pressure on any project to participate. Further, while we would report project participation activity, they could only get assessment results directly from the teams. We began work with their highest-priority projects. Early enthusiasm for the program by both NASA management and the project teams exceeded our most optimistic expectations. Ed expanded the program to include the entire agency.

We engaged distinguished, retired NASA managers at each of NASA's eight field installations to manage our activities. We call these people center program managers (CPMs). They brief team leaders on our processes and schedule *Team Development Assessments* (TDAs). They also debrief TDA reports to team leaders. The team leaders, in turn, debrief the results to their team.

They Voted with Their Feet . . .

From early 2003 to mid-2008, more than 500 NASA teams and 2,000 individuals voluntarily participated in nearly 50,000 assessment events. These included NASA's most important project and engineering teams. These teams launch the Space Shuttle, operate the Space Station, will return humans to the moon, send missions to Mars, study our planet, and operate astronomical telescopes in space.

. . . Because They Realized Results

Figure 5.1 summarizes our NASA teambuilding results over the past five years. Each band displays the scoring of teams beginning in one of five quintiles. The gray diamond indicates the average initial score of teams in each of the five quintiles. Note that gray diamonds are off-center in the center of the quintile because not all of the teams in a given quintile chose reassessments (or were unable to do so because, for example, they disbanded or reorganized).

FIGURE 5.1   198 NASA Team Scores Organized by Initial Quintile

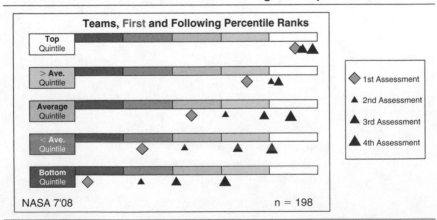

The most important improvement is in the bottom quintile. As I discussed in the introduction, bottom-quintile teams operate at very low efficiency with constant overruns and are the breeding grounds for mission failures. Notice the exceptionally large leap by bottom-quintile teams in the lower left of Figure 5.1. This is, I believe, largely due to our consulting work to address the performance-limiting "Seven Deadly Sins," which we'll discuss in detail in Chapter 18. I believe that these data demonstrate progress toward our goal of reducing or eliminating future Challenger, Hubble, or Columbia mishaps, while increasing team performance across the board.

The result is nearly as remarkable for the next-to-bottom quintile ("< Ave. Quintile"). Again, notice the monotonic improvement of average scores with reassessments.

The upper quintiles show relatively little improvement, as there is little room to grow. However, I consistently find that the upper-quintile teams seem to get the most benefit from workshops. They are already functioning four dimensionally and readily grasp the clarity and potency of this system of thinking. All these NASA teams used customized mixtures of team assessments, workshops, pre-workshop individual assessments, and post-workshop coaching. (Note: We completed the same analysis for 903 NASA team members. The data were similar except for a much larger leap from the grey diamond. Apparently, workshops have much more effect on individual's assessment scores than team scores.)

Systemic Change in First Team Assessments

Is it possible to take an entire organization or business systemically into higher performance? By this, I mean having a positive effect on teams that have never participated directly in a 4-D improvement process but have experienced the indirect effects of an enhanced working environment. I saw hints of this in one of our early flight projects, the Solar TErrestrial RElations Observatory (STEREO) project discussed later in this chapter. I was not, however sufficiently confident to make this claim as there were confounding variables, such as a midstream change in the project manager.

We recently noticed an interesting phenomenon in the team assessment data. The percent of teams scoring their first assessment in the top quintile was significantly higher in 2008 than 2003.

When the study included all NASA teams, over all years, Figure 5.2 revealed an unexpected result.

There was a strong trend of teams scoring higher in their first team assessment with each passing year!

Although the trend is evident (and verified to better than 99.9 percent certain with a Student t-test), I wanted additional evidence that our work, and not some other factor, was creating this effect. (The funny name comes from the fact that a William Gosset published the t-test under the pseudonym *Student*. He wanted to conceal the fact the test was useful in beer manufacturing and that he was working at a Guinness Brewery.) There were supporting anecdotes, such as an engineer in a Marshall Space Flight Center workshop who leapt to his feet saying, "I returned here after an absence of 18 months and noticed immediately that this was a better place to work. I now understand why. It is a result of the 4-D Systems work the engineering directorate did in my absence."

With this in mind, I saw an additional test for the systemic change hypothesis. We had done about twice as much work at Marshall per employee as NASA overall. We then graphed Marshall alone with the results in Figure 5.3. If Marshall had the same rate of improvement as the rest of NASA, something else was in play. The data, however, showed that the rate of improvement in Marshall's first team assessment grew at twice the rate of NASA!

Figure 5.4 plots the two trend lines on the same graph.

I believe that the effect is real. Our work with teams and individuals changed the behaviors of the overall workforce!

FIGURE 5.2   Average NASA Team First Assessment Scores by Year

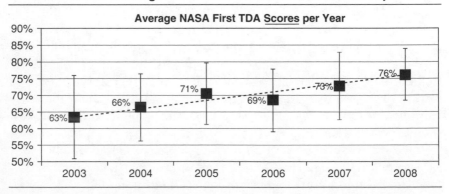

FIGURE 5.3 Average Marshall First Team Assessment Scores by Year

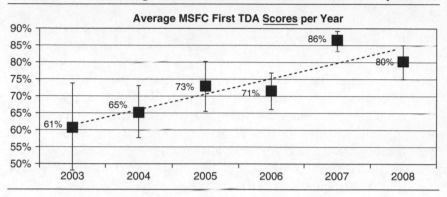

FIGURE 5.4 Marshall and All NASA Compared

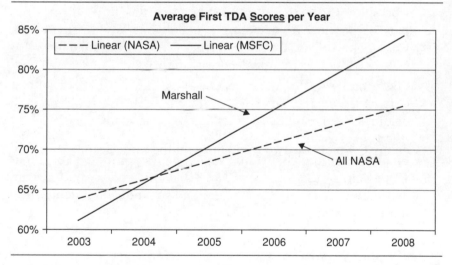

What Level of Engagement Creates Systemic Change?

What fraction of your workforce do you need to engage to see the systemic effects in the charts above? We estimate that about 2,000, or 10 percent, of NASA's employees engaged in 4-D development. About 400, or 20 percent, of Marshall's employees participated in our processes. Note: These estimates are a little high since contractors participated in many workshops and assessments as well.

What Did This Systemic Improvement Cost?

I am averaging costs over the same period as the systemic change in the three figures above. Here are the cost categories:

- The Center Program Managers (CPMs) accounted for about 35 percent of the total cost. They worked with the teams arranging team assessments, debriefing the assessments, and providing limited consulting services. You can do this work as a team leader, with support from human resources, or get our assistance at our web site. (When we refer to "our" or "us," we are actually referring to members of the International 4-D Network.)
- Three-day workshops accounted for about 30 percent of the total cost. Until now, *How NASA Builds Teams* did not exist. You can use the book to substitute for the workshop, use the workshop slides that we provide free (the three diagnostics plus "Expressing Appreciation"), make your own version of the workshop, use our Train-the-Trainer DVDs, or arrange for a 4-D Network Member to provide a workshop.
- Coaching by 4-D certified coaches accounted for about 20 percent of the total cost. If you want, you can use your coaches, whom we will train in 4-D methodology, or you can use our certified coaches.
- Finally, team and individual assessments accounted for about 10 percent of the total cost. Note that the labor costs for team debriefings are in the CPM costs and for individual debriefings in the coaching costs.

The total average cost per year for NASA was about $60 per employee per year or about $600 per participant. Marshall cost about $110 per year per employee at the about the same $600 per participant.

When I saw these costs, I was sure we had made some kind of error. They seemed too low for the benefits realized. I knew that team context shifting was much more efficient than individual training. However, I did not expect so much systemic change for such a low cost. A typical team started with a *Team Development Assessment*. Many, but not all, teams continued with a single three-day workshop. About half of the workshop participants elected coaching twice a month for varying periods. In addition, teams (and individuals in coaching) performed reassessments every four to six months.

Estimating a Systemic NASA ROI

Now we can calculate an estimated return on investment (ROI). To keep this simple, I consider a middle year in the previous graphs. NASA's annual budget is about $17 billion, or $850,000 per employee per year. If we assume mid-period 5 percent productivity improvement, NASA saved about $40,000 per person that year. The ROI is thus $40,000 divided by $60 or 650. (Are your stocks doing this well?) Marshall's ROI would be similar, with twice the cost and twice the benefit. Moreover, I did not include the enormous benefit of reduced mission failures.

Note that I have not included the burdened labor costs (that is, the cost of the participant's salaries including overhead) of participation in 4-D processes. Using reasonable estimates for NASA employees, these would lower the ROI to about 450.

Now, this calculation is included here for fun. Most importantly, these large ROIs are for systemic improvements, not the teams directly using 4-D processes. Their ROI is much larger.

Do 4-D Behavior Assessments Measure Performance?

Our assessments measure behaviors. What do you believe about the correlation of our assessment scores with team performance? It depends on whether you believe that team performance correlates with team members' behavioral norms. I, and everyone I know of who uses these processes, believes in this correlation.

Continuing, I believe it is intuitively obvious that teams and individuals with behaviors that sustain atmospheres of mutual respect, appropriate inclusion, 100 percent commitment, and effective organization significantly outperform teams that do not. (Note: I have cited four of the behaviors we measure in 4-D assessments.) Moreover, the anecdotal evidence is unequivocal. Team leaders consistently report that team performance improves when scores improve.

FIGURE 5.5   NASA and Contractor Data for the STEREO Project

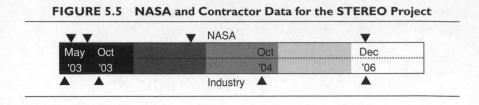

In Figure 5.5 above, the NASA STEREO project and its contractor moved from the bottom quintile to the top quintile in near lockstep over three years as illustrated. The triangles on the top track the government team. The triangles on the bottom track the contractor team.

We assembled these data after the successful launch of this roughly $600 million observatory. It is fascinating to see the two teams, at two different institutions, track so closely over the three-and-a-half-year period. The deputy project manager reported, "Our performance tracked right along with the assessment scores."

Do NASA's Teambuilding Processes Always Work?

The 4-D process of assessments, workshops (or, alternately, this book), coaching, and reassessments are highly effective when the team leaders want the eight core behaviors in their team enough to both advocate them and model them. When team leaders demonstrate burning desire for top-quintile benchmarks in their *Individual Development Assessments*, our processes are also highly effective. When team leaders do not care, our processes are not effective. This is the reason we insisted on voluntary participation. Although, if I had the authority, I would require all projects to use 4-D processes. I would include each team's social context at each design review along with the technical and programmatic status.

A Few Testimonials

In mid-2008, NASA had a pending budget shortfall. Our NASA sponsor, the NASA chief engineer, asked for some supporting e-mails from people using 4-D processes. Within a few days, he received more than 60 e-mails plus phone calls and visits in person by top management. He forwarded a number of the e-mails to me. Here are a few:

> "The value of the 4D program is more than team morale and job satisfaction. . . . Had it not been for the 4D team and individual coaching processes the GSP would not have met critical program milestones and this would have translated . . . into losses in the tens of millions of dollars."
>
> —Robin Pfister, GOES-R Ground Segment deputy PM, manages the most difficult part of a more than $11 billion program.

> "Across my 25 years plus of service to NASA and the federal government . . . I believe the 4D Leadership and Teambuilding Program may be the most powerful and effective I have encountered."
>
> —Ron Brade, director, Human Capital Management, Goddard Space Flight Center

> "I was somewhat circumspect of how well this would work given my previous experiences with this type of thing. I have to admit that it was time well spent and I've really been impressed by the process and results."
>
> —Rick Grammier, project manager of the more than $1 billion JUNO Project at NASA/Jet Propulsion Laboratory

An Application Summary for NASA Results

This chapter summarized the quantitative improvement in behavioral norms for about 200 NASA teams. Further, it showed the systemic institutional improvements by examining teams' first assessment scores. Finally, it correlated the amount of systemic improvement with the amount of 4-D work provided.

If, for some reason, this evidence does not persuade you, try the 4-D processes out. Buy copies of *How NASA Builds Teams* and conduct at least *Team Development Assessments* at regular intervals. See for yourself—you have little to lose.

A Summary of the Role of Each 4-D Process

- *Team* and *Individual Development Assessments*—These quick, repetitive behavioral measurements bring teams and their members' attention to their behaviors and their effects on others. Repetitive assessments are powerful change agents when coupled with *How NASA Builds Teams*.

- Workshops—These three-day events provide forums for work that teams can only perform as a group. Workshops include three team diagnostics that you can download free at www.4-DSystems.com. There are also three occasions when Significant Emotional Events (SEEs) are particularly encouraged. SEEs are powerful change motivators. You know this because you can surely recall events accompanied by your own SEEs, like assassinations of public figures. The three occasions are the experiential appreciation exercise (Chapter 12), the reporting of outcome commitments (Chapter 16), and the reporting of take-aways at the closure.

- Coaching and Consulting—4-D certified coaches specialize in context management with the Context Shifting Worksheet (Chapter 9). Our consultants are experts with organizational management (Chapter 18).

All of these materials (many for free) and services are available through the 4-D Network members at www.4-DSystems.com.

PART III

4-D DIAGNOSTICS

How to Color Code Your Team's Context

The next three chapters explain how to diagnose three key elements of any team's social context:

1. The innate personalities of your teammates, including whether they match their required tasks;
2. The characterization of your team's culture and its match to the larger organization and primary customer's culture; and
3. The mindset (paradigm) that drives your project (if your team is a project team).

Ignoring these elements of context can cause team failure for reasons you never even considered. After you read these chapters, I recommend that you download the relevant PowerPoint charts from www.4-DSystems.com and perform the diagnostics with your team. You can estimate the time required by the number of slides you are using. Our workshop run-rate average is about eight slides per hour.

Quit the BS and Pick Up the Chalk

It is usual for technical teams to have one or more (usually *Blue*, visionary) personalities who resist participating in the exercises. You might relate this story from Frank Martin, a 4-D workshop presenter/consultant, who uses it in workshops from time to time.

Frank has a PhD in physics and preferred technical classes when he was an undergraduate. Nonetheless, he was at a small liberal arts college and required to take humanities courses as well. He chose a course in art history. When he arrived for his first class, he found charcoal and paper on his desk. He had wanted to read about art, not draw it. Grudgingly, he worked with the charcoals, vowing this would be the last time.

When he arrived at the second class, he found pastels on his desk. Frank decided that enough was enough, and he sat at his desk reading the textbook. The professor was walking around the class and noticed Frank just sitting. He said, "Time to do the art." Frank said, "I signed up for an art history class and that's what I intend to do, study art history."

The young professor leaned down and spoke quietly in Frank's ear so no one else could hear, "Mr. Martin, quit the bullshit and pick up the chalk." This shocked Frank, and he began to draw. Many years later Frank gave the commencement address at the college. As he walked around after, he thanked the professor, because at life junctures ever after he "picked up the chalk." Frank also began to notice and appreciate beautiful art created in the professor's classes that showed up all around campus.

CHAPTER 6

Using the 4-D System to Color Your Personalities

A scorpion wanted to cross a river. Scorpions, of course, cannot swim. Just as he was about to give up, a frog swam by. "Hey, Mr. Frog, how about a ride across the river?" he called. Mr. Frog answered, "I don't think so. You might sting me and then we would both drown." The scorpion answered, "Why would I sting you? That would be stupid." Mr. Frog said, "Okay, hop on," and off they went.

About halfway across the river the frog felt the sting in his back and said, "Oh no, you've done it. You have killed us both! Why did you sting me?" The scorpion answered, "Because scorpions do what scorpions got to do." We will now see that people do what their innate personalities drive them to do, even when it does not serve them well. Innate personality trumps reason.

Carl Jung and Innate Personality

Carl Jung posited that our preferences for deciding and information are innate. Innate means present at birth. That is, we each innately prefer to use emotions or logic for making decisions. We each innately prefer to use intuited or sensed information to make decisions. Moreover, we build our personalities on these innate preferences.

The 4-D System illustrates this in Figure 6.1. The diagram shown is for an innate *logical* decider who prefers *intuited* information. This is the personality foundation for a *Blue*, visioning leader. (This happens to be my personality foundation.)

After an overview of the deciding and information preferences, you can use two short quizzes to find your innate preferences.

FIGURE 6.1 **4-D Personality Foundation Tool**

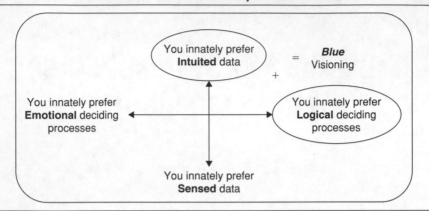

You will then pair your two preferences to find the dimension of your innate personality foundation. Your innate personality foundation will be *Green*, cultivating; *Yellow*, including; *Blue*, visioning; or *Orange*, directing. We now look at an example of how this information might be useful.

Handedness—An Innate Preference

Write your name on a piece of paper. Then put your pen in your other hand and write your name again. You can surely do it, but it is probably slower and more difficult. Is one's handedness innate? Most people believe so. In fact, researchers have identified a handedness gene. Handedness provides a useful analogy to innate personality foundation. Note that handedness is binary for the vast majority of people. We are generally either right- or left-handed, although we all use both hands for many tasks.

Innate personality works the same way, although I am not aware of any discovery of a personality gene. Consider the deciding axis in the 4-D System. We all use logic and emotions in decision making just as we all use both hands. Yet, we each innately prefer to use logic or emotions just as we each prefer to use our right or left hand to write our names.

Does the analogy break down for ambidextrous people? Actually, ambidextrous people tend to retain a handedness preference. Further, most ambidexterity arises from left-handed people who either chose, or were forced, to act right-handed. Interestingly, a similar effect happens with people's personalities as the following story by my colleague Skip Borst illustrates.

Skip Finds His Innate Personality

In an early workshop, my colleague Skip Borst approached me during a break with blazing eyes. "I got it. I got it," he shouted. Then he told me the following. "Since I first learned about this kind of work, I wanted to know where my foundation was located. Therefore, I took the Myers-Briggs tests and the result was what 4-D calls a *Blue*, visioning leader. This did not feel right [note the word 'feel'], so I took the extended Myers-Briggs. The result was the same."

Skip continued, "Just now, I understand. I was born as a *Green*, cultivating leader. Everything else in my life pushed me across the diagonal toward the *Orange*, directing dimension. My father was a hyper-German. I went to the Naval Academy, then into nuclear submarines, and finally nuclear reactor construction. I adapted into the *Blue*, visioning to survive. Finally, I understand who I am and why some work environments at GE were so troublesome for me." Figure 6.2 illustrates Skip's discovery.

I said, "Skip I think you pegged it. Look at what you chose to do the first time you felt free to do whatever you wanted—you became a master certified coach. That's *Green*, cultivating personality stuff all the way."

Two Ways to Decide

About 50 percent of us innately prefer to use logic (for example, rules, rationality, and objectivity) and 50 percent innately prefer to use our emotions (for example, what feels good) to make decisions.

It is extremely useful to know whether a person is an emotional-side or logical-side leader. You can then give them information they

FIGURE 6.2   **Skip's Diagram**

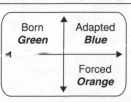

can act on. Logical-side leaders, for example, can act decisively and dispassionately on difficult people issues. In contrast, emotional-side leaders need a lot of encouragement and evidence before they confront people issues. I learned to take emotional-side leaders into difficult personnel situations more gradually and carefully.

The two sides even speak differently. When I was strategic advisor to Larry Singell, dean of the University of Colorado's Business School, he would open meetings with, "I want an outcome that we can all feel good about." Logical-side leaders seldom speak like that.

Notice how others respond to conflict during meetings. Emotional-side leaders tend to focus on the fact that conflict is present. They have difficulty looking at the underlying issue until the tension has abated. The presence of conflict often disorients them. Logical leaders tend to focus on the issues and ignore the tension. They have difficulty with the lingering, unaddressed emotional issues.

Deciding to Buy a House

How do the deciding processes actually work? When I moved to Boulder from Washington, DC, I decided to buy a house. I knew that I was a logical-side decider. When I reflected on how I had made prior home-buying decisions, I realized that I focused on cost per square foot, projected property growth rates, what I could afford, sun angles, elementary school scores, and the like.

This total emphasis on logical-side deciding had one difficulty. I had never bought a house I *liked* using this process. I decided to pick my next house as an emotional-side deciding process. I called a real estate agent in Boulder, Colorado, and said, "I am flying to Boulder next Wednesday night. I want to get in your car on Thursday and visit houses. I intend to buy the first house that feels good. And I intend to have a late dinner in Washington." She was very happy.

As I walked into the fourth house, I heard a small voice saying, "This house *feels* really good. I *think* I'll buy it." I did not yet know if it even had bathrooms. I congratulated myself on switching to an emotional-side decider. "Not so fast," I then thought. As I looked more closely, I realized that I had performed all my usual logical-side analysis. I then noticed how I spoke about my experience. I said, "I *think* I'll buy it." I had not switched my deciding process. I simply allowed an emotion to drop into a logical sequence.

I bought the house and enjoyed it very much. When my emotional-side decider friends (Boulder is chock-full of them) entered my home they would often remark, "This space feels good." At least I got the emotion right.

There is actually an important additional point in this story. I was fully in a life transition that was moving me from a 1-D *Blue* leader to a 4-D *Blue*, visioning leader. You cannot succeed as a leader of people without using emotional deciding when it is required. I address the roles of emotions in Chapter 11, "Manage Your Emotions to Manage Your Team's Energy."

About Your Personality Exploration

The following quizzes may help you locate the personality foundation you were born with—your innate foundation. There is a difficulty with this kind of test instrument. These inquiries require you to imagine some context to form your answer. I suggest that you answer in the context you are most able to be your natural self. For some people, this will be at home. For others, it will be at work.

Jung said that it is one's task early in life to build their personality on their innate foundation. Moreover, that one's task later in life is to complete the process by developing the other three dimensions. (The term "dimensions" is, of course, ours and not Jung's terminology.) Thus, if you are in midlife or thereabouts, you may be focusing on developing one or more of your noninnate personality dimensions. This focus may skew your perceptions. If you suspect this might be the case, try answering from early in life, say as if you were 25 years old. Your innate personality may be more evident at this early stage.

Finding Your Innate Deciding Preference

Indicate your innate deciding preference by placing a check on whichever side seems truer for you in Figure 6.3 on page 64. Then sum the check marks to get a total for each side. Circle the preference with the higher score. There is no right or wrong answer. Each process is equally valid.

FIGURE 6.3　Innate Deciding Preference Quiz

EMOTIONAL DECIDER	Check		LOGICAL DECIDER
Harmony is intrinsically valuable?			Harmony is a means to an end?
Prefer to act on "what feels right"?			Prefer to act on "what's logical"?
Consider the people first?			Consider the task first?
Prefer harmonious relationships?			Prefer being right?
Decide through consensus?			Decide with my own thinking?
First, trust my heart?			First, trust my head?
Intolerant of conflict?			OK with conflict?
Total – Emotional Decider			**Total – Logical Decider**

What Information Do You Prefer to Use?

Imagine an automobile accident that a sensor and intuitor observe. When the police asked a sensor what he or she saw, they replied, "Well, I saw that green 1998 Chevy enter the intersection at about 35 miles per hour. I noticed that the driver seemed to be looking to the left . . . " The sensor continued with a highly detailed account. The police are very happy. They now turn to the intuitor who said, "Yes, of course I saw the accident. You know, if you synchronized these stoplights these kinds of accidents would not happen." Intuitors leap past details into the big picture.

Finding Your Innate Information Preference

This is analogous to the similar test for the innate deciding preference that we discussed earlier. Mark how you prefer deciding, totaling the check marks on each side in Figure 6.4.

Where Is Your Foundation?

Now, use your deciding and information preferences to locate your innate personality foundation.

FIGURE 6.4   Innate Information Preference Quiz

INTUITED INFORMATION	Check		SENSED INFORMATION
Rely on my inner knowing?			Rely on my observations?
Think more about "what could be"?			Think more about "what is"?
Prefer creativity?			Prefer common sense?
Act on flashes of insight?			Act on careful analysis?
Prefer wrestling with concepts?			Prefer wrestling with facts & data?
Prefer holistic perspectives?			Prefer details?
Love big ideas?			Love established reality?
Total – Intuited Information			**Total – Sensed Information**

Look, for example, in the upper right corner of Figure 6.5. If your quiz showed an innate preference for logical deciding and intuited information, your foundation is a *Blue*, visioning leader. The process is the same for the other three personality foundations.

The two quizzes are, I believe, better than 90 percent accurate. How do I know this? I have used these quizzes with more than 2,000 workshop participants. They don colored badges displaying their results. If they have it wrong, their teammates quickly tell them. Moreover, as I listen to them I tell them if their badge is incorrect.

FIGURE 6.5   Finding Your Innate Personality Foundation

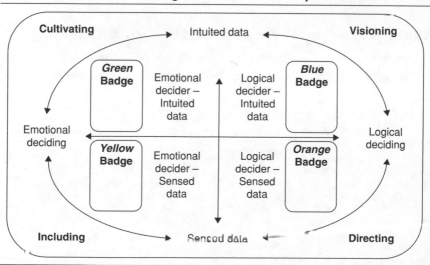

However, if your scores on either or both of the quizzes were close, here are a few other ways to look for your foundation:

1. Educate a friend, colleague, or spouse about this material and see where they think your innate personality resides;

2. Ask yourself, "What would I do if money was no consideration?" Your choice of profession might give you some insights. (Recall Skip's story.)

3. Look at what is most difficult or challenging for you. This is usually diagonal to your innate strength.

   a. Organizationally challenged ➔ *Green*, cultivating foundation.

   b. Conflict intolerant ➔ *Yellow*, including (relating) foundation.

   c. Human relationships difficult ➔ *Blue*, visioning foundation.

   d. Tend to see people as objects ➔ *Orange*, directing foundation.

Make your own colored badges or go to www.4-DSystems.com and download a free PDF file with the four badges. Print this sheet, cut out the badges you need, get them laminated, and have your team members wear them for the duration of this exercise. Many put this badge beneath their normal work badge and have fun with it later. They can show their badge and say, "I'm a *Green*, cultivating people-builder—meet me where I am."

Tasks Where You Have a Natural Advantage

Is any one of the four personalities preferred? It totally depends on the situation. We summarize the four personality types and their preferred work situation in Figure 6.6.

FIGURE 6.6 Strengths of Each Leader Foundation

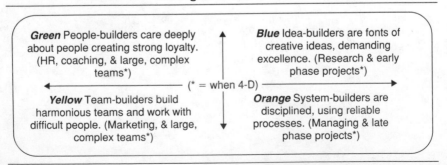

Green People-builders care deeply about people creating strong loyalty. (HR, coaching, & large, complex teams*)

Blue Idea-builders are fonts of creative ideas, demanding excellence. (Research & early phase projects*)

(* = when 4-D)

Yellow Team-builders build harmonious teams and work with difficult people. (Marketing, & large, complex teams*)

Orange System-builders are disciplined, using reliable processes. (Managing & late phase projects*)

An Example of Why Innate Personality Must Match Task

Working with proposal teams in aerospace companies dominated my early post-NASA consulting practice. My NASA background as a director of a multi-billion-dollar budget (when you included the support services such as shuttle launches) was very useful when advising contractors bidding for major NASA systems procurements.

Here is a case where we did the analysis in this chapter just in time. A client asked me to help with a major proposal for a nuclear space propulsion system. I met with the proposal team and began by charting the personalities of the team members. As we worked, it became apparent that the proposal team leader, Tom, was innately a very *Blue*, visioning leader, a personality invested in creativity and invention. I used the adjective "very" because Tom had a gift for creativity. His office was full of plaques for his patents.

This would have been fine except that NASA saw this program as strategically urgent. They were rushing into development rapidly in case the president's party changed in the upcoming election. Hence, they would want *Orange*, directing leadership to move the program ahead quickly with discipline, process, and certainty of result.

We then analyzed the project lead on the NASA side as innately an *Orange*, directing leader. The proposal team suddenly understood why the personal interactions between their *Blue* leader and NASA's *Orange* leader had gone so badly.

I turned to Tom and said, "I'm sorry, but you are the wrong person to lead this proposal team. We need an experienced *Orange* leader if we expect to win." The proposal team understood and quickly agreed. We then used the 4-D System to identify the personalities of *Orange* candidates to replace Tom and quickly closed on the perfect replacement.

I followed Tom back to his office to see what he would say about what I had done. I was concerned that he might be angry. He closed the door and said, "Charlie, I cannot thank you enough. I would have been a disaster in that job. Your analysis provided a much needed and painless exit." The contractor installed the recommended *Orange* leader and won the proposal competition. I believe that if they had continued with the *Blue* leader, Tom, they would have lost the competition no matter what else they did. How important is this insight?

"Who's on the Bus?"

I suggest you lead your teammates/colleagues through the material in this chapter. You can obtain the workshop slides that accompany this chapter at www.4-DSystems.com. You can then graph "Who's on the Bus" as in Figure 6.7. The entire process will probably not take much more than a few hours depending on how lengthy your discussions are.

It is useful to see who is on the team and examine their personalities' match to task and customer.

It is interesting to explore why teams deviate from the averages of 50–50 emotional-logical deciding and 70–30 sensing-intuiting. There are two recurrent patterns. Teams of technical people tend to have most members on the right logical-side. Teams formed from scratch often have a large cluster in the team leader's home dimension. We tend to prefer people like ourselves. This is generally okay if the leader's innate personality matches the task. It is not okay if the leader's innate personality does not match the task, and it is deadly if the leader's innate personality is diagonal to the task.

Whom Do You Need on the Bus?

Imagine building a house or adding a room to your house. You would want a free-ranging *Blue* innovative architect during the planning phase. Of course, you would have your *Orange* manager/builder review your design to confirm efficient and doable construction. Once the design is complete, you would turn the job over to your *Orange* manager for the construction phase.

FIGURE 6.7   Who's on the Bus?

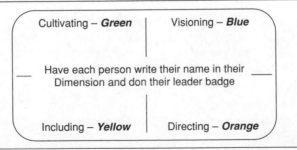

Cultivating – *Green*	Visioning – *Blue*
Have each person write their name in their Dimension and don their leader badge	
Including – *Yellow*	Directing – *Orange*

Similarly, early phase project teams should be mostly *Blue*. These creative idea builders perform trade studies to compare alternatives with out-of-the-box thinking. The team's majority population then must shift to mostly *Oranges* during the implementation phase.

What do *Greens* and *Yellows* provide to technical project teams? Their deep values and relational skills help people work together. They offer important diversity in thinking that improves decisions. Further, many of the greatest project managers that I have known are 4-D *Green* or *Yellow*. The reason is that the higher you rise in management, the more important people abilities become. You can delegate *Orange* work to the next level. However, you cannot delegate your cultivating or including work to others. You must learn to do this yourself.

No matter what your home personality color, *you need to be 4-D able*. How does one become 4-D able? You study *How NASA Builds Teams*, especially Chapters 12 through 18, and use the assets at www.4-DSystems.com, especially the team and individual behavior assessments.

Application—The Project That Could Not Complete

A NASA project manager for a large flight project asked me to provide a three-day workshop for his team including his contractor. The project was in its implementation phase—the design was (supposedly) complete. The challenge now was to build the hardware and software on cost and schedule. Here's how the project manager explained his presenting dilemma: "They can never seem to close anything out. The same problems are reopened and reworked over and over again."

As I presented the workshop, I realized I was feeling unusually fatigued. Moreover, I could not move the team through the material in an orderly way. By the second night, I was so tired that I went to bed very early. I woke at 5 AM the following morning with a deep insight. I was having the very same problem with the team as the project manager!

I looked at the personality analysis performed earlier and immediately understood the problem. These people were temperamentally unable to do the work this project phase required *within the project's social context*. Under stress, we become more of who we already are.

The majority of the team members were *Blue*, visioning leaders who became 1-D *Blue* in the stress field of the project. 1-D *Blues* do not perform efficiently in an *Orange* project phase.

The root context problem was that the contract was "cost plus" in a "cost-capped" program. Cost-plus means that the contractor was to implement technical changes directed by NASA technical managers and would receive fee (profit) on NASA approved change orders. Cost-capped means that NASA headquarters established a ceiling on the project's total cost. NASA's solution to the dilemma was to use the contractor's profit as budget reserve and gradually spend it to solve problems. Unprofitable projects tend to receive lower management support and priority than profitable ones.

Two steps would conclude this project successfully:

1. NASA should clamp down on the change orders—some were more a matter of taste than technical necessity; and

2. NASA should fund the project to do the job right and not one cent more.

It has become fashionable in NASA to manage project costs by threatening cancellation. I do not believe this motivates people to work more efficiently. If fact, I am proud that I never cancelled a single project in my 10 years as director of astrophysics and funded many painful overruns, including the mission that won John Mather's Nobel Prize. Further, the data do not support this threat and rigidity. Underfunding (or insufficient schedule) creates team social contexts that cause mission failures (Bearden, 2007).

Chapter 16 discusses creating high-performance projects.

1. The Contractor should tell NASA the truth about the unfunded issues and real cost-to-go. Demand your fair profit and give the project the management support it needs.

2. The Contractor should compassionately begin relocating the bluest of the 1-D *Blues* to jobs they can do naturally and well. Put 4-D able *Orange* leaders into key positions such as project manager and lead systems engineer.

This project has a cost near a half-billion dollars. There is no excuse for not doing the job right.

Never Use This Information to Limit

The radius of each arc in Figure 6.8 represents capability in a dimension. I urge you in the strongest possible terms to avoid using this information to limit yourself or others. Recall the *Blue* project team unable to execute that I used to introduce this chapter.

Clearly, you need a strong *Orange* ability to bring the project to completion. Would you only consider leaders with *Orange* foundations? Look at Person A in Figure 6.8.

Their foundation is in the right place. Now compare them to Person B, with a *Yellow* foundation (that you cannot see in the image), who is much more developed. Not only are they more able in the *Orange*, directing dimension, you get the dividend of great *Yellow* teambuilding abilities as well.

The *Green*, Cultivating Personality's Innate AMBR

- **A**ttention: These people naturally attend to people's needs and universal values;
- **M**indset: We are here as stewards—for others, family, for our religious/spiritual values;
- **B**ehavior: Supporting others in being happy and successful; and
- **R**esults: Success without damaging people.

Of course, their diagonal challenge is the discipline/organization of the directing dimension.

FIGURE 6.8   Comparing Two *Orange*, Directing Leaders

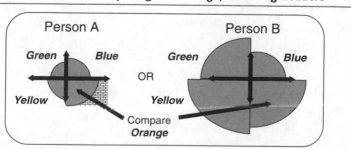

A workshop I provided for the Colorado State Mental Health Board provided my deepest immersion into a team of *Green*, cultivating leaders. The group included both people who are mentally ill and people who care for them. When I began this section on personality, one woman raised her hand and said, "Which personality do you want, I have several of them." They had a great sense of humor.

Can you guess how the group's personalities distributed in 4-D? Yes, they were overwhelmingly in the *Green*, cultivating dimension. The obvious exception was their three attorneys, who were all in the *Orange*, directing dimension.

They engaged us because they could not organize themselves. This is, of course, because the directing dimension is the diagonal of the personality foundation for nearly all of them—no surprise here. They described their biggest problem as securing funding from the state government. I asked, "What do you say to the state legislature?" They easily answered, "We tell them how heartfelt this work is."

Can you guess the color of the foundational dimension of governments? Government cultures are overwhelmingly *Orange*. I advised this *Green* team to find an *Orange* leader who shared their values and put them in charge. Can you see why this would be difficult? We prefer to associate with people who are like us. The term for this tendency is homophily.

Incidentally, a few months later I heard that the U.S. Congress finally passed the federal omnibus mental health bill. The lawmakers delayed the bill for two years until the sponsors provided the metrics that they demanded. *Green* cultivators must meet *Orange* directors' needs to get what they want from them.

The issue for *Green* badges on technical teams is that they must be sufficiently able in one of the two logical-side abilities (visioning or directing) to contribute when they are doing work. Moreover, they need strategies to function above threshold minimums in their directing diagonal dimension. Business cultures are more than 80 percent *Orange* demanding organized behavior. Here's the good news. *Greens* who achieve 4-D dimensionality tend to rise to the highest levels of management. They are superb leaders creating loyal followers because they show they deeply and innately care about other people.

We now pause in our discussion of *Green* leaders to examine the need to address all four dimensions. We shortly return to *Greens* with a demonstration of 4-D dimensionality by Gandhi.

The Highly Effective (4-D) Pattern

My colleague Skip Borst came up with this compelling statement about the need to address all four dimensions: "When dimensions are omitted, people under stress fill them with their most toxic emotions and most pathological story lines." Not only is it important to address all four dimensions in important communications, there is a necessary sequence: cultivating, including, visioning, and then directing.

Most of us have experienced trying to loosen a frozen bolt. Applying only directing is equivalent to using ever-larger wrenches and turning the bolt as hard as you can. It is more effective to lubricate with WD-40. Our context managing processes begin by lubricating with appreciation followed by including. It is this simple. You can never go wrong with authentic appreciation.

Presidential speechwriters know this intuitively. Try tracking an important speech with the 4-D System. Many politicians spend the first half of their speech lubricating the audience with appreciation and including. When they cannot authentically appreciate another person or entity because they are angry with them, they appreciate the circumstances. "I really appreciate the difficulty we face together in . . ."

I analyzed one of Bill Clinton's State of the Union addresses. Many hailed this speech as one of his finest. He began by appreciating Sonny Bono (recently deceased) and members of Congress. He was angry with the Republican Congress so he could not authentically appreciate them. Therefore, he appreciated the difficulties of the problems they mutually faced and included by offering to work with them. He then included veterans, the handicapped, and minorities by noticing them out in the audience. For the first 28 minutes, he walked around the two emotional-side dimensions and then articulated his vision of a better America. Finally, he made his first move into the directing dimension by taking a stand on Social Security.

Did you notice how President Bush included in his 9/11 speech? He put on the firefighter's badge and recognized the wife of the man who said, "Let's roll" on the airplane that crashed in a Pennsylvania field on that ill-fated day. That's inclusion writ large.

Some years ago, President Bush made a speech at Kitty Hawk, NC, advertised as an announcement for a new space policy. Unfortunately, the policy was not ready. It was fascinating to watch him appreciate and include for 25 minutes. I observed no real substance.

I called people who heard the speech to see what they thought. Everyone reported enjoying the speech. Appreciation and inclusion are so pleasant that no one found the lack of substance troublesome.

Did these speechwriters secretly attend a 4-D workshop? No, they probably built the speech using intuitive abilities developed with trial and error over the years. You have the benefit of a simple organizing system to guide you to do just as well.

We now rejoin our investigation into *Green* leaders with 4-D action by Gandhi.

Gandhi Demonstrates 4-D Leadership

Anyone familiar with Gandhi's life would likely deduce that he is a *Green*, cultivating leader. Moreover, the fact that he was an attorney, effective in the *Orange* diagonal, suggests he was 4-D capable. There is a scene in the movie *Gandhi* that illustrates his 4-D abilities as he urges resistance to a British law demanding Indians provide their fingerprints. The 4-D analysis of a scene demonstrates Gandhi lubricating before directing.

He opens with a big including statement (with British army officers present): "I want to welcome you all, every one of you. We have no secrets." He then describes General Smut's new law requiring fingerprinting all Indians like criminals. He adds that the British officials could enter Indian homes without knocking and adds that under British law they are not legally married. "Under this law," he says, "our wives are whores and every man here is a bastard." He is using emotions to energize the crowd.

Members of the crowd make angry statements advocating killing a few British and expressing willingness to hang for their actions. Gandhi praises their courage (appreciation as more lubrication). Gandhi, then makes this remarkable statement: "But, my friends, there is no cause for which I am prepared to kill. Whatever they do to us, we will attack no one, kill no one, but we will not give our fingerprints, not one of us. They will imprison us, they will fine us, they will seize our possessions, but they cannot take away our self-respect if we do not give it to them."

His next statement amazed me, as I did not expect such a powerful visioning statement from an emotional-side leader. He says, "I am asking you to fight, to fight against their anger, not to provoke it. We will not strike a blow, but we will receive them, and through our pain, we will make them see their injustice. And it will hurt, as all fighting hurts. But, we cannot lose. We cannot. They may torture my body, break my bones, and even kill me. Then, they will have my dead body, not my obedience."

Now, he goes back to including (more lubricating) stating that they are all Hindu and Muslim, children of God. Gandhi then asks them to "Take a solemn oath in his name that, come what may, we will not submit to this law."

After a pause, the audience applauds in unison. Then an old man stands, signifying taking the oath. A young boy follows, and then everyone else quickly stands. The movie scene closes with a humorous inclusion action. Gandhi leads the singing of "God save our gracious King." The Indians are already all standing. The three British officials now stand up with them!

Gandhi overthrew the British using his deep *Green* values supported by effective action in the other three dimensions. I believe that if he was less than 4-D able, he would not have succeeded.

The Effective Cultivating Leader

Jerry Garcia of the Grateful Dead summed up the *Green*, cultivators idealism and inability to organize with "It's hard to get your thing together if your thing is paradise on earth."

The *Green*, cultivating personality performs best in jobs where caring about people matters most. They frequently provide training and coaching, and are excellent team leaders when they are also four dimensional. If they are only *Green*, they cannot organize (directing dimension) sufficiently to lead.

When 4-D *Green*, cultivating leaders support their innate strength with the other three dimensions, they behave like the left side of Figure 6.9 on page 76. When they lack any of the three supporting dimensions, there are holes in their capabilities. Their behaviors morph into the 1-D set in the right-hand side of the chart. Idealistic turns into victim, and so on.

FIGURE 6.9   Comparison of 4-D (left) and 1-D (right) *Green*, Cultivating Leaders

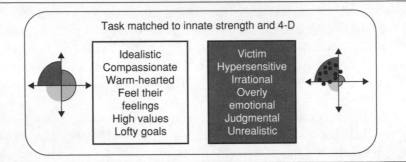

Task matched to innate strength and 4-D

Idealistic Compassionate Warm-hearted Feel their feelings High values Lofty goals	Victim Hypersensitive Irrational Overly emotional Judgmental Unrealistic

The *Yellow*, Including Personality's Innate AMBR

- <u>A</u>ttention: These people naturally attend to teamwork and relationships;
- <u>M</u>indset: We are here to work together;
- <u>B</u>ehavior: Facilitating teamwork and collaboration; and
- <u>R</u>esults: Success through harmony.

Of course, their diagonal challenges include acting on difficult personnel problems and tolerating the conflict that *Blues* so often enjoy.

Eisenhower as an Including Leader

For years, I could not find a good illustration of an including personality in action. Then one night, while I was making dinner, I had the History channel on TV in the background. I heard the announcer say, "The reason that Eisenhower was chosen to be supreme allied commander is that he was so likeable. He was the only general who could work with Montgomery."

I dashed to the TV. Could it be true? Did I finally find my including personality in a general? I rushed out to find any videotape I could about Eisenhower. I found one and expected to have to sit through tons of material looking for good snippets.

The Speeches of Dwight Eisenhower (1988) opened with a scene of Ike speaking at the British Royal Military Academy, Sandhurst. Here is a 4-D analysis of that speech.

As you might expect, Eisenhower naturally lubricates with an inclusion statement: "Any person, whether he is at the plow in the field or with gun at the front, that fails to do his full duty every day, every hour, must forever bear on his own conscience . . . that he's contributed . . . to the agony . . . our two countries must endure."

He continues to direct the cadets to include: "You must know every single one of your men. It is not enough that you are the best soldier in that unit, that you are the strongest, the toughest, the most durable, the best equipped, technically."

His direction to include continues: "You must be their leader, their father, their mentor, even if you are half their age. . . . That cultivation of human understanding between you and your men is the one art that you must yet master. And, you must master it quickly."

I find this amazing. Here we have a general downplaying toughness in combat in favor of comradeship and human understanding. Innate personality trumps logic.

Do you remember Ike's presidential campaign slogan? It was, "I like Ike." Think about it. Can you imagine "I like Al Gore" buttons? I make this joke with the greatest respect for Al Gore. It is just that he is a *Blue*, visioning personality and naturally disadvantaged in popularity contests.

The Effective Including Leader

I know no better summary of the including leader's perspective than this from Dwight Eisenhower: "Some of my friends are for it. Some of my friends are against it. I am for my friends."

Yellow, including leaders are great in jobs where relationship and teamwork matter most. I believe including leaders are the best leaders of the largest and most complex project teams (when they are also 4-D).

When *Yellow*, including leaders are 4-D, they have characteristics like those on the left side of Figure 6.10. When they lack any of the three supporting dimensions, there are holes in their capabilities morphing their behaviors to the corresponding 1-D behaviors on the right.

**FIGURE 6.10   Comparison of 4-D (left) and 1-D (right) *Yellow*,
Including Leaders**

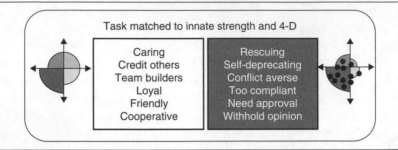

The *Blue*, Visioning Personality's Innate AMBR

This quote from Donald Trump nicely captures the *Blue*, visioning leader's mindset: "As long as you are going to think anyway, think big."

Here is *Blue* AMBR:

- Attention: These people naturally tend to ideas, concepts, and being the best;
- Mindset: Big, novel ideas are the deal;
- Behavior: Generate and then promulgate their ideas (often faster than anyone can respond to them); and
- Results: Success through excellence and innovation.

Of course, their diagonal challenges include joining teams as collaborators. In addition, *Blues* often have high attention needs. In teams, they offer their opinions often, sometimes to the detriment of orderly progress.

At a technical conference, I observed an overdone 1-D *Blue*, visioning leader. He picked up his viewgraphs (this was some years ago), briefly glanced at the audience, and presented his material facing the screen. When he finished, he glanced back, then walked backward to his seat with his eyes still mostly on the screen.

When I ask, "Was he in relationship?" most people answer "No." They give this answer because they are thinking only of relationships with people. Actually, he was in relationship with his ideas. This is the danger for deep *Blue*, visioning leaders. We *Blue* leaders can experience our ideas as more seductive than human relationships.

I know this all too well. For many years, I was an overdone *Blue*. I lived in my head, ignoring my emotions and, more problematically, discounting other people's emotional needs. One day, I asked myself "Why is work not more fun for me?" Slowly, I got it: It's about your human relationships, stupid. Many call me "the new Charlie." How do I sustain the quality of my relationships? I have others reassess my behaviors every four to six months with our online *Individual Development Assessment*. All my behaviors consistently score in the upper part of the top quintile. I must score there to present this work and be in integrity. Where attention goes, power flows.

The Amazing Howard Hughes—A One-Dimensional *Blue*, Visioning Leader

The movie, *The Amazing Howard Hughes* (1977) caricatures the overdone visioning personality brilliantly. I have no idea how accurately the film portrays Howard Hughes. It does not matter for our purposes.

Here are a few scenes that typify the 1-D *Blue* leader. Hughes says, "I'm going to be the best at whatever I do. Then, one of these days, they're going to wake up and discover that Howard Hughes is the richest man in the whole wide world." Being the best is a typical *Blue* value.

Later in a conversation regarding the release of a movie, Hughes says, "Hell, that just shows he's got no brains, he's got no guts. It's bad enough when a novel ends that way, it's even worse for a motion picture, Cruickshank. We're going to have to change that ending." This demonstrates another characteristic of an overdone *Blue* leader—capriciousness, changing his mind so frequently that no one can complete anything.

Hughes continues, "It's a most peculiar world, Cruickshank. Now, that is, most people are supposed to take an interest in their fellow man, but for some reason, however, I just don't seem to be as interested in my fellow man as I am in other things." Cruickshank asks, "What other things?"

Hughes continues, "Well, I guess you'd have to say those things that are all around us. The earth and what the earth is made of, the sky and the universe beyond. I have more real interest, you see Cruickshank, in why we get from winter to summer than I'm ever going to have in understanding my next-door neighbor. I'll tell you the truth, Cruickshank, most people just bore me and I don't want to get involved with them." Overdone *Blues* have such strong relationships with their ideas that there is little room for relationships with people.

The Effective Visioning Leader

Visioning leaders excel in tasks where concept mastery and creativity matter most. Here is the visioning leader's diagram, 4-D on the left, 1-D on the right in Figure 6.11.

The *Orange*, Directing Personality's Innate AMBR

- Attention: These people naturally attend to task, process, and certainty;
- Mindset: Plan the work—work the plan;
- Behavior: Execute with discipline and rigor; and
- Results: Success through processes and consistency.

Of course, their diagonal challenge is seeing people as people with legitimate personal needs.

Hoosiers—The Mono-Style Directing Leader

The 1986 movie *Hoosiers* caricatures the mono-style directing personality beautifully. By mono-style, I mean that while Coach Dale is 4-D, he uses his directing style in each dimension. His slogan more likely

FIGURE 6.11   Comparison of 4-D (left) and 1-D (right) *Blue*,
Visioning Leaders

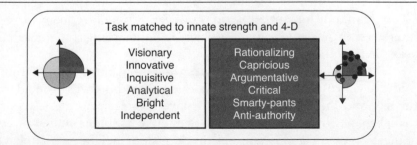

would have been "My way or the highway." He demands control (his) and consistency.

The team has a star shooter, Ray, who can make baskets from anywhere. Coach Dale wants the team to pass four times before shooting. When the team falls behind, they feed Ray the ball. He shoots immediately, making the basket. The crowd is cheering, and the coach is furious.

Coach Dale screams at the team during halftime in the locker room, exhorting them repeatedly to pass four times. As they come out for the second half, Ray dribbles the ball down court and shoots, making the basket. Coach Dale benches him and sends in his last player, the diminutive Ollie. Soon, another player fouls out, and Ray leaps up to enter the game.

Coach Dale stops him with "Sit down!" Ray asks, "What do you mean? We've got to have five out there." Coach Dale, "Sit down! SIT!" The referee comes over, "Coach, need one more." Coach Dale points to the team and says, "My team's on the floor." The mayor looks at the coach and asks, "What are you trying to do?" What is he trying to do? I think it is obvious. He is making the point that obedience and discipline are more important than winning this game.

The Effective *Orange*, Directing Leader

Michael Winner provides this humorous insight into *Orange* leaders' mindsets: "A team effort is a lot of people doing what I say."

Orange people excel in tasks that require management abilities as in plan, organize, direct, and control. In Figure 6.12, a now familiar diagram, 4-D is on the left and 1-D is on the right.

FIGURE 6.12 Comparison of 4-D (left) and 1-D (right) *Orange*, Directing Leaders

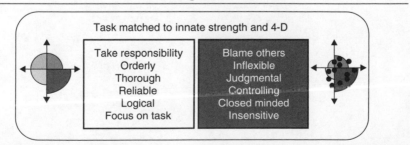

Task matched to innate strength and 4-D

Take responsibility	Blame others
Orderly	Inflexible
Thorough	Judgmental
Reliable	Controlling
Logical	Closed minded
Focus on task	Insensitive

Innate Personalities Alter Our Perception

Figure 6.13 maps some representative books on teams and leaders in our 4-D space. These books, and most people, tend to speak about what matters from a single (1-D) perspective. Their chosen perspective almost surely springs from their innate personality foundation.

You now have the gift of knowing that building teams and developing leaders requires all four dimensions. You now know that no single dimension is sufficient. This is a potent insight, and one that I hope you will remember the next time you read a book or article about leadership.

We Examine a Few Well-Known Public Figures

So you can see how easily you can characterize your colleagues, we will practice with a few presidents and candidates. We will make a guess about their home base and look at the strength of their diagonal to see how 4-D they are. This is not about politics—only our capacity to categorize well-known figures. Which innate personality characterizes Jimmy Carter, Al Gore, Barack Obama, and George W. Bush?

This big *Blue* held many of his pre-election events at universities. He authored three popular books. He bungled being *Yellow* with an inappropriate kiss and dancing to a Spanish song. This is, of course, Al Gore, who we might thus conclude was less than 4-D able. He demonstrated *Blue* after he lost the election by lecturing around the

**FIGURE 6.13 Authors Emphasize "One Thing" When Success Requires
All Four**

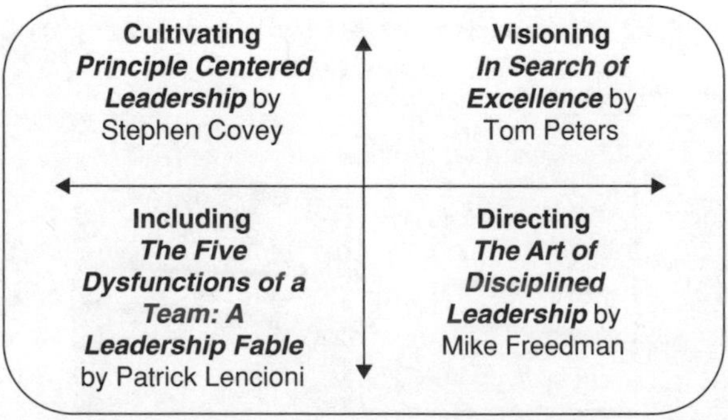

Cultivating ***Principle Centered*** ***Leadership*** by Stephen Covey	Visioning ***In Search of*** ***Excellence*** by Tom Peters
Including ***The Five*** ***Dysfunctions of a*** ***Team: A*** ***Leadership Fable*** by Patrick Lencioni	Directing ***The Art of*** ***Disciplined*** ***Leadership*** by Mike Freedman

country and creating a movie about the environment. He won the Nobel Peace Prize in 2007.

This *Green* farmer and Sunday school teacher was an unpopular president. I recall him looking haggard and distressed as he tried to be *Orange* and manage a deepening economic crisis. I suggest that he was less than 4-D as well. His work after his presidency honoring his *Green* values brought him great success, including the 2002 Nobel Peace Prize. This is, of course, about Jimmy Carter.

This generally likeable *Yellow* personality had great difficulty tolerating internal conflict. His *Blue* intellectual talents were so limited that people published joke books about his speaking. We can conclude he is not 4-D. We are speaking, of course, about George W. Bush, one of America's least popular presidents. He is leaving office as I write this. Like the others, what he does when he is no longer president, when he can do whatever he wants, will confirm my classification, or not.

This *Green* turned down big corporate jobs to perform community service in Chicago. Interestingly, he shows no weakness in the diagonal *Orange*, at least in his presidential campaign, which showed tight organization. His choice of an apparently *Orange* chief of staff shows he is aware of his potential softness in this area and is attempting to compensate for it. Overall, President Obama looks 4-D. Time and crises will show if he is 4-D able or not.

Are You a Competent or Incompetent Manager?

When I was in the University of Colorado Business School's Management Department, colleagues would bring me articles from time to time. One day, I received an article on industrial psychologists' assumptions about the "base rate of managerial incompetence" in a typical American business. The article reported the percentage of managers deemed incompetent at their jobs by these psychologists (Clark, 1990). What is your guess?

I ask this question in workshops and am amazed that people generally guess 60 percent to 90 percent of American business manag ers are incompetent. Managers are the most powerful and influential people in business organizations. How can this be? Could a restaurant succeed if over half of the cooks were incompetent at what they do?

These guesses are surprisingly close to the assumptions of industrial psychologists. The number cited in the article is 70 percent! Industrial psychologists assume *a-priori* that 70 percent of business managers are incompetent.

However, I have good news for people who work in aerospace. I found a PhD thesis (Milliken-Davies) written about a large aerospace company. Only half of the aerospace managers were incompetent at their jobs. (Is this good news?)

How to Join the Ranks of the Competent 30 Percent

The 4-D System provides an important insight into managerial competence. Planning, organizing, directing, and controlling are common elements of management. Notice that this is what the 4-D System names directing leadership. I was most pleased to discover this. Many writers claim management is a limiting ability that one must transcend to be a great leader. In our 4-D System, management is integral to leadership. I will tell you that you had better be able to plan, organize, direct, and control to succeed at NASA or in a typical business.

What is causing people to name management as incompetent? The root cause, I believe, is their desire for authority figures to meet their emotional needs, on the emotional side of the x-axis in the 4-D System. The most basic of these needs are feeling authentically appreciated and feeling included. Of course, people also need to believe in a realistic and promising future. They need their management to be four dimensional.

What is the message for you? Do you want people to name you in the 30 percent of competent managers? If so, you must master 4-D leadership!

4-D Employee Recruitment

The difference between project managers who fail and those who succeed is an interesting inquiry. As a NASA director, I needed my projects to be successful. I would have a project moving forward more or less on budget with good teamwork only to have the successful project manager leave for one reason or another.

I was frustrated that the replacement project manager was successful only about half the time. This was not good enough. What were we missing in our selection of project managers? Looking back, I see that we did not know to look for 4-D abilities. My perspective was one dimensional, the directing dimension. Mainly, what had the person done before?

If you wanted to inquire about the other three dimensions of a prospective project manager, what would you do? You would ask the applicant about how they showed the people who worked for them they cared about them. You could inquire into how they shared information. You could ask about the depth of their commitment to team success. In other words, you inquire into their capabilities in the other three dimensions—cultivating, including, and visioning dimensions. Then, you would check their statements with people who worked for and with them.

An Application Summary for Innate Personality

It is enormously rewarding to find out who you are at your core and why you behave as you do. Here are three strategies:

1. Use the quizzes in this chapter as instructed. My experience with literally thousands of workshop participants is that the quizzes are about 90 percent accurate. I make this claim because our workshop participants all wear color-coded badges; we can all see if they are behaving in ways that are consistent with their color.

2. Teach this material to someone who knows you well and have him or her select a badge for you. Or, even better, download the slides from our web site and go through the material with your team. If you are unsure, ask your colleagues to help. They usually can "badge" you.

3. Once you have a tentative choice, look at these two additional verifications:

   a. Ask yourself what you would do if money were no consideration. If it matches your badge, you probably have it right.

    b. Look at the diagonal to your choice. Is it particularly challenging for you? Do you have special coping mechanisms for working in that dimension?

For example, one of our workshop presenters is 4-D *Green*. He goes to great length to make sure that his innate limitation in *Orange* does not disrupt the event by testing everything the night before and bringing backup computers and projectors.

Chart your teammates' innate personality distribution. If your team is a general management team, you might see a distribution that matches the population at large: about 50–50 left-right (emotional-logical) and about 30–70 top-bottom (intuitor-sensor). My experience is that technical teams populate more on the right (logical) side.

What is the best distribution? I like the dominant population to match task or project phase, as discussed previously, with a mix that includes all four of the personality foundations. This helps provide diversity of perspective when you make decisions.

Will You Stand Up?

Recall the scene where Gandhi asks the Indians to take a solemn vow that they will not obey General Smut's new law. After some hesitation, an old man stands up. Then, a young boy stands up. The entire crowd then follows. This is how leadership actually works. Gandhi surely played an essential role in setting up the opportunity. However, unless someone took the crucial leadership action of standing up, his speech would have been for naught.

You are poised to stand up for your quality of life and work experience. Above all, this book is about changing you, not other people. Commit today to be 4-D able. Study this book and use the *Team* and *Individual Development Assessments* and other assets at www .4-DSystems.com.

Next, we apply the same 4-D characterization processes to examine culture.

CHAPTER 7

Using the 4-D System to Analyze Cultures

Franz Kafka said, "In a fight between you and the world, bet on the world." I say, "In a fight between you and the culture, bet on the culture."

This is the second of three *social context diagnostics*. We saw in the previous chapter how innate personality informs what we are most likely to do well, both at the individual and team level. We now use similar methods to analyze the personalities of teams and organizations, commonly called cultures. Cultures flow from the leader and team members' personalities, historical events, and the larger organizational context.

Asch's Experiment—Context Alters Perception

I have been presenting a simplified summary of Dr. Solomon Asch's work from the 1950s for many years. His experiments were wonderfully elegant. He showed subjects two cards, as seen in Figure 7.1. One card had a single line. Another card had three lines, one of them the same length as the line on the first card.

FIGURE 7.1 Asch's Cards

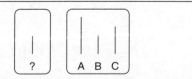

He asked people to name the line in the second card (A, B, or C) that was the same length as the line on the first card. A child could do this repeatedly without error. However, Dr. Asch arranged to have seven accomplices precede the subject's report with the same wrong answer. After this, how many of us would give an answer that was plainly wrong? The result is astonishing. One-third of the subjects gave an obviously incorrect answer. I had assumed that these people knowingly gave wrong answers to fit in.

A more recent repeat of the experiment (Blakeslee, 2005) used MRI to see what was happening in the subjects' brains. Different parts of our brains are active if we are choosing to lie or if the context is altering what we are actually seeing. "The researchers found that when people went along with the group on wrong answers, activity increased in . . . an area devoted to spatial awareness. There was *no activity in brain areas that make conscious decisions*." (Italicized for emphasis.)

The study showed that we see reality as the group context defines it. We are not nearly as independent of others as most of us would like to believe. Social context strongly drives Space Shuttle launch readiness reviews, jury trials, and elections. This chapter analyzes your team or organizational culture, another manifestation of social context. You can manage this aspect of context and thus improve team performance.

The "Culture as a Field" Metaphor

Magnetic fields are invisible and only observed by their effects on other magnetic materials, for example, dropping iron filings on a piece of paper covering a bar magnet. Culture fields are invisible and only observed by their effects on people. For example, the Asch experiment established a culture field that changed people's perception. People can no more resist the force of the culture than the iron filings can resist the force of the bar magnet. Thus, you must manage your team's culture field direction to align with your customer's culture and your task.

The Four Cultures

The 4-D System reveals four cultures, *Blue* (visioning), *Green* (cultivating), *Yellow* (including), and *Orange* (directing). Each perceives reality differently. Each has different driving core values. Each includes others differently. Each has a different vision of success. Finally, each directs and organizes differently.

For these reasons, like our innate personalities, teams and organizations tend toward one of four culture foundations. Cultures without a dominant and stable foundation tend to experience chronic, ongoing tension and confusion until a lead or dominant culture emerges.

The upper-left *Green*, cultivating foundation icon in Figure 7.2 suggests connection to deep personal values and caring about people. We find this culture in business's human resource organizations and non-profits such as churches and charity organizations.

The lower-left *Yellow*, including icon suggests harmonious group relationships. We find this culture in small service businesses. These cultures excel in giving customers customized products and services that are exactly what they want. This is the small home remodeling contractor who wants to build exactly what you want.

The upper-right *Blue*, visioning foundation icon suggests researchers working independently. We find these cultures in research laboratories and research universities.

The lower-right *Orange*, directing foundation's icon suggests process and efficiency. This is the culture of most companies since most consumers buy lowest cost or best value. I believe that more than 80 percent of business cultures are *Orange*.

FIGURE 7.2   Icons for the Four Cultures

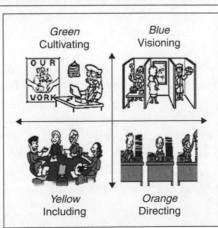

Green
Cultivating

Blue
Visioning

Yellow
Including

Orange
Directing

Note the communications style in the icon of the visioning foundation and compare it to the diagonal including culture's icon. Which prefers e-mail? Which prefers face-to-face communications?

I worry that the world is moving evermore to an exclusively *Orange*, directing culture every year. We increasingly buy commodities, goods that are largely undifferentiated except by price. I can remember when it was interesting to travel around the United States and visit different shops. Now, the same mass-market shops are in every airport, every mall, and every country. As the 4-D diagrams display, we seem to be losing *Green* core values, such as empathy for others, in favor of *Orange* greed. The change will come, and I cannot foretell how.

The *Blue* Project Team That Could Not Complete

Recall the story of the late-phase NASA contractor project team that could not bring project activities to closure. The root cause was that the project's *Blue*, visioning leaders were acting out their attention needs and resistance to closure.

Later in that workshop, I used the material in this chapter to diagnose the team's culture. Not surprisingly, their culture was also overwhelmingly *Blue*. I started the third workshop day saying, "I have felt really tired during this workshop, and I want to talk with you about why. This is going to take about ten minutes and I am asking you not to interrupt me until I finish. I am not sure that all of you are able do this, but I am asking."

Heads nodded and I continued, "Every time I try to move this workshop forward, one of you raises your hand and interrupts me in the middle of a sentence or the middle of a slide. It feels like hitting a barrier that drains my momentum." I demonstrated this at the same time by walking across the room and after a few steps, pretending as though I was actually hitting a wall. "I was losing all my energy in pushing this workshop forward in the face of sustained interruptions."

I pointed to their culture diagnostics, which we recorded on flip charts. "This is your trouble. You smart, energetic, and talented *Blue* people are stuck in your *Blue*, visioning culture when your team should be moving to the *Orange*, directing culture. You are resisting this change just as surely as you are resisting my attempts to advance the workshop flow."

I continued: "I understand your problem in completing this project. You are just doing what visioning personalities do in visioning cultures. You are busy showing each other how smart you are, while resisting *Orange* management control and authority. I know this is true because it is what I experience from you also. I have made these assertions to see if my diagnosis is correct." You could have heard a pin drop. Nobody said anything. I had nailed it.

After a pause, I continued with the workshop materials. The interruptions ceased. I felt myself gaining energy steadily and felt great by the time the workshop finished. Our overall "smiley sheet" score was 8.9 on a 1-to-10 scale. The NASA project manager gave us a 10. (These scores are not important, although they feel good when they are high. What really matters is how our work raises *Team* and *Individual Development Assessment* scores.)

This is very interesting. I provided a strong dose of *Orange* and the overdone *Blues* stopped acting out. I provided a brief prescription for success in a prior chapter. The project's drama played out pretty much as I expected. The problems continued, management removed the leader, and placed the team under extreme *Orange* organizational leadership. Slowly and painfully, the culture moved *Orange* and the project moved toward orderly completion.

Some Culture Inquiries

Just as in our innate personality work, we need to locate the dominant or lead dimension of the culture. We can then investigate the following questions.

- Does your team's culture foundation match your customer's foundation? If not, competitors that match your customer's culture will take business away from you.
- Where does the culture foundation of your home institution (that is, the larger company) lie? If your team or organization's culture does not match your home institution's culture, you must take special effort to feed the institution's culture or you risk annihilation.
- If everything matches up, that is great! The danger, however, is that your lead dimension becomes so overdone that your diagonal

shrinks, limiting performance. You must be vigilant in protecting the diagonal. If, for example, your culture is *Blue*, visioning,
you risk collapsing the *Yellow*, including dimension. People then
relate in ways that alienate others and impede collaboration. If
your culture is *Orange*, directing, you risk collapsing the *Green*,
cultivating culture. People then feel treated like objects.

Blue or *Orange* Culture Foundation

Teams doing the work of business organizations and government
entities like NASA have their culture leads in the *Orange* or *Blue*.
Therefore, you can use the following questionnaire in Figure 7.3 to
locate your culture's lead. As with the personality foundation exploration, choose how things actually are (not how you would like them

FIGURE 7.3   *Blue or Orange* **Culture Diagnostic**

1) Our team grants the most power to:	
Exceptionally capable thinkers/ wizards	Managers at the top of the org chart
2) Our collaboration processes are:	
Argumentative without concern for ruffled feelings	Organized by our processes and management systems
3) Our team most values:	
Creativity and excellence over process and certainty	Process and certainty over creativity and excellence
4) Our team's decision processes are driven by:	
Our technical experts	Our management
5) Our office management/admin processes are:	
Haphazard and disorganized	Rigorous and documented
6) Our member's personal behaviors are:	
Chaotic and sometimes frustrating	Disciplined and tightly organized

FIGURE 7.4   Lead Culture Results Table

Results Summary	Team A Blue	Team A Orange	Team B Blue	Team B Orange
1) Our team grants the most power to:				
2) Our collaboration processes are:				
3) Our team most values:				
4) Our team's decision processes:				
5) Our office management/admin processes:				
6) Our member's personal behaviors are:				

to be) in your current team or organization. Draw a circle around your choice. Notice that *Blue* is on the left, and *Orange* is on the right.

Then transfer your results into the "Team A" column in the Figure 7.4 table.

Now, repeat the scoring for your sponsor/customer placing the score in the "Team B" column. If you have mismatches, compare the two columns to find your highest-leverage change opportunities.

Drawing Your Team's Culture Diagram

Begin by drawing your lead as *Blue* or *Orange* with a large arc as in Figure 7.5. The example on the right is for an *Orange*, directing culture. Next, assume that the other logical-side foundation is strong as

FIGURE 7.5   Sample Culture Diagram

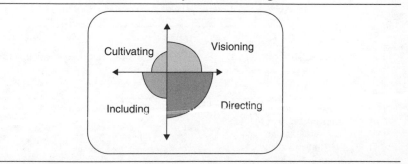

well, so we draw the next largest arc in the *Blue*, visioning dimension in the diagram.

Now, it is a safe assumption that the diagonal *Green*, cultivating dimension is the weakest. Finish with an intermediate-sized arc in the including dimension.

If your score was *Blue*, perform the same process with the largest arc in the visioning dimension. We now investigate the characteristics of each of the four culture foundations. For many years, we independently measured all four dimensions with more complex tools. When the results never departed from the pattern of *Blue* or *Orange* with the weakness in the lead's diagonal, we simplified the measurement. Fundamentally, the location of the lead is most important.

Green, Cultivating Cultures: Accommodate Members' Values

My only teambuilding experience with a *Green*, cultivating foundation culture was in a workshop for the Colorado State Mental Health Board, which I described in the previous chapter. Interfacing with the *Orange*, directing culture of the government's funding organizations was the biggest challenge for this *Green* culture.

The challenge for these cultures found in non-profits, churches, and business human resource entities is the diagonal *Orange* organization. There is a discussion later in this chapter on enhancing *Orange* in a culture. Figure 7.6 illustrates 4-D analysis of cultivating cultures.

The organization chart's tilt in the lower right conveys weak management control typical of these cultures. Churches, for example, often depend on volunteer labor.

FIGURE 7.6   4-D Analysis of Cultivating Cultures

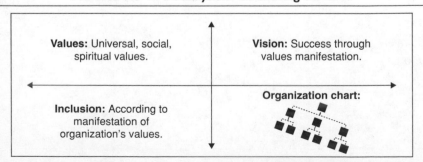

Values: Universal, social, spiritual values.

Vision: Success through values manifestation.

Inclusion: According to manifestation of organization's values.

Organization chart:

Yellow, Including Cultures: Accommodate Group Relational Needs

Some years ago, I joined a group of consultants who wanted to intentionally build an including culture. We thought this would help us attract consulting clients. Our meetings were monthly in Denver. We spent the first hour chatting about whatever people wanted to talk about—the Broncos, the skiing, where outdoor clothes were on sale. This was maddening for me. This *Yellow*, including context did not fit my (diagonal) *Blue*, visioning personality. Figure 7.7 illustrates 4-D analysis of cultivating cultures.

After several meetings, I became frustrated with our lack of progress. One day, just before lunch, I walked up to a flip chart and drew a standard hierarchal organization chart. I began to place roles and assignments in each box with another person as the head of the entire organization. Some of the meeting participants became visibly distressed. I thought I heard one say, "control freak," under his breath. I suggested we break for lunch while I pondered what to do.

After lunch I said, "Let's give this another go." I drew the circular organization chart in the previous figure, and began to fill in the same roles as before. Everybody was happy. In the circular configuration, the discomfort of hierarchy was gone.

Ricardo Semler wrote a most interesting book about an including business culture (1995). He describes a Brazilian company that manufactured customized pumps. This product matched the culture foundation. Employees rated their supervisor's performance, which is opposite from the usual practice. People took turns being CEO. The company was very successful until the Brazilian economy collapsed, according to Mr. Semler.

FIGURE 7.7   4-D Analysis of Including Cultures

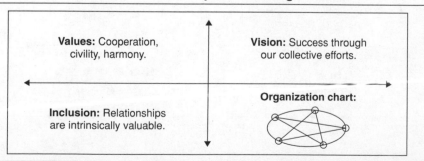

Of course, the challenge for these cultures is in the diagonal *Blue*. They need to develop greater tolerance for dissention and conflict.

Blue, Visioning Cultures: Accommodate Individual Experts' Needs

My direct experience with a *Blue*, visioning culture was as faculty in the University of Colorado's business school. Their culture diagnostic scored almost 100 percent in the *Blue*, visioning dimension. When I first arrived at the university, a NASA colleague was simultaneously leaving. He said to me, "The hardest thing for you to deal with is that the organization chart is upside down. The wizards have the power here. I am so frustrated in getting anything done." Indeed, it was surely true. I watched the dean or president take a position on some matter. The most prestigious faculty would often oppose the action and a deluge of e-mail would ensue. By the end of the day, the idea was dead. Figure 7.8 illustrates 4-D analysis of visioning cultures.

In addition to my teaching duties, I was strategic advisor to the dean. I asked him to describe the dean's role. He said, "The president's job is to make speeches, and the faculty's role is to think. The dean's job is to make sure that the faculty doesn't make speeches and that the president doesn't think."

FIGURE 7.8   4-D Analysis of Visioning Cultures

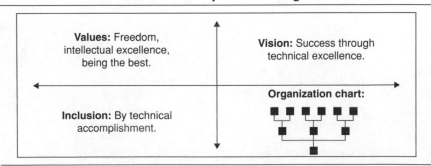

Orange, Directive Cultures: Accommodate Management's Needs

In Boulder, Colorado, where I live (the very *Green* People's Republic of Boulder), there is great concern about large *Orange*, directing culture companies displacing local favorites. Nearby, in Superior, the simultaneous construction of a Home Depot and Lowes closed a 150-year-old hardware store. People worry that Barnes and Noble and the like will close the locally owned Boulder Book Store. Figure 7.9 illustrates 4-D analysis of directing cultures.

The airline industry interests me as I fly many thousands of miles per year on United Airlines. Airlines are an extreme example of the directing culture. Numbers and process drive everything. Ask a flight attendant why he or she is on a particular flight doing a particular service. They will say, "My choices are all governed by my seniority number."

Is the directing culture the right culture for an airline? Would you fly on Innovation Airlines? What if the pilot announced, "We aren't sure if these new engines will work or not. But, if they do, we will arrive 30 minutes early." We would scramble to get off the plane.

What is the diagonal weakness of the directing culture? One-dimensional directing cultures fail to see people as people and do not empathize with their needs. I do not often have an opportunity to speak with people on strike. During the summer of 2000, United's pilots went on an informal strike with a devastating slowdown.

FIGURE 7.9   4-D Analysis of Directing Cultures

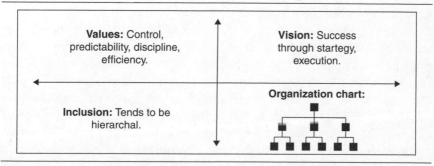

I frequently went into the cockpit and talked with the pilots before the flight. I asked, "What's this slowdown really about?" Their answers were always the same: "It's not really about the money. It's about a lack of trust with the management and feeling unappreciated." (Do you recall what people most want at work?) United's culture apparently is one dimensional with the same performance limitations as 1-D directing leaders.

In contrast, similarly *Orange* Southwest Airlines uses fourdimensionality to create competitive advantage. Jody Hoffer Gittell writes (2003), "Southwest's most powerful organizational competency—the 'secret ingredient' that makes it so distinctive—is its ability to build and sustain high performance relationships among managers, employees, unions, and suppliers. Shared goals, shared knowledge, and mutual respect characterize these relationships . . . organizational processes build and sustain strong relationships among those who are critical to the organization's success." Three of Southwest's 10 practices are 1) lead with credibility and caring; 2) invest in frontline leadership; and 3) hire and train for relational competence.

Give the Directing Culture What It Craves

The directing culture dominates both the business world and projects in the implementation phase (where most of the money is spent). Moreover, 80 percent of American CEOs are *Orange* personalities. The reason is obvious. Cultures reward people who manifest their values. The directing culture is all about control. Control is so important in this culture that it is essential to appear to be in control. One way to demonstrate control is by having deep knowledge readily available. I recall an old Bob Newhart joke that may be useful.

A man agreed to take care of his neighbor's dog while he was on vacation. After the neighbor left, the man opened the door and walked into the kitchen. A giant dog suddenly appeared, leaping behind him and blocking the only exit. The dog approached menacingly, snarling and drooling. Terrified, the man backed up slowly as the dog advanced. He reached back, felt a bag on the counter and reached inside. "Thank god," he thought when he realized the bag had dog biscuits inside. He threw one to the dog who quickly ate it. A few seconds later, however, the dog advanced again. He threw another and another.

The situation was now under control. There was, however, a problem. He was running out of biscuits.

Here is the relevance of this story. You must never run out of data biscuits to feed the directing culture's data dog! You must provide the endless detailed data that the culture requires to sustain the appearance of control.

A colleague told me about a speech the head of NASA Space Science made to the Jet Propulsion Laboratory staff when satellite launching resumed after Challenger. Reportedly, he said, "Here's what I most ask of you. Never make me say, 'I didn't know.'" It is interesting that he chose these words instead of "Here's what I most ask of you, succeed." He said what he did because he knew that they would do all they could to succeed without him asking. Moreover, the culture could tolerate his failure, but could not tolerate the appearance that he was not fully knowledgeable and, by inference, not in control.

Building *Orange* from the Bottom Up

The vast majority of business cultures are *Orange*. Ford, Microsoft, United Airlines, you name it, all are *Orange* at their core with an emphasis on providing consistent, price-competitive products. There is, of course, an obvious exception: Entrepreneurial, start-up companies all start *Blue*, necessitating transition to *Orange* as they grow and mature. This transition requires shifting power from the geniuses who created them to the broader staff using organizational charts, delegated authority, and processes. Trust me; this is much more difficult than it appears from afar. I worked to *Orange* up a *Blue* financial firm. It took many months to get broad agreement on an org chart with clear, unambiguous lines of authority. Early versions had 45-degree lines and many boxes with multiple lines.

In fact, we often find implementation projects, businesses, and proposal teams that need to *Orange* up to succeed. For example, a proposal team for a very large program contacted me early in the process. Then, I heard nothing for a year. Surprisingly, with two months remaining, they called and asked me to begin work with them. The team's personality measurements revealed that the proposal manager and many members were *Green*. Moreover, the leader's personal disorganization showed that he was not just *Green* but 1-D *Green*. Recall how the positive personality traits of personality foundations morph into undesirable ones when people are one dimensional. For example, he rescheduled our planned teleconferences repeatedly up to the day before. Interestingly, the widely held view in the industry was that this company was sure to win.

After the culture analysis above showed total incoherence about whether the team had a *Blue* or *Orange* culture, I concluded their culture lead must be *Green*. I brought their leadership team together and said, "You are going to lose. In this stressful environment, you have no possibility of winning because you will offer a *Green* proposal to one of the deepest *Orange* cultures in NASA. Your only hope is an immediate change of team leader to a 4-D *Orange* personality." They would not act. Moreover, they forbade me from discussing the situation with upper management. They continued to work a vast army of people to prepare their proposal, and I went back to Boulder.

I was in Europe as the announcement of the winner of this huge program drew near. The International Herald Tribune reported daily that the announcement was imminent. They also predicted that the company I had worked with would win. Finally, a headline story reported their loss as a big surprise. I was not surprised. I am guessing that they spent $50 million to $100 million on the proposal.

If I had started work earlier and they changed out the team leader and other key positions, I would have worked with them using our standard processes to *Orange* up at three levels:

1. Personal level: Disciplined, controlled, organized; showing up on time; performing their work on time; avoiding crises modes, working the number of hours per week within their informal contract; maintaining clean home-work boundaries;

2. Administrative level: Clear, documented roles, accountability, and authority; communicated administrative processes with designated owners for all resource allocations including compensation; and

3. Creating customer value level: Driven by processes with named owners (e.g., project management processes, customer interface management processes, and R&D processes).

Of course, you must build *Orange* in a way that protects and sustains the *Green*, *Yellow*, and *Blue* subcultures. An *Orange* organization will yield few benefits with employees who do not feel appreciated or included, and lack the hope of a realistic and positive future.

Supporting Vital Subcultures

Just as leadership effectiveness requires four dimensionality, every team or organization needs to sustain the other three subcultures. *Orange* organizations, for example, need to avoid the tendency to make subcultures adopt *Orange* values and processes.

- You require *Blue* subcultures for research, generating new products and processes. *Orange* management methods would limit their creativity.

- You require *Yellow* subcultures for marketing, building good customer relations (and congressional relations). Too much *Orange* will sour them and their important relationships.

- You require *Green* subcultures to develop teams and individuals. Companies often name these organizations' "human resources." (Can you see how *Orange* that name is?) Too much *Orange* will frustrate these cultures and the *Green* personalities within them. The best people will leave if they can.

On the other hand, these subcultures must adequately feed the *Orange* culture foundation's data-dog to survive. Meeting *Orange* culture's demands is most difficult for the diagonal *Green* subcultures. My clients commonly complain about lack of timely response from human resource organizations. One joked about a human resource person, "The reason Fred never gets anything done is that he's always so busy." Awareness and acceptance of the valuable differences across subculture interfaces is essential for all parties to succeed.

Finally, I note that the good alignment of four core organizational functions (HR/employee development, marketing, new product development, and management) with the four dimensions is another nice corroboration of the validity of the 4-D System.

4-D Organization of Proposals

Jack Welch said, "If you can't create competitive advantage, don't compete." I say, "If you can't match cultures, don't compete." During 4-D System's early days, a friend asked me to visit his aerospace company. He explained that he had formed a committee of the best and brightest scientists to help them choose which proposals to submit into a broad competition. He had assured his management that their proposals would rank very high and that NASA would select at least two. These proposals were for $400 million science missions.

When the results came in, NASA had selected none of their proposals. Further, their rankings were very low. His vice president was extremely angry and directed him to get a new group of scientists for the next round. He told me he was proposing me as a candidate for this group and asked if I would meet with the VP. He warned me that I should expect a hostile reception.

On the bright side, a limo would take me to and from the airport, and the company would wine and dine me in style. 4-D Systems was just beginning, with start-up costs using all the revenue. On balance, this trip looked good, so I agreed to go. True to his word, the night before the meeting we ate and drank like gluttons in a very fine restaurant. I woke up at 3 AM wondering what in the world I would say to this hostile VP. I thought, when in doubt apply the 4-D System to the situation, and went back to sleep.

I opened the meeting by drawing the 4-D System on the whiteboard and said, "Tell me about the four proposals you submitted." Each was a scientific marvel pushing the budget envelope even at this early stage of definition. (I learned to multiply this kind of early estimate by π to see the end cost.) As they described each proposal, I made a large "X" in the upper right indicating a deep *Blue*, visioning proposal.

Then I said, "Tell me what the government selected." They went on about "how stupid the selections were" with "off-the-shelf hardware," "limited science," and "low probable-cost estimates." I was making a large "O" in the far lower right *Orange*, directing Dimension as they described each winning proposal.

I continued, "Do you see what happened? You proposed 'science excellence,' and the government picked 'certainty of result.'" They were in awe of the power of this simple analysis. Then I asked, "Do you know why you did what you did? You followed the advice of your very *Blue* science advisory panel."

They responded as losing proposal teams usually do. They blamed the customer saying, "NASA lied to us." I came back with the greatest mantra of all time: "So what." "Look," I continued, "You basically have two choices. You can market the customer adequately to determine how to write a proposal that will match the decision maker's culture, or place two proposals in *Blue*, visioning and two in *Orange*, directing.

The VP was actually delighted, and I subsequently supported many of his proposal teams. I found I could spend an hour or so with the diagnostic tools in *How NASA Builds Teams* and reliably predict if they were going to win with what they were doing or not. Much more important, I could tell them how to win. My clients found this incredibly valuable. Everything you need to match your culture to your customer is in this book.

Matching Proposal Team Culture to Customer

The following case studies demonstrate how winning can be nearly impossible if your proposal team's culture does not match your customer's. As the adage says, "The fish can't see the water." In each case, the critical error was selecting a leader with an innate personality misaligned with the customer's culture. The leader then staffed with many same-color people. Under stress we tend to do what we know how to do and we choose to do it with people just like us. We thus, consciously or unconsciously, build the invisible magnetic field that changes how we perceive reality. Under stress, we choose actions that match the context of our team culture, not our customer's culture. Let us examine the perils of failing to align your local culture with your customer's.

Case Study I—A Space-Based Laser Proposal

Here is a case study of a space-based laser proposal—a satellite using a laser beam to destroy enemy missiles. To practice recognizing customer cultures, look at each statement below and identify its dimension. I have provided the easy answers in italics. I have made you the client in each case, evaluating your prospect.

- You are feeling good about proposing; you have the world's greatest laser wizards/scientists in your company. *(Visioning Dimension)*
- Mr. Congressman wants a demonstration of "flaming wreckage" ASAP, and you hear he may insert himself into the selection process. *(Directing Dimension)*
- Mr. Congressman pressured your customer, Mr. Air Force, to fund this demonstrator. Mr. Air Force believes other items are of

higher priority. He wants the demonstration as cheap as possible and has staffed with managers focused on cost/schedule performance. *(Directing Dimension)*

- You quickly charge your Mr. Leader to form a proposal team comprising your brightest and most innovative people. *(Visioning Dimension)*
- You hear that your competition has put a seasoned manager in charge, Ms. OC, who is pushing a plain-Jane approach. *(Directing Dimension)*
- You have the advanced technology for the 21st-century system. However, no financially viable model for an operational system exists. *(Visioning Dimension)*
- Your people are confident. The Air Force technical wizards love your advanced, large deployable system concept. *(Visioning Dimension filter)*

What is the root problem here? You selected a (1-D) *Blue*, visioning personality to lead your team. He then selected *Blue* people like himself to staff the team. The proposal team built a *Blue* culture field and happily wrote a *Blue* proposal.

However, the decision makers totally align with your competition's team, leaders, and design approach in the *Orange* culture of the directing dimension. The team members understood the mismatch at some level, lowering the social context and exacerbating the behaviors toward 1-D *Blue*. Can you win this competition? I believe you cannot, unless your competitor stumbles badly. You surely cannot count on that. Their cultural alignment with the customer gives the other team an overwhelming advantage.

When I presented my analysis with the 4-D diagrams, my client understood immediately. They approached the competition and negotiated a technology role in a partnership. Then, together they convinced the sponsor that a national team (that is, both contractors working together) was best for the country. Then my client received the *Blue* work they wanted all along, and the other company received the *Orange* leadership role they wanted. The alternative was to spend a lot of money on a losing bid.

Case Study 2—A Telescope Proposal

Let us try another one.

- Mr. Customer wants an 8-meter cool (30 degrees Kelvin) telescope in deep space for $500 million. (Hubble was 2.4 meters, room temperature, and cost $1.7 billion!) *(Visioning Dimension)*

- The best and brightest scientists populate Mr. Customer's team. They have intellectual air superiority in the project. *(Visioning Dimension)*

- You really want to win this contract, so you put your Mr. Manager, who recently finished a complex astronomy telescope, in charge. He selects experienced engineers for his team. *(Directing Dimension)*

- Mr. Customer sees advanced technology as the only path to success. Conventional design solutions are backups. *(Visioning Dimension)*

- Your team knows better. Proven approaches are the right ones. *(Directing Dimension)*

- Your team believes the most detailed technical proposal will win. Although the details increasingly show the financial implausibility of the customer's vision, you press ahead. *(Directing Dimension)*

- Your competitor puts a scientist with no hardware experience in charge. He is promoting risky, high-promise solutions. *(Visioning Dimension)*

- You are sure that these will not appeal to the customer and that he will soon come to his senses and choose your expensive conventional design. *(Directing Dimension)*

Can you win? I think not. You have gathered a team of *Orange* people, just like yourself, and created an *Orange* culture.

Your customer and your competition are both *Blue*. Therefore, you will not win unless they stumble badly, which they are not likely to do. My client, the *Orange* proposal team leader, told me that he understood and thanked me for my analysis. He then asked me to brief the teammates. I did and everybody confirmed my viewpoint. We agreed that the proposal would offer *Blue* innovative, low-cost solutions as the baseline with *Orange* conventional methods as back ups. I went off to do other things for a few months.

The team leader called me when the proposal was nearly complete and asked me to participate in a *"Red team"* review. *Red* teams compare proposals with the customer's requirements as stated in the request for proposals. As I read what they had written, I was astounded. They had written it with the *Orange* conventional solutions as the baseline, with lip service to *Blue* innovative approaches as back-ups. "What are you doing?" I asked. "You wrote it backward. You will lose." They had no comprehension of what I was saying. "Do you remember the 4-D analysis I presented to you?" They said, "Of course we remember it." Yet, they could not see their misguided approach.

This was so interesting. Their *Orange* culture was so strong that they could not see the difficulty. Apparently, their culture had altered their perception more powerfully than the Asch experiment. I had to show them the problematic statements line-by-line with a *Yellow* highlighter. Then, they changed their approach and won that program phase.

There was one more final competition in this process for the ultimate development contract award. The project's culture was moving from *Blue* to *Orange* at a rate impossible to determine from outside. We decided on a hybrid strategy that offered greater performance to *Blues* with more conservative design margins for *Oranges*.

The lesson is that you must match your proposal team culture to your customer's to assure a win. Proposal teams are short duration and ad-hoc. The most effective approach is to choose a leader with a personality aligned with the proposing customer's culture. For technical work, the culture must be *Blue* or *Orange*. You can always use the simple test instrument in Figure 7.3 with the table in Figure 7.4 to measure your proposal team's culture.

Cultures Must Change as Projects Mature

As discussed earlier, projects, be they space missions or new home construction, move through similar distinct phases. Projects begin with a formulation phase, advisedly led by *Blue* architects performing *Blue* culture's trade studies. As the project matures, they must adopt an *Orange* builder's culture. We occasionally encounter project teams in the midst of this transition.

Teams in transition experience low-grade, chronic conflict. The *Blue*, visioning culture is reluctantly yielding power to the *Orange*, directing culture. Spokespersons for each culture aggressively challenge the other. The *Blue*, visioning culture people say, "If you think we scientists will agree to anything less than the best you can do, you are nuts." The *Orange*, directing culture people say, "If we managers don't freeze the requirements now and get on with this, the project will be canceled as the cost estimate rises." After a while, these conversations turn personal. The gift of 4-D insights is recognition that the argument is not personal, but structural. If you removed a troublesome person speaking for one side or the other, someone else would step up. You have a culture foundation in conflicted transition.

What happens when a directing culture contracts for work with a visioning culture that never transitions? I mentioned that Hubble had one exceedingly difficult system specification. This was to point the body axis of the telescope to an arbitrary location in space with a stability of 0.007 arc-seconds for 24 hours at a time. Recall that seven milli-arc-seconds is the angle a 25-cent coin makes at a distance of 200 miles.

My predecessors told me that the technical requirements were so daunting they feared that no contractor would submit a bid. What culture would sign on for such a difficult task? A deep *Blue*, visioning culture would sign on, of course.

How Hubble Launched with a Flawed Mirror

Marshall Space Flight Center in Huntsville, Alabama, has a Germanic tradition. Wernher von Braun, the developer of German rocketry during World War II, was the first center director. Thus, the culture of the center surely tends toward *Orange*, directing culture.

The company PerkinElmer (P-E) won the contract for the optical telescope assembly (OTA), including the very challenging fine guidance sensors that pointed and stabilized the telescope. The only people who would be comfortable tackling such a difficult technical job would be *Blue*, visioning leaders and culture.

Therefore, the Hubble project began in 1977 with an overdone *Orange* culture at NASA/Marshall working with an overdone *Blue* culture at P-E. As is typical of early phase projects, everyone is happy to be under way and stress is low. NASA told P-E, "You won!" P-E responds with "Thanks."

As in *all* large, complex projects, Hubble's costs were underestimated. The growing overruns drive everyone's stress dramatically upward. How do you imagine the overdone directing culture responds to increasing stress? Do these directing-mindset people say to the *Blue*, visioning contractor (where people are doing most of the real work), "We see that you are struggling? Would it help if we were to get off your back and let you work?"

As you know, nothing of the sort occurs. Under stress, we become more 1-D of who we already are. The directing culture unknowingly and thoughtlessly expands into more directing, ignoring the other three dimensions. The data-dog's hunger increases dramatically. Criticism of the contractor becomes ever more aggressive.

How does the overdone visioning culture respond to the perceived attacks and demand for more food for the data-dog? Do they say, "You now want a lot more data? We are happy to give it to you. Generating a lot more management data seems like a good use of our time. We are glad to help." You know better; this does not happen.

As Hubble's technical and cost problems increased so did frustration (a nice word for anger) through the NASA chain of command. Marshall then dropped the thermonuclear bomb on P-E. They told them that if they did not complete the mirror on cost and on spec, they would put Kodak's back-up mirror in the telescope. This was deeply insulting to P-E.

P-E took protective action. At that time, the overwhelming majority of the Danbury, Connecticut, plant's work was highly classified. This was at a peak of the Cold War. The three-letter agencies (CIA, NSA, NRO . . .) did not like having NASA people around. NASA classifies almost nothing, and NASA people speak openly about anything and everything. Very few NASA people had the clearance that these classified programs required. It was easy for P-E to make plant access difficult for NASA personnel. I recall feeling uncomfortable when I visited the P-E plant. It was a bit spooky.

Time went on, costs grew, and P-E just could not seem to complete the optical telescope assembly. Finally, we dispatched a large team from Marshall to take residence in the P-E plant and manage the people. Jerry Richardson led this effort. I called him after he was there for a while and asked him what the problem was. He said, "Our problem is that we can't get people, paper, and parts in the right place at the right time." Is there a better statement regarding lack of an *Orange*, directing culture? The OTA finally finished and went to Sunnyvale, California, to integrate with the Lockheed spacecraft.

The most important message in this story is that we talked frequently with the P-E management about a culture mismatch. We tried many things. We changed out managers doing unnecessary damage to them and their careers because we did not understand the potency of culture as context. This seems almost childish given the understandings in this book.

At one point, P-E named an including personality as the NASA interface. Clearly, this was not the answer. If we had had 4-D diagrams back then, we could have saved hundreds of millions of dollars. We would have grasped the real problem in minutes. All we needed was to place strong P-E *Orange* directing leaders in charge of their effort. Then, they could inexorably move the P-E culture to where it needed to go—to *Orange*, directing. If we had the whole 4-D System back then, we would have assessed the teams and individuals, tipped them back to healthy functioning, and never had a flawed mirror!

As I said earlier, NASA held me blameless when we discovered the flawed mirror because I was not working in Astrophysics when P-E manufactured the flawed mirror. It took me several years to realize that I was as culpable as the technician who spaced the null corrector incorrectly. I was in charge of NASA Astrophysics during the period when P-E withheld the measurements that suggested we had a mirror problem. I was a full party to creating Hubble's flawed social context.

An Application Summary for Cultures

Every team or organization has an unseen force that acts on members of teams and organizations as surely as magnetic fields align iron particles. Fortunately, we can use the 4-D System to characterize cultures into one of four types analogous to individual's innate personalities.

The leader's innate personality often defines the culture of ad-hoc teams like proposal teams, as we tend to choose to associate with people like ourselves. Project team cultures need to be *Blue* in early phases, and move to *Orange* as projects mature if they are to work efficiently. Founders' personalities and core marketing strategy drive the culture of large organizations. Business cultures are predominately *Orange* because consumers mostly buy products differentiated by price or value.

You have several options to change your culture. First, use the material in this chapter to select the culture you need to succeed—cultivating, including, visioning, or directing. Then proceed on two fronts.

1. Select leaders and team members with innate personalities that match the required culture. Then, use the culture characterization tool in this chapter to check the alignment with *Blue* or *Orange*. Technical teams usually have one of these logical-side cultures.

2. Look at the scores for each of the six factors you measured in Figure 7.3. Then, work on the factor most out of alignment. For example, Factor 1 is "Who you give power to." Your choices are *Blue*, the wizards, or *Orange*, the hierarchal leaders.

If you want more *Orange*, develop the infrastructure—organization charts, assigned and delegated roles, accountability and authority (RAAs measured in both team and individual assessments)—and operate that way.

If you want more *Blue*, deemphasize structure and reward people more for technical excellence than hierarchy in the organization.

Finally, work toward more *Blue* or *Orange* on three levels as discussed in the previous section on becoming more *Orange*: the personal level, the administrative level, and the creating customer value level.

CHAPTER 8

Incoherent Project Mindset Colors? Update Your Resume

How important is this short chapter? I put it this way: If you get this wrong, customers will name you incompetent no matter what else you do. John Casani, one of NASA Jet Propulsion Laboratory's greatest project managers, showed me a presentation on this subject some years ago. He began with, "I wanted to explain why some project managers are fired when cost goes from $400 million to $410 million and others get medals for projects that go from $350 million to $750 million." (Note: John's presentation was based on a 1993 NASA study called Science Systems Contract Study by CSP Associates.) I adapted his ideas into the 4-D framework.

Our work emphasizes projects because this is where most organizations, from aerospace to drug companies, create value. Simply put, projects are activities with start and stop dates that produce products in distinct, usually defined, phases. If you have little interest in projects, you might skip ahead to the next chapter.

Basic Project Management

Figure 8.1 shows the Project Manager's Triangle with *Blue* performance on the top and an *Orange* base with cost on one side and schedule on the other side. In the simplest terms, project and program managers trade cost, performance, and schedule within an envelope of acceptable risk.

FIGURE 8.1 Project Manager's Triangle

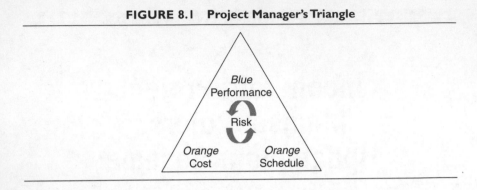

Project Mindsets Drive Project Structure

Technical teams adopt an *Orange*, directing or *Blue*, visioning mindset early in a project by choice or default. This choice is very important as structures and procedures that work for one mindset are inappropriate for the other. Here are some areas that are markedly different for each of the two mindsets:

- Definition of success: for *Orange* it is meeting cost (and schedule) commitments, and for *Blue* it is breathtaking performance;

- Risk acceptability: *Orange* projects are more willing to risk ultimate performance in favor of cost control than *Blue* projects;

- Process ownership and control: *Orange* projects tend to have more managerial oversight and process imposition (e.g., earned value management) than *Blue* projects;

- Incentive structures/performance evaluation criteria: *Orange* projects have more incentives for cost and schedule, and *Blue* projects have more incentives for meeting or exceeding requirements; and

- How participants communicate: *Orange* projects have well-documented and rigorous documentation processes. Compliance with these processes and the hierarchical management structure is absolute. *Blue* projects value transmission of information above process, and informal channels are routinely used.

The *Blue* Performance Mindset

In the *Blue* mindset, performance is in the driver's seat, cost trails along behind, and schedule is flexible unless set by other factors such as a planetary launch window or the need to replace a failing weather satellite. The *Blue* performance mindset freely spends money to reduce risk.

Sponsors grumble and often fire project managers for overruns. The money, however, keeps coming. Cost growth over the life cycle of a *Blue* major space program of a factor of two or three from early estimates is usual. Sponsors see the result as worthy of the ultimate cost. Cost is the dependent variable because cost increases to meet (or sometimes exceed) performance requirements.

Hubble, for example, began with an initial budget estimate of about $450 million and finished at $1.7 billion! The people involved experienced a lot of discomfort with an occasional firing. There was never any serious thought to canceling the program or increasing risk by, for example, omitting system tests. *Blue* customers and their desire for maximal returns were firmly in the driver's seat.

The *Orange* Cost/Schedule Mindset

In the *Orange* mindset, cost is in the driver's seat while maintaining performance at the lowest acceptable level. Management minimizes schedule, as this minimizes cost. Risk creeps upward to save money if necessary. Sponsors of *Orange*, directing mindset projects fire project managers and cancel projects for relatively small cost growth. The sponsor's budget and concern for opportunity costs are in the driver's seat.

Consequences of a Confused/Wrong Mindset

Invite your team members to vote on how different stakeholders see the mindset of your project using 3×5 cards for confidential voting. (As stated previously, you can download the PowerPoint slide set for this chapter at www.4-DSystems.com.) Tally the votes and place them in a display like Figure 8.2, adding more columns if necessary for additional sponsors, teammates, subcontractors, and so on.

FIGURE 8.2   Performance vs. Cost across Stakeholders

	Our Team	Our Customer	Other
Performance			
Cost			

Occasionally some will argue for making schedule a third category along with performance and cost. I prefer not to do this because managers minimize schedule in the cost mindset and allow the schedule to be whatever is required in the performance mindset. However, occasionally people push hard, so then include it.

Participants do this exercise in 4-D workshops. The results are always interesting and often provocative. When I first introduced this simple diagnostic into our workshops, I thought it was rather benign. On the contrary, it has produced more drama than any other activity, as you will see in the examples below.

Incoherent Mindsets Risk a Large Space Program

I was working with the program office and two contractors on a multi-billion-dollar space program. Each participant filled out 3×5 cards as in the exercise above for all three entities. The results were shocking. Overwhelmingly, the group at large saw the two contractors as *Orange*, directing and the government program office as *Blue*, visioning. (We had identified the government's lead personality foundation as *Blue* earlier.) At this moment, everybody saw that the program would experience sustained overruns. He was a powerful personality driving his *Blue* mindset throughout his management team. Requirements would creep up and budgets would increase. Moreover, given the very large scale of the program, there would be massive, painful political consequences. That is exactly what happened until larger powers changed key personnel. (And, I presume put an *Orange* leader in charge.) Congress would surely have canceled the program except that it addressed an essential national need.

Incoherency Incites Drama

A project workshop was proceeding in an orderly manner until we performed this exercise. Interestingly, the project team scored themselves as mixed between *Blue* and *Orange*. One senior manager stood up and said, "I want to know who in this room believes the paradigm for this project is *Blue*, because I manage the most expensive part and I am 100 percent *Orange* in my actions." His boss, the project manager, stood up and said, "I scored it *Blue* because that's how I see it." Shouting ensued, and the senior manager left the workshop. (He returned later after several phone calls.)

The other senior manager began shouting as well, and he then went to the back of the room and lay on the floor acting as if someone was crucifying him. (I am not making this up.) These events attracted management attention and ultimately resulted in the replacement of the project manager. Once more, we see the incredible power of simple diagnostics to reveal underlying social context.

Under new management, the team's reassessment score moved up several quintiles. I do not believe, however, that the project ultimately survived. Perhaps, if we had done this work earlier, they would have had ultimate success.

An Application Summary for Project Mindsets

This exercise is very easy and revealing. Brief your project's teammates using the PowerPoint slides for this chapter that you download from www.4-DSystems.com.

Draw the diagram in Figure 8.2 on a flipchart, filling out the names like "customer" and "other" with the actual names you use. For NASA projects, I would likely label these "headquarters" (the customer), "project" (the NASA project office), and any contractors (separately identified by each contractor's name, especially if they have members present). Then give each person a 3×5 card and ask him or her to draw the same image. Then, ask them to vote putting an "x" in each location according to their view of the governing mindset/paradigm. Collect the cards and tally the (anonymous) votes on the flip chart. Rich discussions will surely follow.

PART IV

SHIFTING THE CONTEXT

These nine chapters are about how to improve your team's social context, and hence performance.

Chapter 9 explains the holistic Context Shifting Worksheet (CSW) discussed in the introduction. The CSW applies the entirety of the remainder of *How NASA Builds Teams* to ad-hoc situations.

Chapters 10 and 11 begin with the analysis of attitude into two manageable components. Chapter 10 is about how to manage your most powerful means to influence others, your expressions of thoughts. You will learn that most of what you say is not the truth since it is arguable. Therefore, you learn to speak *Green story-lines*. (no relation to the *Green* of the cultivating dimension). Chapter 11 teaches you how to categorize emotions into one of five groups. You can bring your team the energy it requires by expressing emotions from the appropriate group.

Chapters 12 through 18 teach mastery of the eight behaviors measured by team and individual assessments. The behaviors are:

- Chapter 12—Expressing Authentic Appreciation;
- Chapter 13—Addressing Shared Interests;
- Chapter 14—Appropriately Including Others;
- Chapter 15—Keeping Your Agreements;
- Chapter 16—Expressing Reality-Based Optimism and Being 100 Percent Committed;
- Chapter 17—Resisting Blaming and Complaining (and Rescuing or Rationalizing); and
- Chapter 18—Clarifying Roles, Accountability, and Authority

CHAPTER 9

The Context Shifting Worksheet (CSW)

4-D Senior Coach Alexandra Ross called me and said, "Charlie, I need to tell you that the CSW is the most amazing thing. I use it in more than 70 percent of my coaching calls."

This simple tool works amazingly well by shifting people's attention and mindsets for ad-hoc situations. I will take you through a real example. Figure 9.1 shows the CSW.

FIGURE 9.1 The Context Shifting Worksheet

Context Shifting Worksheet

1: SET THE STAGE:
• The Situation: _____
• The desired Outcome: _____
• My/our *story-lines* in play: _____
• Their *story-lines* in play: _____
• My/our feelings about this Situation: _____

2: CULTIVATING DIMENSION –Being Grateful	4: VISIONING DIMENSION –Being Creative
☑ What can I/we appreciate about the people/ situation?	☑ Any truths that need to be stated to move from optimism to hope?
☑ What do they want that I can want for them also?	☑ Outcomes we are 100% committed to?

3: INCLUDING DIMENSION –Being Authentic	5: DIRECTING DIMENSION –Response-able
☑ Who do we need to include in working this?	☑ Any drama states we need to avoid/exit?
☑ Agreements I we are committed to keeping? Broken agreements that need processing?	☑ Any individual/team-level RAA issues we need to address?

Specific actions/Requests I will take/make: _____

©4-D® Systems, 2009

CSW—A Proposal Team Prepares for Orals

Some years ago, I supported a contractor in a tough competition for a $1 billion contract. They were preparing for their final, oral presentation to the customer. My client asked me to take them through the Context Shifting Worksheet as preparation. I dialed into a telephone bridge at the agreed time. I had expected my client and perhaps one or two others. I realized that there were about 15 people on the teleconference, many of whom had no familiarity with 4-D.

I talked them through the Context Shifting Worksheet as follows.

- They described their situation as "We are in a very tough competition for a very large NASA program. Our competitor has had a virtual monopoly for years in this area."

- Next, they described their desired outcome as "We want to win." Then after a little prodding, they said, "We also want a good contract, one where we can please our customer, enjoy the working environment, and make a reasonable profit for our company."

- They named their *story-lines* in play (Chapter 10) as "We can win this with the right proposal—and it will not be easy."

- They named their customer's *story-lines* in play (also Chapter 10): "They see us as arrogant, and this does not help." We talked for a while about how to tone down the arrogance a bit.

- Their feelings about the situation were stated as follows "I guess we feel a bit anxious as this competition draws to a close." (You will learn in Chapter 11, "Manage Your Emotions to Manage Your Team's Energy," to categorize this as a scared-group emotion.)

I then had them draw a horizontal and vertical line on a piece of paper and explained the four dimensions. Here is an abbreviated summary of the work we did for the rest of the hour.

Beginning, as always, in the *Green*, cultivating dimension, I asked (Chapter 12), "What can you authentically appreciate about the customer?" The team lead quickly answered, "Nothing." I said, "Let me see if I have this right. You are making a presentation to gain a multiyear working relationship. Do you not think that they will discern that you do not value or appreciate them?" The team understood my message and after a few minutes we all wrote, "We appreciate the thoroughness and fairness of your evaluation process" in the *Green*, cultivating dimension on our papers.

We continued in the cultivating dimension with the shared interests inquiry, "What does the customer want that we can want for them also?" Soon we wrote, "A contractor who values the science from the mission as much as they do." (This led to a page in the written proposal with photographs of the bidder's key personnel with personal statements about valuing the mission's science returns.)

In the *Yellow*, including dimension, I asked, "Is there any way we can more appropriately include the customer (Chapter 14)?" Nobody had any instant ideas, so I then asked, "Do you have any broken agreements that you have not processed?" It took a few minutes to identify these. People took actions to process these using the back-into-integrity process described in Chapter 15.

In the *Blue*, visioning dimension, I asked, "How about some creative problem solving?" The team leader quickly spoke, "We don't have time for creativity. What's next?" Before I could say anything, a team member said, "Not so fast, I want to give this a try." I then asked, "Is there an uncomfortable truth that you have been unwilling to address?" Someone answered, "This is a very tough mission thermally, and our thermal engineers are not as good as the customer's." Someone else spoke saying, "I remember having a similar situation on a proposal. We acknowledged this and said that immediately after we won, we would bring our thermal team to meet with theirs and share knowledge. It worked then and it should work here." "Wow," I said, "You combined an 'inclusion,' an 'avoids truth withholding,' and 'appreciation' in one action!" We all continued to write. We continued to work through the remainder of the CSW, but I believe you get the idea.

So, how does the CSW process actually shift the context? The briefers make essentially the same briefings they prepared all along. However, they had powerfully shifted their *Attention* and *Mindsets*. For example, in the area of appreciation, they had filled an empty space with an authentic appreciation for the customer. I knew for sure that most of these shifts would reveal themselves in the natural course of events.

In fact, the orals went great. The customer selected my client in spite of having an essentially even technical score and higher probable cost. Proposals are the same as nearly everything else human.

We adopt a mindset and then select evidence that supports it. I believe that customers, more often than not, know which proposal they will select before they open the document. Here is another example.

Recovering $3 Million of Denied Fee

My industry VP friend, Jim, called me and asked for assistance. He was very upset. He had just returned from a meeting with a customer at the conclusion of a successful space mission. The reviews of his team's work had been favorable, although not perfect. There was $3 million of award fee remaining, and he expected to receive most if not all of this profit. The customer told him there would be no fee because they just discovered that a higher-than-expected roll rate in the satellite made the data more expensive to analyze. He asked my advice. He called me because he knew I had a long and excellent relationship with his customer. I suspect that what I told him surprised him. I said that it would be more effective to shift his frame of mind, or mindset, than my intervening with his customer. I explained how frames/mindsets trump facts in human dialogue. He had no hope of avoiding a power struggle in his current frame. (Charlie's two rules: 1) Avoid power struggles, and 2) Never power struggle if you do not have the power.)

He understood this and began work with one of our supercoaches, Alexandra Ross. They talked for an hour on the following Friday using the CSW. He received some weekend action items. They spoke for an hour the following Monday. The customer meeting took place on Wednesday. Jim left a message on my cell phone, "This is magic. I have most, if not all of the fee and a deeper relationship with the customer." (Alexandra's internal nickname ever since is "Magic.")

Applying the CSW to Your Situations

You can download PDF copies of the CSW (the same as the image in Figure 9.1) for your use from www.4-DSystems.com. You can also request a 4-D certified coach or consultant to guide you through the process or do it yourself. I believe that if you have read and internalized the core messages in *How NASA Builds Teams*, you can easily take your teammates through the CSW process.

Here are some typical applications:

- Any interpersonal difficulty;
- Any time you want to influence another entity (person or organization) to give you what you want (recall the previous examples regarding garnering profits and winning proposals);
- Any time you want to give a powerful speech (recall the analysis of presidents' speeches);
- Any time you want to deliver bad news (recall Skip's message: "When Dimensions are omitted, people under stress fill them with their most toxic emotions and most pathological *Storylines*."); and
- Any time the situation seems irresolvable and includes some kind of personal or organizational interface.

CHAPTER 10

Red Story-Lines Limit Team Performance

What Matters for Leadership Effectiveness

Several years ago, I read the following by Warren Bennis (1976): "The accumulated research . . . suggests there is not one single trait or characteristic that has any value in predicting leadership potentials, none, not even intelligence." This is interesting. If leadership effectiveness does not correlate with anything, how can we build effective team leaders? Is our quest hopeless?

Try this exercise. Write the names of great leaders that you admire on a sheet of paper. These people can be historical figures, relatives, colleagues at work and so on. It does not matter who you write, as this is only a set-up for the next step.

Next, make a list of several attributes that make (made) these people great leaders. Workshop participants generally write similar attributes, such as honest, courageous, visionary, good communicator, decisive, trustworthy, disciplined, organized, and compassionate.

Now, without a lot of thought, characterize each attribute as more about skills or more about attitudes. What do you discover? If you are like most people, you find that attitude is overwhelmingly more important.

I observe that most leadership training is about skills development. This is why people say, "Leaders are born, not made." Leadership development that focuses on *skills* when leadership effectiveness is about *attitudes* is unlikely to succeed. So, why don't more trainers teach attitude? I suspect that it is because they do not know how. Attitude is a somewhat mysterious, elusive notion. (We use the term "mindset" for attitude.) We will use the 4-D System to simplify attitudes/mindsets into two manageable components: thoughts and emotions.

He Just Could Not Delegate

When I worked at NASA Headquarters, the subordinates of one of my branch chiefs repeatedly complained to me that their boss never delegated work to them. The branch chief wanted to do everything himself, complaining at the same time about overwork. I spoke to him about delegating, and he promised to do better. There was, however, little improvement.

Therefore, I sent him to a class about delegating. The improvement was short lived. Then, I sent him to a longer class about delegation and management. The result was the same. Then, I sent him to a longer (six-week) course. The result was the same. (I am reminded of the adage, "The definition of insanity is doing the same thing over and over and expecting different results.")

Finally, I got it. The problem had nothing to do with his intellectual understanding of delegation. He was a bright scientist. It had to do with his *Attention* and *Mindsets*. Unfortunately, I did not have the technology at that time to shift them. We do now, using the 4-D System.

4-D Organization of Mindset

Once more, we use the 4-D System to simplify a vague notion like mindset into two entities we can characterize and manage. The result of placing the 4-D System on mindsets, displayed in Figure 10.1, reveals the underlying components as emotions and thoughts. The image conveys another important idea: We generate and manage our thoughts in the thin covering on top of our brains called the cerebral cortex. Emotions, in contrast are body sensations that often correlate with specific body locations. Stress, for example, can manifest in tightening of one's jaw.

We begin with words, which is how our minds form and express our thoughts.

FIGURE 10.1   4-D Analysis of Attitude

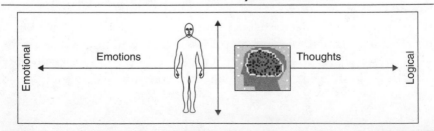

How Powerful are Words?

Stories, formed from words and then expressed, are your most powerful means of influencing others. From the Gospel according to John, "In the beginning there was the Word, and, the Word was with God, and the Word was God."

As Miguel Ruiz (2001) wrote, "It is through the word that you manifest everything. The word is the most beautiful tool you have as a human; it is a tool of magic."

Finally, there is this from Howard Gardner (1995): "Leaders achieve their effectiveness chiefly through the stories they relate."

Story-Lines and Truth

Here is a brief overview of *story-lines*. The logical path is tight so I present it in outline form:

- Webster's defines "story" as, "the telling of a happening, true or fictitious, with the intent of informing or persuading;"
- We define "truth" as that which is indisputable;
- We define *story-lines* as thoughts and expressions that seem true to us, but are in fact arguable; therefore,
- Although our *story-lines seem* true, by definition *they are not*.

You will find that the vast majority of our expressed thoughts are *story-lines*—true for us, but not necessarily truth for others. Nonetheless, *story-lines* powerfully influence us when we think them (self-talk) and influence others when we speak them. Many people are inexhaustible fonts of *story-lines*. I find these people wearying; we have some effective methods to deal with them coming up.

How We Process *Story-Lines*

Once more, in bullet form:

- Because our *story-lines* are arguable, they may or may not be truth for others.
- *Story-lines* we agree with sound like the truth when we hear them. A small voice whispers to us, "That's the truth," meaning I am in agreement with you. We prefer to associate with people who run similar *story-lines*, a tendency called homophily.

- *Story-lines* we disagree with sound wrong. A small voice whispers, "That's just their *story-line*." We feel compelled to argue with them.

I encourage people to respond to *story-lines* they agree with by facetiously saying, "That's the truth." Conversely, respond to *story-lines* that they disagree with by saying, "That's just your *story-line*." It is fun.

Are World Religions Truth or *Story-Lines?*

The religions of the world are interesting because they illustrate *story-lines* that believers are sure are God's truth. We tend to attack people who run *story-lines* we disagree with. Most incredibly, we wage war on people who run religious *story-lines* we find disagreeable.

Mark Twain puts it this way:

Man is a religious animal.

He is the only religious animal.

He is the only animal that has the TRUE religion.

Several of them, in fact.

He is the only animal that loves his neighbor as himself and cuts his throat if his theology isn't straight.

He has made a graveyard of the globe in trying his honest best to smooth his brother's path to happiness and heaven. (Twain, 1962)

Religious *story-lines* are deep truth for those who share them and conflict provoking for those who do not.

Your *Story-Lines* About Motivations Are Wrong

For the first five or so years of developing the 4-D System, I spent about half of my time consulting. One day, I received a call from a favorite client, "Can you come out right away? A NASA center director wants to cancel our contract, and we need your help."

We met a few days later and I asked, "Why does he want to do this?"

- **Bruce (these are not their real names) spoke first:** "Our competitor got to him again. Every time we beat them, they go running to the customer and try to take our work away."
- **Sam:** "Harry has never liked our company. I don't know why, but he just doesn't."
- **Shirley:** "All he cares about is politics. Harry is always looking for some way to advance politically."
- **Fred:** "He's getting orders from above. The NASA administrator is making him do this."

I said, "This is very interesting. We would respond to the center director in very different ways depending on whose *story-lines* we believed. I am suspicious about your perceptions. I have worked with all of you for some years and notice these things about each of you:

- Bruce, you always see that competing company behind every tree;
- Sam, you comment frequently about someone who doesn't like the company;
- Shirley, you are unusually political; and
- Fred, you have never liked the NASA administrator since you had a run-in with him years ago.

"These *story-lines* are more about each of you than they are about the center director. Psychologists call this projection. Each of you is attributing your own undesirable thoughts/emotions to others. Imagine that you have a big movie projector on your head flooding the scene with your worldviews and biases."

Then, I asked, "Did anybody ask him why he wants to do this?" Shirley said, "I did." I asked, "What did he say?" "He said he wanted the flexibility to accommodate budget cuts." "Well, that makes total sense to me. He was in headquarters when we had all the big overruns in science programs because of the post-Challenger launch delays."

After a brief discussion, we decided to build our response on what the center director had said. Fortunately, my clients had a good story about adapting to budget reductions. After they met with the director, they called me and reported, "The meeting went really well. He admitted that he wanted to cancel the contract. He said that our strategy to adapt to budget reductions is so impressive that he could not possibly cancel the contract now."

Months later, I attended a presentation at Ball Aerospace by Robert K. Cooper. He cited research that *story-lines* about other people's motivations are wrong 95 percent of the time! Would you bet heavily on something important with only a five percent chance of being correct? When you notice you are running *story-lines* about the motivations of others, stop them immediately.

Managing Your *Story-Lines* with AMBR

This is the four-step *story-lines* AMBR process:

1. **A**ttention: Notice and name *story-lines* *Green* or *Red* according to the behaviors they cause; *Green story-lines* (no relation to the *Green*, cultivating dimension) sustain high performance. *Red story-lines* inhibit your performance.

2. **M**indset: You and your team need *Green story-lines* to perform well;

3. **B**ehavior: Only express *Green story-lines*; and

4. **R**esult: You thoughtfully manage your team context, and hence performance.

Story-Lines Can Drive Industries to Success or Ruin

A major American industry did not shift *story-lines* until a foreign competitor passed 65 percent of U.S. market share. You probably can guess the industry. American car manufacturers ran a *story-line* that "improving quality means higher costs." What behavior does that *story-line* create? A tiny Japanese company, Toyota, ran a *story-line* that "improving quality is the best way to lower costs." What behavior does that *story-line* create? Which *story-line* supports success?

PRACTICE "COLORING" THESE *STORY-LINES*

I like this quote commonly attributed to Henry Ford, "Whether you think you can do it or think you cannot, you are right." Try assigning *Red* or *Green* to these *story-lines*. It is easy to do, and it may build your confidence.

1. Improving my effectiveness is in the "too hard" category.
2. Anyone with burning desire can live in the top quintile.
3. The social condition of my team matters little.
4. Unaddressed social conditions were root cause of Hubble, Challenger, and mishaps of all sorts every day.
5. There is no excuse for keeping good people in bad places.
6. We will address our management/structural flaws later.
7. What we are doing is not important enough to do well.
8. We have no excuse for less-than-excellent performance.
9. Nobody prioritizes anything here.
10. I am responsible for prioritizing my work.
11. I cannot get my boss to listen to me, so I will not try.
12. I am committed to communicating until I feel understood.

Answers: 1 is *Red*; 2 is *Green*; 3 is *Red*; 4 is *Green*; 5 is *Green*; 6 is *Red*; 7 is *Red*; 8 is *Green*; 9 is *Red*; 10 is *Green*; 11 is *Red*; and 12 is *Green*.

Choosing *Story-Lines*

So I summarize. We all have thoughts that we express to others (and ourselves). These expressions powerfully influence behaviors. Most are arguable and therefore not the truth, although they seem like the truth to us. These are our *story-lines*.

Since our *story-lines* are not the truth, we are free to choose them as we wish. The only thing that really matters is the context our *story-lines* create for our teammates and ourselves. We name *story-lines* that create high-performance contexts *Green*. We name *story-lines* that create low-performance contexts *Red*. You can decide today to run only *Green* *story-lines*.

Let Go of Bananas That Trap You

I have heard that in South America people catch monkeys by attaching woven baskets to trees with a banana inside. The monkeys smell the banana, reach into a basket's narrow neck, and hold on. They cannot extract their hand while gripping the banana. Collectors walk from basket to basket scooping up the monkeys who cannot let go of the banana.

Story-lines that limit us can be like these bananas. It can be hard to let them go, especially if they are lifelong or from childhood. Some may be impossible to release without working with a coach.

Troublesome *Story-Lines* in Technical Teams

Technical organizations are full of 1-D *Blue* personalities whose preferred communication style is argument. Moreover, many of these people are fonts of *story-lines* they want to argue with you. While you may find their argumentative style annoying, they are enjoying themselves.

In addition, as we will describe later, people in drama states will try to enroll you in their shared *story-line* "clubs". Victims, for example, want you to buy in to the notion that the situation is hopeless. Thus, you validate their helplessness. Blamers want you to join them in making another person "bad."

So, what is your best strategy to deal with troublesome *story-lines* you do not share? Should you try to argue people out of their *story-line*? This rarely works, and in some cases engages you exactly as they want, wasting your time and energy. What if you said, "That's just your *story-line*" to the person? This will surely be provocative. I have found that the most effective response is this simple, "If we acted on your *story-line* (or you can name it "proposition" or "notion," if they are unfamiliar with our terminology), what result would we realize?" The following exercise is useful for surfacing and shifting *story-lines* in play.

A Team/Organization *Story-Line* Exercise

All teams run *story-lines* about themselves, their customers, their management, and so on. Surfacing and discussing *story-lines* is particularly useful when we have two teams who need to work together both in a workshop. For example, we frequently have a government team together with their contractor team.

If you have an organizational interface that is problematic, try this exercise. Bring representatives of both parties into the room. For NASA teams the two parties are most often the NASA project team and their principal contractor. Have the people on your side write the *story-lines* the others run about them on flip charts. People are much more willing to tell the nasty *story-lines* they believe the others are running. This exercise usually brings humor into the room. The fun part is that everyone sees that these *story-lines* are not the secrets they thought—everyone knows them. Then, have the participants color the *story-lines* on the charts *Green* or *Red* according to the behavior they create.

This characterization is sometimes ambiguous as the context of the *story-line* is important. For example, "Working with NASA project managers is difficult" could be either color depending on the intent. If the intent was "so, we must find better ways," the *story-line* is *Green*. If the intent was "so, we'll just give up," the *story-line* is *Red*. During workshops, we clarify by asking the intent of the person who offered the *story-line*.

Here are a few examples. We begin with the NASA team relating the *story-lines* they believe the contractor runs about them:

- NASA does not want us to make a fair profit as they can then use our profit to fund overruns. (This is a *Red story-line* as it sets up an adversarial relationship.) The NASA people shift it to a *Green story-line* saying, "This simply is not true. We understand that you need a fair profit to do business with us. Just do good work and you will get your fair profit."
- NASA beats us up inappropriately when we bring bad news. (This is another *Red story-line* because it motivates the contractor to withhold troubling information.) The NASA team responds, "There has been some truth in this. If you will be completely open and honest with us, we will be more reasonable." This shifts the *story-line* to *Green*.

Continue this process until you have surfaced 5 to 10 *story-lines*.

Now, switch and have the contractor tell the *story-lines* the NASA people run about them. Again, here are some examples:

- "You call us money-grubbing contractors behind our backs. This is offensive to us." Can you see that this is *Red* also? Do you remember how often *story-lines* are incorrect? They are incorrect 95 percent of the time. They add, "The truth is that we care just as much about this mission succeeding as you. We are proud people, too." NASA responds, "We believe that what you say is true, and we will stop running that one."

As I walk past offices after workshops, I frequently hear "If we ran that *story-line*, what result would we get?" This pleases me greatly.

Story-Line Shifting Saves the Project

The $1 billion project was already under heavy stress when word came from the customer to advance all the technology milestones and reduce the budget. The customer offered no additional details except that the new direction came from a meeting with the NASA administrator and the customer would come out in 10 days to review their response. The project manager was furious: "How could he have done this to us? This was already nearly undoable, and now he is just trying to make us miserable. We cannot get a break from this guy. I feel like quitting right now."

Greg, who had 4-D awareness, spoke up and said, "Boss, I notice two things about your *story-lines*. First, they are *Red*, and second, you are making assumptions about our customer's motivations. Such assumptions are wrong 95 percent of the time. Further, if we open our customer conversations with these *story-lines* in play we will appear unresponsive and angry. (Do you remember Charlie's two rules about power struggles? 1) Avoid power struggles, and 2) Never power struggle when you do not have the power.) Who has the power here? The customer has the power."

The boss responded, "Greg, you are right. How can we switch these to *Green*?" Greg said, "Let's decide to run these *Green story-lines*. He must have made these concessions to the administrator to save the program, and we should be grateful to him for that.

Further, it shows great confidence in our abilities and commitment. We need to thank him for that vote of confidence."

The boss held the *Green story-lines* during the upcoming meetings, and the customer confirmed they were truth for him. This *story-line* shifting was part of a larger process using the Context Shifting Worksheet, resulting in a fee increase from 67 percent to 96 percent of the available profit pool.

Animals Run *Story-Lines*, Too

I used to travel frequently to Moab, Utah, to mountain bike. One day, I drove over a steel cattle guard with spaces in between rails. Apparently, cows will not cross for fear of hurting their legs.

A few seconds later, I crossed a similar painted version. There were no rails, only painted lines on the pavement. I stopped and asked the rancher whether they were equally effective. He told me, "Yes, the painted version works equally well." I thought the reason might be that cows had poor eyesight or poor cognitive abilities—that once they had experienced discomfort from the real version, they transferred that experience to the painted form.

Knowledgeable people tell me that cows that have never seen the real version will still not cross the painted version. I am not sufficiently interested in the psychology of cows to pursue the matter. The point is that humans, like cows, run limiting *story-lines* that we have no real reason to fear releasing.

Avoid Argument with the Indisputable Truth

Most of us know people whose primary relationship mode is argument (usually *Blue* personalities). Would you like to communicate with them in a way that precludes argument? It is this simple: Tell them an indisputable truth. The simplest indisputable truth is the truth of your experience.

Let us illustrate this with some simple examples. Which of these statements is truth (indisputable) or *story-line* (arguable)?

- "This room is too hot."
- "This room feels too hot to me."

Or,

- "Your comment was stupid and unnecessary."
- "Ouch, your comment hurt!"

Or,

- "Your child's behavior is unacceptable."
- "I am feeling uncomfortable with your child's behavior."

Can you see how the indisputable truth opens a space for communications? Telling the truth of your experience conveys what you want without provoking argument.

The Difficult Workshop Participant

The project was extremely challenging technologically, and the team was under very high stress. Many team members were what I call "wizards" (for example, *Blue* PhD physicists) from Stanford University. These technical geniuses are often unaware of how they affect others emotionally.

The *Team Development Assessment* for the team indicated one particularly troublesome individual. There were many negative comments about "Ben." I was not particularly concerned. I have done this workshop 100-plus times and have seen everything. So I thought.

Ben had his hand up, it seemed, all the time. I felt relentlessly challenged throughout the day, with Ben occasionally abetted by his friend, Jack. Then, I showed a slide describing Einstein as an overdone intuitor. The example I cited claimed that Einstein ignored Edwin Hubble's papers on expansion of the universe in favor of his intuitive sense of a steady state universe. I had read this somewhere a long time ago.

Ben launched a devastating argument about cosmology. I tried to push back. It soon became clear that Ben knew far more about cosmology than I did. I was embarrassed. Now off-balance, I had difficulty focusing on the material. After a while, I recovered, finishing the day reasonably well.

During dinner, I thought about the coming day. I did not want any more of this. Clearly, Ben wanted to argue, and I wanted to help this team perform. So, I decided, since I did not want to argue, I would open the following morning with an indisputable truth.

I began with the truth of my experience. I said, "I have taught this class over a hundred times and never experienced anything as personally unsettling as yesterday. For a while, I felt off balance and confused. I also noticed that I was feeling anxious." I did not have to name Ben. Everyone knew who I was addressing.

As I paused to take a breath, Jack leapt up and launched a lengthy discourse claiming what I had experienced had not happened. I listened until he finished then asked, "Jack, are you trying to get me to discount my own experience?" Jack quickly said, "No." Then he realized he actually was and sat down quietly.

I then addressed the team leader, "I know Ben is bright and technically valuable. However, in my experience he is detrimental to your team's social context. The only way you can build this very difficult sensor is with excellent teamwork. You have to decide whether Ben provides net value to your effort." There was no further trouble from Ben or Jack. The workshop continued in a productive and orderly manner. At the next break, the team leader spoke to me: "Wow—that was one of the most amazing things I have ever seen—thank you very much."

Over the ensuing months, I heard from others that Ben had dramatically changed, displaying a new sensitivity to the effects of his social behaviors. I received an e-mail, "I know this is hard to believe, but in a recent meeting, Ben was the one who brought the group together."

Some months later, I was preparing for a workshop with another team using the same technology. I noticed Ben's name in the attendance list. I wondered what this would be like.

The workshop was fine. Ben caused no trouble. Then during an appreciation exercise where each person speaks, Ben said, "I want everyone to know that a previous 4-D workshop changed my life. Until that day I had no idea how my behaviors affected people. I've recognized that I needed to change, and I have." Wow, I thought, the 4-D processes did it again.

To avoid an argument, tell an indisputable truth.

An Application Summary for *Story-Lines*

You have two tasks. The first, noticing and naming your *story-lines* can be difficult. However, try to notice and name your *story-lines* as such. I make this easy for myself by assuming that every thought and statement I make is a *story-line*. Thus, I cultivate the habit of thinking and expressing *Green story-lines*. I have habituated thinking and expressing thoughts that take others and me to the outcomes I want. With a bit of practice and help from your colleagues, you can do this too.

The second task is to notice and name other people's statements as *Green* or *Red* depending on the behavior they create. This is much easier than noticing your own *story-lines*. When you find another person running *Red story-lines* that would cause performance-limiting behaviors, you have some choices. You can try confrontation, which will almost surely engage you in argument since *story-lines* are, by definition, arguable. This has never produced a useful result for me.

I have had much better experience in asking, "If we ran the *story-line* you just stated, what behavior would result and where would that behavior take us?" We now can focus on the behavior and nearly always switch to a *Green story-line*.

In a recent teleconference, a 4-D staff member said, "I don't know why you are writing a book because nobody reads anymore." I responded, "If I buy into that *story-line*, I would stop, and then how would we take the benefits of the 4-D System into the world." After some more discussion, he understood, and we moved on.

I suggest you also adopt the practice of never permitting yourself to take action on any *story-line*, yours or others, about someone's motivations. The reason is that you are going to be right only about 5 percent of the time. It is an even better practice to notice these *story-lines* as they are developing and immediately stop them.

All these actions are easier if you are with a group of people who understand these ideas and are mutually supportive and reinforcing.

A Team Activity

Finally, be sure to bring your teammates together and perform the *story-line* surfacing exercise described above. I now describe the exercise as we would perform it for NASA and a principal contractor in the room. (This seems easier than using "Sub-team A" and "Sub-team B.") Begin by having the NASA people describe the *story-lines* that the contractor runs about them. You must be rigorous about letting only NASA people participate. Have a helper record these on a flip chart with the label on the top of the page.

Then, do the same process with the contractor. My experience is that everyone has lots of fun with this exercise. The reason it works is that nobody tells the *story-lines* they are running about the other party. This would deteriorate into blaming and ill will. I think the reason people find it humorous is that they imagine that the *story-lines* are secret and unknown when, in fact, everybody knows them.

If there are other parties (organizations) present with several members, for example the customer, go ahead with a third or more cycles.

Then, review each set of *story-lines* and have the group members categorize each as *Green* or *Red*. As I mentioned earlier, you might have to ask the person who offered it to clarify the intent or context in order to assign the color. Then have the group replace any *Red story-lines* with *Green*.

When you are finished, have someone type the results and provide them to the participants.

CHAPTER 11

Manage Your Emotions to Manage Your Team's Energy

How important is your management of emotional expressions? Consider this quote commonly attributed to Carl W. Buechner: "They may forget what you said, but they will never forget how you made them feel."

Emotional Intelligence Is More Important

Dan Goleman caught my attention in 1995 with his remarkable book, *Emotional Intelligence*. This came from a Goleman article three years later (1998): ". . . psychologists asked senior managers to identify the organization's most outstanding leaders. They used objective criteria such as profitability to differentiate star performers. Emotional intelligence proved to be twice as important as technical skills and IQ for jobs at all levels. Moreover . . . emotional intelligence played an increasingly important role at the highest levels."

You already know this if you work in a technical organization. You have seen people promoted to leadership positions because of their technical brilliance but who are clueless about how to manage people. You even have a colloquial name for emotional intelligence; you call it "people skills."

Naming Emotions So You Can Manage Them

When we are able to name or categorize things, we can begin to manage them. You can categorize emotions into five kid word groups: glad, mad, sad, scared, and love. (Note: There is actually a sixth group, surprised, which we will ignore going forward—it is a bit player.) We now examine each emotion group.

Glad—How Do You Use Glad at Work to Uplift?

Do you celebrate accomplishments and victories? Technical organizations tend to look for problems to solve. They focus so intently on problems that they can lose sight of accomplishments and fail to celebrate them. I used to assign the newest person in my division to interview everybody and generate a summary of the past year's accomplishments. We were always astounded at our wonderful achievements. (I did this right before senior executives' bonus ranking and took the summary to my boss. I did well.)

Can you bring humor to difficult situations? This is surely a gift and something I wish I could do more competently. I believe that meetings tend to continue with the moods they start with. To bring glad-group emotions into our 4-D Systems meetings (held weekly as a teleconference), one or two people tell a joke before we do any work. This brings a nice, uplifting energy to the entire meeting.

Mad—How Do You Use Anger to Motivate People?

There is a great scene in the movie *Patton*. The general's aides inform him of bad news about the weather. More snow is coming. This means that there is no air cover, and one suggests that they pull up and wait for better weather.

Patton speaks with angry passion, "There are brave men dying up there. I'm not going to wait, not an hour, not a minute. We're going to keep moving. Is that clear? We're going to attack all night. We're going to attack tomorrow morning. If we're not victorious, let no one come back alive."

An aide says to him that the others cannot tell when you are acting and when you are not.

Patton replies, "It's not important for them to know. It's only important for me to know." Is Patton demonstrating mastery of this powerful emotion, anger? His comments indicate that he is intentional in his application.

How do you use mad at work? This emotion is a powerful motivator. Notice how often the most moving speeches use anger. However, overdone anger irrevocably damages relationships.

Sad—Ever Use Sadness to Mourn a Loss?

In the midst of the tragic fallout of Hubble's flawed mirror, Ed Weiler, the Hubble program scientist, said to me, "Charlie, you have to do something. The astronomy community is tearing themselves apart. They are spewing hate and venom in their e-mails."

The American Astronomical Society was meeting in Philadelphia in about two weeks. I called the society's president and asked for time to address the community. He said "good idea," and referred me to the conference chairperson. The chairperson said, "All the available time is booked already. I am not willing to displace a researcher to give you time. However, here is what I can do. I will put you on at dinnertime and use posters to let people know that you will be speaking. I do not know how many people will come, so I will place your talk in an expandable room. That way if only a few people choose to attend, you won't be embarrassed." This was fine with me.

I began to think about what I would say riding on the train from Washington to Philadelphia. Then, it struck me. This was about a loss, and the proper response to a loss was mourning. The work that these technical people required was on the emotional side.

I arrived in the small room about 30 minutes early. Only a few people were present. As 6 PM neared, the room filled and filled. As promised, the hotel removed the partitions making the room larger and larger. It looked to me as if everyone at the meeting was coming to hear NASA's astrophysics director speak about Hubble.

I walked up to the podium and said, "We need to be clear about what's happening here. We have all suffered losses. I have lost my reputation for competence and embarrassed NASA and my country in the eyes of the world. Many of you bet your careers on this telescope. Many graduate students bet their degrees on Hubble. We have all suffered losses. The proper response to a loss is to mourn it. So let's take a few minutes to feel our sadness and properly mourn this deep loss."

I bowed my head and felt my own sadness. I heard sobbing throughout the room. I waited for what seemed like a very long time but was probably a minute or two. Then I blinked my eyes to clear them and said, "Complete this process in whatever way you need to. I will now tell you my plan to fix the telescope with a space repair mission." I finished my speech and took a late evening train back to DC. The next afternoon, Ed walked into my office and said,

"I don't know what you did but they are settled down." I said, "Ed, it's simple. We just took the time to mourn our loss."

Scared—Fear Can Be Incredibly Powerful

Richard Nixon once said, "People react to fear, not love. They don't teach that in Sunday school, but it's true." (Safire, 1975).

An honest expression of fear can mobilize action. I might say, for example, "If we don't immediately descope this mission by 40 percent, it will be canceled. Have you ever used fear to motivate in this manner?

One of my bosses said to me, "Charlie, you are the most fearless person I have ever known." I said, "Thank you, but it's not so. I feel lots of fear. I just have a *Green story-line* that I habitually run. Whenever I feel fear, I ask myself, 'What would I do if I had no fear?'" I do not always act on my answer to that question, but at least I know. I suggest you try running that *story-line* when you feel fear.

Misperceptions of Risk

I have been interested for years in the near-total lack of connection between perception and reality of fear. If you think about this, you can easily find many examples. About 3,000 people died in 9/11. Forty-two thousand Americans die on our highways each year. How proportional is our government's response? It is far more deadly to have your children visit a family with a swimming pool than one with guns in their house (Levitt and Dubner, 2006).

Before the attack, the base commander at Pearl Harbor removed the fuel and armament from the planes, then lined them up in a field. He was most afraid of the Japanese Americans living in Hawaii.

Each year, 36,000 Americans die of flu, and an Asian bird pandemic could far exceed the worldwide flu epidemic of 1918, which killed more than 20 million people, including 500,000 Americans. What are we doing to prepare for a flu pandemic compared to the war on terror? (What are you doing?)

Love—At Work

When I mention love at work, people snicker, thinking this is about romantic love. It is not. We are speaking here of love for work, for life, and affection for teammates. I loved working for NASA. I love the work described in this book, and I have no problem saying so.

Manage Your Team's Emotional State

You are probably already actively managing the emotional states of others without conscious thought. We will illustrate the process with an imaginary day.

You start the day with a short, stand-up staff meeting. Knowing that meetings tend to continue as they start, you use a joke to surface glad-group emotions making the meeting more enjoyable for everyone.

Next, you learn that a contractor ruined a flight mirror by continuing polishing a month after meeting specifications. (This actually happened.) You listen quietly when your people tell you about this, saving "mad" for the contractor's management. Your *story-line* supporting mad is that, if the facts are correct, mad will maximize their motivation to offer their fee (that is, their profit dollars) to solve the problem.

You next hear that one of your people just lost their father. Your *story-line* is that by sharing sad with them, you can support them in their grief. You visit them and empathize, having had a similar loss earlier.

You meet next with the scientists and managers of a project that has continuous overruns. You are authentically concerned that any additional cost escalation will result in cancellation. You carefully try to instill as much fear as needed. You want them to look for descoping options to reduce the cost before they lose everything.

You close your day with a speech at a local school about NASA's exploration program. Your *story-line* is about "300 Million Explorers"—when the sense of ownership in the space program touches nearly every American. You convey your passion for the space program by speaking from your heart about your love for NASA and its mission.

Managing your expression of emotions is, frankly, not difficult with a little practice. It does help, however, to slow down and experience your emotions, at least occasionally, which we now examine.

Time and Our Culture

What is your experience of the drumbeat of our society? Is it moving faster and faster? We used to write letters to each other. Then, we moved to e-mail. Now, even that is not fast enough. My colleagues and I all use instant messaging, and cell phones have text messaging.

Ask someone, "How are you doing?" and notice how he or she responds. In the United States, people often respond with some version of "Good, I'm really busy." I first noticed this with my students, who consistently answered with some variation on busyness. It is interesting that this is so firmly rooted in young people. Recently, someone greeted me with, "I hope you are really busy."

I experiment with cultures when I travel.

- In Japan, they ask, "O genki desu-ka?" (How is your life energy?) The standard response is "Genki-desu." (I am "genki," or "My life energy is good.")

- The inquiry in China is "Tsai fon le mayo?" with the response, "Fine, I ate today."

- On a vacation to Ireland, I noticed people respond to "How are you?" with, "Fine, the weather is good," even when it is not.

Where are we rushing to as we hurry through life? Is our society collectively using busyness to avoid feeling uncomfortable emotions? (Note how close "busyness" is to "business.") I believe this is the case.

What does busyness have to with experiencing emotions?

Try this. Imagine a waterfall. Imagine a car. Imagine a mountain. Imagine an ocean. Can you make the shift? Most of us can quickly visualize images.

Now, feel sad. Feel glad. Feel mad. Feel scared. We need more time to experience changes in emotions. This is because we experience emotions in many parts of our bodies while thoughts only involve a part of our cerebral cortex. When we are rushing constantly, we cannot experience our emotions. Is our habitual busyness a strategy for avoiding feeling our feelings?

Expand Your Experience of Time

If you would like some respite from busyness's time starvation, begin by running a *story-line* that this has more to do with your daily choices than your work context. For many of us, this is not easy—busyness contexts are powerful. However, you must choose this *story-line* to avoid the helplessness of victims. Surely, you have seen one person overwhelmed by a job, which another person later assumed with apparent ease.

Think of James Taylor's song lyric, "The secret of life is to enjoy the passing of time." Then, take these actions.

- Limit multi-phasic activities, like typing e-mails during phone calls. Over time, it will make you crazy. (There is actually no such thing as multi-phasing. There is only quick, inefficient serial phasing.)

- Before you answer the phone, take two deep breaths. Then close your eyes for the conversation. Nobody will know you did it except through a deeper experience of feeling heard.

- Practice little time-expanding rituals. Pause before meals and take five minutes of quiet time before important meetings. I would take 10 to 15 minutes of private time to relax and clear my mind before all important decision meetings.

- Name waiting as found time and enjoy it. This includes traffic jams and waiting in doctor's offices. People report to me years later that this works really well for them.

- Schedule time for yourself on your calendar. In Japan if a person opens an office door and sees someone sitting alone, he or she will quietly excuse himself or herself. However, they easily interrupt groups. In America, it is just the opposite. As a culture, we do not value time spent alone. At NASA there were enough people wanting to see me every day that if I permitted it, my meeting calendar would completely fill every day. Therefore, I had my secretary fill 20 percent of my time with appointments with myself. This had two advantages. First, when people called for appointments, she would only schedule new meetings in blank spaces protecting my time with myself. Second, when people called she would say, "He's in a meeting" and take a message. She did not reveal that I was meeting with myself, only that I was in a meeting.

- Take an occasional snow day. Snow sometimes closes cities for days at a time (especially Washington, DC). Then, people come back to work, and life goes on.

- Try scheduling weekly quiet time for your team. A team (contractor) building a satellite for NASA has three hours of quiet time each Wednesday morning. For that period, there are no meetings, no phones answered, or e-mail read. People describe how wonderful it is to just think without interruptions.

Costs of Using Busyness to Avoid Feelings

When I was at CU, one of my undergrad students showed me a graph in a psychology textbook. The vertical axis was suicides per 100,000 people and the horizontal was age. The suicide curve for white females was low and flat ending at 8.4 suicides at age 85-plus. The curve for white males rose quickly to about 25 suicides and was flat until about 60. At 60 it began rising to about 30 suicides at age 70. The curve rose again at age 70 and maintained a steep upward slope to 73.6 when the curve ended at age 85-plus. What is happening at the inflection points in the white men's curve at 60 and 70 years old? They are retiring. Warren Farrell (1994) argues that the same process of disciplining and repressing emotion many believe to be necessary for professional and economic success causes suicide. (Note: The curve for black men and women is similar to the white female curve, low and flat.)

I suggest another explanation. Like most males, I learned early in life to repress physical pain. From sports to war, our culture expresses admiration for male pain tolerance. We applaud, for example, football players who continue to play with painful injuries. In my confusion, I extended my ability to repress physical pain to emotional pain. Yet, as Karol Truman (1991) suggests, this strategy does not work over the long haul.

So, what is happening to men in retirement? Out of work they are unable to stay in work's busyness and sustained time starvation. Having slower lives with more time, they experience uncomfortable emotions. With no practice, this can be very stressful.

Practice Experiencing Your Emotions

Blaise Pascal puts it this way: "All human evil comes from a single cause, man's inability to sit still in a room." For me, these are the most powerful words in the Bible: "Be still and know that I am God." "For you are in me and I am in you."

In many parts of the world, people are comfortable just sitting. One sees this, for example, in the Middle East, Caribbean, and Asia. Modern Americans are not. This permits us to design an experiential activity to practice feeling your feelings.

Try this:

- Commit to doing nothing for 10 minutes. Set some kind of timer if you want.

- Notice the emotions that come up and see if you can locate them on your body. Emotions are body sensations that the mind experiences as feelings. Anxiety is most likely. I experience anxiety in my chest.

- Then relax into your emotions by belly breathing. The breath is the only involuntary physiological rhythm that you can change at will. The muscle of breathing is the diaphragm, which separates the lungs from other organs. Place both hands on your stomach. Breathe with your diaphragm, feeling your stomach expand outward and contract inward.

- All great athletes belly breathe. I was watching the Olympics some years ago. The U.S. women's swimming team won a gold medal and went immediately to the awards stand. All their tummies were moving in and out behind their thin bathing suits as they continued breathing.

- Try grounding your feet to the floor. This brings your energy out of your head and into your body. Being grounded, you suck anger out of hostile others just as a grounded lightning rod takes lightning's energy harmlessly into the ground. I once worked for a *Blue* senior manager who directed people to implement idea after idea. Some of his ideas were great, and some were disastrous. Confrontation was difficult as he frequently expressed himself with intense, emotional outbursts. I decided that it was a matter of duty to confront him when I thought he was about to do the wrong thing. Before telling him this, I would belly breathe and ground my feet to the floor. Just as lightning does little damage when the resistance to ground is low, these outbursts would conduct through me for the most part. It was unpleasant but tolerable.

Be patient with yourself as you experiment with quiet—this may be much harder than you thought. However, noticing and casually naming your emotions is a core emotional intelligence ability.

An Application Summary for Expressing Emotions

I want to provide a team exercise for each chapter. However, I cannot imagine gathering a group of hard-core, logical-side, technical people to talk about emotions. (Technical teams do this activity in workshops with no problem. It is a different context.) Therefore, I recommend that you do this work on your own. Many technical people run *story-lines* like, "Emotions have no role at work; people should check their emotions at the door when they come to work." Can you color this *story-line* based on the behavior it supports? It is, of course, *Red* because it removes your capacity to use emotions as energy management tools. The *Green* substitute is "Emotions are a primary source of team energy. I can and must manage my expression of emotions."

To help you make the shift, perform the following exercise. Write occasions when you have expressed emotions from each of the groups (glad, mad, sad, scared, and love) and describe the effect on others.

Closing the "Attitude is Thoughts and Emotions" Segment

Perhaps you are beginning to appreciate the simple, yet holistic view the 4-D System presents. Without an organizing system, you might have read for example, Howard Gardner's *Leading Minds,* and thought team and individual effectiveness were only about cognition and stories.

Alternatively, you might have read Dan Goleman's *Emotional Intelligence* and thought team and individual effectiveness were only about emotions. The 4-D System calls our attention to both *story-lines* and emotions.

Now we move onward into eight behaviors measured in team and individual assessments, two in each of the four dimensions.

CHAPTER 12

People Need to Feel Appreciated by You

We work through the eight behaviors in the following chapters. The sequence is the same as the Context Shifting Worksheet's, which is our preferred order of application. We begin with the "express authentic appreciation" behavior (Figure 12.1).

When workshop participants name their most powerful take-away from our workshops, they choose "expressing authentic appreciation" most often. The experiential exercises in this chapter are memorable. Download the PowerPoint slides for this behavior, and take your teammates through the material in this chapter.

Consider the following: "In the financial world, we use the term appreciate to mean growing in value. When you master habitual appreciation, you and everything around you grows in value." Mother Teresa is commonly credited with saying, "There is more hunger for love and appreciation in this world than for bread."

FIGURE 12.1 Appreciation, the First of the Eight Behaviors

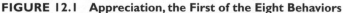

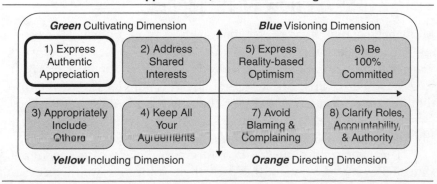

What Is Most Important to People?

The U.S. Chamber of Commerce (1986) reported that employees name appreciation as what they most want at work. I know the reference is a bit dated, but it does not matter. The result would be the same at any time in human history once people had food and shelter. We all need to feel appreciated. Notice the word "feel." Are you skeptical? If so, reflect on what it was like to be in a job where you did not feel appreciated. Can you recall a personal relationship where you did not feel appreciated? What was that like?

Attention: What Do People Most Want at Work?

Many observe that 20 percent of the workers in a typical business organization are giving all they can to their work. Thus, nothing you can do will make them give more. Another 20 percent of the people are giving as much as they are willing to give. They will not give more to their work, no matter what you do. (You probably are already familiar with the Pareto principle that about 80 percent of the effect comes from about 20 percent of the causes.)

The 60 percent in the middle say that they would give more to their work if there were more in it for them. What do they most want? They want to feel appreciated by you! What does it take for you to give them that? It requires that you pay attention to the *Mindsets* and *Behaviors* that support authentic appreciation. Appreciation will then become natural and habitual. It may or may not take more of your time. If it does take more time, you probably will not notice it.

How about Money?

Many believe that what people most want is more money. Money as a sign of appreciation is surely valuable. However, most business workers make enough money to provide the essentials for life. According to a Washington Post article on money and happiness, "A wealth of data in recent decades has shown that once personal wealth exceeds about $12,000 a year, more money produces virtually no increase in life satisfaction" (Vedantam, 2006).

The article continues, "'People grossly exaggerate the impact that higher incomes would have on their subjective well-being' said

Alan Krueger, a professor of economics and public affairs at Princeton University and an author of the study." The problem is that once people get past the level of poverty, money does not play a significant role in day-to-day happiness, Krueger said. It certainly can buy things, but things do not usually address most of the troubles people experience in daily life—concerns about their children, problems in intimate relationships, and stressful aspects of their jobs.

Therefore, money is much less important than our emotional needs. People *need* to feel appreciated and included. Money itself will not motivate most of us for very long. (Although, I would be willing to do the experiment if someone would give me a sufficiently large amount.)

Finally, if I have not persuaded you, ask yourself whether you would prefer to make $100,000 per year as a tollbooth collector or $75,000 per year as an aerospace engineer.

Whose Needs Are You Meeting?

The following dialogue appeared in a Scott Adams' *Dilbert* cartoon. Tina, the tech writer, approaches Dilbert working at his computer and says, "You wrote last year's date on this report. Ha-Ha! Swift." Tina continues, "I enjoy pointing out your mistakes because it makes me feel better about myself." Dilbert says, "I wrote this last year." Tina responds, "This will go faster if you say you didn't."

Is this why so many of us have difficulty with expressing appreciation? Do we feel better about ourselves when we point out other people's mistakes?

The Dilbert cartoon triggers inquiry into the unintended consequences of only addressing our own needs while ignoring other people's needs. In such a context, it is unlikely that we will get our own needs for appreciation met—and never know why.

Reflect on the following. How do you identify, and then meet, the appreciation needs of people you are in a relationship with? How do you get your appreciation needs met in important relationships?

Two years before the Hubble mirror flaw, I found myself in a self-initiated, unexpected, and hostile divorce. My ex said to me, "I don't know why you want to leave this marriage because I love you." I replied, "I want to leave this relationship because I don't feel loved." I engaged a psychologist to explain this apparent contradiction. I learned that we only feel deep appreciation when someone appreciates us for something we valued about ourselves.

My sense was that my ex valued me for being a dependable parent and provider. I valued my creative, adventurous self. I valued my successful leadership of one of the largest research programs in the history of man. She did not know or care about what I did at work. Keep this example in mind when you express appreciation for others. Knowing their personality foundation color can also be helpful. For example, *Yellows* value different things about themselves than *Blues*.

Gratitude's Mindset Provides Authenticity

When we speak to people about expressing appreciation, their first concern is usually authenticity. We jokingly tell the salesperson's mantra: "Authenticity is most effective when you learn how to fake it." We believe that the most effective way to express authentic appreciation is to first experience it. The mindset that supports your experience of appreciation is gratitude. It is easy to live in a continuous mindset of gratitude. Just bring your attention to the gifts in your life.

Living in Gratitude

As a consultant, I often found myself with workgroups that were grumpy and discouraged because of some setback. Losing an important competition, for example, plunged them into despair. I would say to them, "Let's pause for a minute and reflect on what we are grateful for about being on this team (or, in this company)." I then go around the table asking each person to say what he or she is grateful for to the others. The mood shifts dramatically positive and work resumes. Try this the next time you are with gloomy teammates. The transformation is remarkable.

The great German writer, Goethe, is broadly credited with saying: "Ingratitude is always a form of weakness. I have never known a man of real ability to be ungrateful." Actor, comedian and economist Ben Stein put it this way in his commencement address at

Ithaca College: "We are all heirs and heiresses to a society of freedom and plenty that most of us did absolutely nothing to earn."

Commit now to writing what you are grateful for (at work, about your family members, and in your life) on a word processor and then printing it out. Place the printed information in plain view in your office, in a desk drawer, or on your bedroom night-stand. Meditating on what you are grateful for is a wonderful way to end your day. Decide now to live your life in the state of gratitude.

Habitual Appreciation Enhances Longevity

Did you know that habitual appreciation is good for your health? The following is from Dr. Dean Ornish of the University of California Medical School. "Regarding appreciation, I am not aware of any other factor in medicine—not diet, not smoking, not exercise, not stress, not genetics, not drugs, not surgery—that has a greater posi-tive impact on quality of life, incidence of disease, fitness, and pre-vention of premature death" (Ornish, 1998).

We sometimes use *Heartmath*® instrumentation in our work-shops to display heart rate variability. Heart rate coherency is a state of quiet alertness that enhances health and cognition. We are able to demonstrate that authentic appreciation can change heart rate vari-ability from incoherent toxicity to coherent alertness in less than a minute.

I heard this once on the radio: "Departing CEOs of Fortune 500 companies cited lack of appreciation as the primary reason for leaving their jobs." Wow, these people have it all. I will tell you a small secret—appreciation is a business word for love. We all need it.

Ask your bosses if they experience more or less appreciation when they moved up. I believe you will find that they experience less appreciation the higher they rise. Why are we reluctant to appreci-ate bosses? There are some vernacular terms for this. Most people are familiar with the term "sucking up." Do you realize that bosses need appreciation as much as anyone else does? Many seldom receive it. If you appreciate authentically, nobody, including the boss, will experi-ence or name it sucking up.

Mastery through "HAPPS" Appreciation

From the emotional state of gratitude (glad-group) use "HAPPS" to express appreciation.

- Habitually—Appreciate as a matter of habit. Habits are our personal bureaucracy. Once authentic appreciation becomes habitual, you won't experience it as onerous or time consuming;

- Authentically—Live in the mindset of gratitude to support you in *experiencing* what you appreciate in others; this is the key to authentic expression;

- Promptly—The closer in time to the valued behavior, the better;

- Proportionally—Make the statement of appreciation (verbal, financial, paper) proportional to the behavior; and

- Specifically—Your expression of appreciation will have more power when it is specific. Avoid repetitions such as "good job" as a matter of routine.

  (Note: If you chose to perform assessments at our web site www4-DSystems.com, you saw the material shown here as our assessment standard for this behavior.)

I frequently work with 4-D clients as consultants before workshops. I observed a boss who habitually said "good job" to everyone who exited his office. During a workshop, in his presence, I asked his team what this was like for them. They said, nearly in unison, "We hate it." He seemed surprised and soon totally understood. When it is rote, it has no meaning for anyone. Do not do this.

Is it okay to express appreciation in e-mails? Many *Green* personality trainers urge people to appreciate very personally because that is how they would give appreciation. This issue illustrates why our 4-D System's approach is essential. Appreciation modalities must be compatible with both the appreciator's personality type and the organization's culture. In *Blue* or *Orange* cultures, people may feel uncomfortable if appreciation is too personal. People will not behave long in ways that their culture opposes. Recognizing this, I suggest that any modality you feel comfortable with is okay. You can appreciate with e-mail, voice mail, or even leaving notes. I occasionally get an award in the form of a simple color page thanking me for my participation in a proposal win. I love receiving these impersonal appreciations.

Exercising Appreciation Muscles

You have probably used some kind of exercise machine or weights, at least briefly. As you developed muscles, the same activity surely became easier. Do the following exercises with your teammates (or family) to develop their appreciation muscles. I suggest you download and project this chapter's PowerPoint slides from our website. At the indicated place in the projected slides:

- Invite each person to stand up and say what he or she is grateful for about being on this team. (Where attention goes, power flows.) In hundreds of workshops, nobody has ever had difficulty doing this. You must, however, move through the group in some systematic manner, with a talking stick for example, so people cannot hide from the opportunity by simply being silent.

- Then, having encouraged the mindset of gratitude, systematically move again through the group, asking people to express authentic and personal appreciation for someone they work with. Ask them to stand up, look at the person, and then speak directly: "(Name), I appreciate you for . . ." The process completes when the appreciated person looks at the appreciating person and says, "Thank you."

This might look scary. However, once you get past the first few people, everyone enjoys this exercise. Interestingly, many report that it is much more difficult to receive the appreciation than give it. This suggests a way to enhance appreciation on your team—graciously accept appreciation others give you.

Learn from 9/11—Do It Now!

I was speaking to an FBI agent shortly after he returned from the World Trade Center 9/11 disaster site. I asked him what he learned. He said this: "Many words were spoken into the ears of the dead that they yearned to have heard while they were alive." This is important enough to repeat: "Many words were spoken into the ears of the dead that they yearned to have heard while they were alive." Appreciate someone you deeply care about now. Do not wait.

We ask workshop participants to appreciate someone they care about and report what happened the following morning. The reports are interesting. Many are about spouses who say something like, "I am really glad that you are in that workshop."

On one occasion, a person raised his hand and said, "That was a really bad idea." I asked him to continue. He said, "Well, I stopped on the way home and bought my wife a dozen roses. I knocked on the door, handed her the roses and appreciated her just as we learned in class yesterday. She then gave me a nasty look and said, "Forget it—you are not getting any tonight, buster." Authentic appreciation from her husband was so rare that she believed he was manipulating her.

Story-Line and Emotion Synergy

We now integrate expression of your thoughts and emotions to manage your team's context in Figure 12.2.

Begin by bringing your attention to the gifts in your life. This should promote a glad-group emotion. Feeling happier, you can bring up a thought about gratitude for another's behaviors. Feelings of gladness will increase more. Now, public expression and grateful acceptance promotes more glad feelings.

FIGURE 12.2   Glad Group Emotions and *Story-Line* Synergy

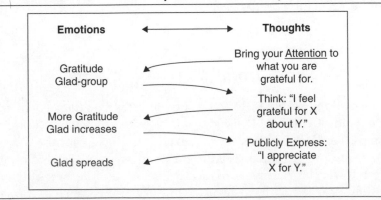

Excess Criticism Tips Teams into Death Spirals

Gladwell (2002) writes, "The Tipping Point is that magic moment when an idea, trend, or social behavior crosses a threshold, tips, and spreads like wildfire." Can teams tip into dysfunction? What might trigger it?

Consider the following all-too-typical scenario. A team receives approval for a new important project and selects their supplier. Everyone is in good spirits and optimistic. Then, it becomes apparent that the funds are insufficient. The customer angrily chastises the supplier's project manager. (Too many managers confuse toughness with meanness.) Many technical managers have black belts in finding fault that they learned during graduate school. Consider the run up to Challenger. The Thiokol managers named the Marshall engineers the "bad news boys" because they were so adept at highlighting contractor shortfalls (Vaughan, 1997).

1. Excess criticism initiates the tipping cycle displayed in Figure 12.3.

2. The suppliers become weary of these beatings and delay or omit problem reporting.

3. Despair and misery prevail.

4. Participants mount the stage as victims and blamers. The situation, of course, deteriorates, and the cycle continues with the context and performance spiraling downward. The project team is now broken. (Note: I omitted the 4-D System axes because the picture had so many other arrows.)

FIGURE 12.3   Criticism Tips Teams Downward

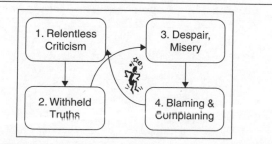

I was presenting this material in a 4-D workshop when a manager leapt up and ran out of the room. "Where are you going?" I asked. "I have to intercept a letter I put in today's mail to my contractor." We are happy when workshop participants convert the knowledge to action so quickly.

Appreciation Tips Teams Back to High Performance

Can these now bottom-quintile teams tip back toward high performance? Yes, they can, as illustrated in Figure 12.4 and the following five steps.

1. We begin by remedying whichever of the "Seven Deadly Sins" are in play. You can read about the sins in Chapter 18, "Don't Put Good People in Bad Places."

2. We then teach our client's management to shift their mindset to look for behaviors to appreciate. They use the HAPPS methodology: Habitual, Authentic, Proportional, Prompt, and Specific to express authentic appreciation. An atmosphere of mutual respect grows. The context becomes more positive, launching the tipping process. The potency of this authentic appreciation cannot be overstated. Listen to this statement broadly credited to G. K. Chesterton: "I maintain that thanks are the highest form of thought, and that gratitude is happiness doubled by wonder." The context slowly shifts to one of mutual respect. As people experience authentic appreciation, they are more motivated to express it.

FIGURE 12.4   Appreciation Tips Team Upward

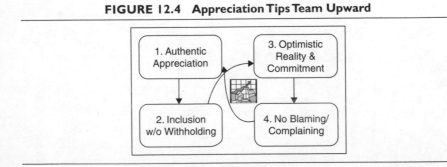

3. Both sides make and honor agreements about problem reporting, for example. They agree to report all problems within 24 hours. This improved context eliminates drama-inducing truth withholding.

4. Mutual understanding replaces argument about the difficult realities of the situation, providing a platform for creativity. There is more about how this works in Chapter 16, "Creating the Future You Want."

5. Responsible action replaces blaming and complaining.

When is Replacing the Leadership the Only Option?

I wrote earlier about the attribution error of firing project managers for overruns that they did not cause. When we engage with broken teams as described previously, management often solicits our advice on whether changing leadership is necessary.

Gladwell (2005) describes an instant diagnostic of whether people can repair relationships: "Gottman could eavesdrop in a restaurant and tell in five minutes whether a couple should hire lawyers and divide custody of the children." He listens for the Four Horsemen: Defensiveness, Stonewalling, Criticism, and Contempt. Of the four, contempt is by far the most powerful. Contempt comes from a superior plane; it is hierarchal. Examples of contempt expressions include, "You're scum," or "You're beneath me." Contempt and disgust are about rejecting someone from the community, that is, dis-inclusion. Once a person expresses contempt, relationships may be irrecoverable. We agree. If leaders have expressed contempt across the customer-supplier interface, there may be no recovery option. In this situation, it may be in everyone's best interest to change out the leadership.

Abundance Mindset

I love this quote from a greeting card because it directly confronts a *Red story-line* our society ubiquitously runs: "If you are not happy with what you already have, how could you be happier with more?" (One of our workshop participants noted that it would make a good birthday card; you could use it to give a cheap present.)

My last job at NASA was charting its post–Cold War strategy. I worked closely with Administrator Daniel Goldin, a man who could be difficult. I wanted to do my absolute best in what could be a stressful environment. As part of my process to center myself, I examined my purpose and my legacy from my time on the planet. In the first version, I wrote that I wanted to be wealthy. Then I realized that during the time in my life when I had the most material wealth, I felt the poorest. This is because I placed my attention on accumulating wealth. I changed my life vision to live in the experience of abundance in the spirit of Epicurus, 300 BC: "Wealth consists not in having many possessions but in having few wants."

Comedian Ben Stein is frequently credited with, "I cannot tell you anything that, in a few minutes, will tell you how to be rich. But, I can tell you how to feel rich, which is far better, let me tell you firsthand, than being rich. Be grateful . . . it's the only totally reliable get-rich-quick scheme."

The way to experience abundance is to run the *story-line* that "I have enough, so I can give things away." I will share a little story to illustrate this. One day I noticed my friend Ron Billingsley's birthday in my Outlook calendar. Ron has been a good friend since we worked on leadership together in the early 1990s at the University of Colorado. I had not seen or talked to Ron in several years. Ron was a professor in the English department, which had lower salaries than the sciences or even the business school. Ron, however, has a few expensive tastes. One is pricey Cordon Rouge champagne. I bought two cases and left them anonymously on his doorstep on his birthday.

The next morning he called and could not stop laughing. I tried to play dumb, but he was not buying it. He had busted me. "How did you know it was me?" I asked. The Billingsleys have lived in Boulder many years and have a large network of friends. He said, "Well I first made a list of all my friends who knew when my birthday was. I then circled the ones who knew I loved Cordon Rouge. I then asked who would be crazy enough to do this, and it was surely you." I will tell you that giving that champagne has brought me much more pleasure than drinking it.

Thinking in terms of opportunity cost is another path to abundance for me. I suggest that this is the only real cost of anything. I take my children and relatives on trips to foreign countries. Supporting five people for three weeks in France, for example, puts some big numbers in the VISA bill. What, however, is the real cost?

The proper question is this: What do my wife and I need that we cannot have because we funded these vacations? What can we not have because we bought Ron some champagne? The answer for my wife and I is nothing. Therefore, the cost of these gifts is nothing.

An Application Summary for Expressing Appreciation

As a statement of my appreciation of you for buying and reading *How NASA Builds Teams*, I have provided the workshop slides for this chapter free at www.4-DSystems.com. I believe that the slides and the written material in this chapter provide sufficient context so you and your team can perform the two experiential exercises described herein.

Workshop participants are uncomfortable until the first two or three people express appreciation. The momentum then builds and everyone finds expressing authentic appreciation is fun. Your team should have a similar experience. If you are timid about trying this with your team, just recall these words: "Mr. Martin, quit the bullshit and pick up the chalk."

Most important, use recurrent *Individual Development Assessments* and *Team Development Assessments*. These will bring your *Attention* and *Mindsets* to expressing authentic appreciation. Moreover, reassessments track your progress and your team's progress, providing encouragement to continue your authentic expression of appreciation.

CHAPTER 13

Mine the Gold in
Your Shared Interests

Can you recall how we tend toward homophily? We prefer to be in relationship with people who share our *story-lines*. "Shared Interests" is the same phenomenon (Figure 13.1). We are most comfortable with people who want for us, the things that we want for ourselves. These common interests are always present.Human's tendency to focus on differences rather than what we can want for each other causes much of the conflict in the world. This 4-D work is about habituating you to bring your attention to the shared interest inquiry: What do they want that I can want for them also?

Some years ago, a NASA exccutive called me, "Charlie, this center director and I just can't get along. Can you help?" We went off-site with an abbreviated 4-D workshop. On the second morning, we paired the people into two groups: his staff and the center people.

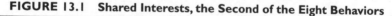

FIGURE 13.1   Shared Interests, the Second of the Eight Behaviors

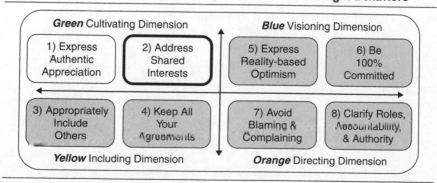

Each group addressed the inquiry "What do they most want that we can want for them also?"

The center people reported first: "We want for you to be totally successful." My client responded, "Really, why would you want that?" "Because," they answered, "If you aren't successful, then we won't be successful either. We are totally dependent on your success for the funding we need to survive."

Later my client said, "You have an interest that I do not share. You want to grow your institution. This could only come at the expense of others who I care about." The center people said, "Where did you get that idea? We only want stability, not growth." (Do you recall the percent of the time that our assumptions about other people's motivations are incorrect? We are wrong 95 percent of the time.) The process went back and forth for a few hours with each side identifying what the other wanted that they could want for them also. This surfaced *Red story-lines* that were in play and eliminated them. I could feel the tension palpably recede. It surely seems trivial when we lay it out, but it is hard work in the midst of conflict.

Using Shared Values to Defuse Power Struggles

Several years ago, I was in Huntsville preparing for a workshop at the Marshall Space Flight Center. As I walked into the Marriott, I saw my colleague Jim Odom sitting in the lobby. As I mentioned earlier, Jim is the best project manager I ever worked with. "What are you doing here?" I asked. "Waiting for you," he answered. He went on to tell me that he had just finished meeting with the center director and saw my name on his calendar earlier that day. As we had not spoken for several years, he wanted to meet with me. He guessed that I would stay at the Marriott, the best hotel in Huntsville, so he sat in the lobby for a few hours waiting for me to walk by. (He was a corporate vice president at the time.)

We talked for a few hours trading Hubble war stories. Jim told me about his first meeting with the Hubble Science Working Group. Recall that I said that they were the nastiest people on the planet. They were until Jim began managing Hubble. The telescope scientist, a very important person, walked up to Jim and said, "Odom, I'm going to make you miserable." Can you see the invitation to power struggle with the energy flowing into the directing dimension?

Jim intuitively took all the energy back to the center with a simple, diagonal action into the cultivating dimension. He said, "No, you're not because we want the same thing." You can see the change in the diagrams in Figure 13.2 moving from left to right.

I have only two rules ("Charlie's rules"):

1. Avoid power struggles.
2. Never power struggle if you do not have the power.

Shared Interests with Japanese Scientists

We tend to focus on positions rather than interests (see Fisher, Ury, and Patton, 1991). When I became NASA's director of astrophysics in 1983, I thought it would be interesting to collaborate with the Japanese, as we had with Europe for many years. A colleague told me not to bother—the Japanese were impossible to work with. Moreover, they would not share their data with foreigners.

I approached my Japanese counterpart, Yasuo Tanaka, and he said, "I cannot believe this. I have been trying to cooperate with NASA for years and no one would talk with me." I soon learned that the scientific part of Japan's space program was an offshoot of the University of Tokyo, the only space program the United States would allow after World War II. Moreover, they built their own rockets and spacecraft. This looked ideal, as I preferred to spend NASA science money on instruments and detectors than spacecraft.

When the topic turned to data sharing, I did not talk about their position, which I knew was to retain data longer than NASA's policies

FIGURE 13.2   Odom Addresses Values to Avoid a Power Struggle

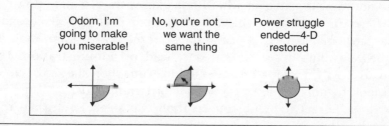

permitted. I asked instead about their interests—the reasons under-neath their position. Yasuo explained that, unlike NASA scientists, they had to do everything themselves including tracking the satellite after launch. If they made their data public, foreign scientists would pub-lish their results while they were still busy with satellite operations. I asked him, "Don't you prefer to publish in English language journals?" "Of course, they are the really prestigious journals," he answered. "Isn't that difficult given that your native language is Japanese," I asked. I think you can see how the conversation continued.

I thought about our shared interest—scientists analyzing data and advancing knowledge. I then suggested, "How about this. I will start a visiting scientist program. If you provide the rocket and spacecraft, and we jointly develop the instrument, I will sponsor six American scientists to visit Japan and jointly write papers with you and your colleagues." This was a good arrangement for everyone. Our sci-entists had opportunities to advance astrophysics with data that would be otherwise unavailable. The Japanese scientists authored papers with top English-speaking scientists. Acting on shared interests is easy if you just look. (Yasuo later received special recognition from the Japanese Emperor for our first mission together, YOHKOH [SOLAR-A].)

Shared Interests and the Hubble Hire

One afternoon, as I gazed out my office on Independence Avenue, I wondered, "What part of the Hubble servicing mission might we have overlooked?" The new instruments were straightforward. The replacement wide-field camera and corrective optics looked much easier than building the original instruments. What about the opera-tions when the astronauts change the Hubble instruments in space? What perils are there? This does not look harder than changing a transmission in space. However, I had no idea how hard that is. I did not want to trip over what I don't know that I don't know.

I set out to hire a space operations expert. We placed ads in aerospace magazines. A candidate from Martin-Marietta, Tim, applied. I went to see Karen, our head of administration. I had scarcely finished saying I wanted to hire Tim when she said, "No way. You look for any angle to grow your program, and it will not work this time. Forget it!" Our conversation was over. I returned to my office, fuming.

After a time, I acknowledged to myself that there was some truth in what she had said. I had done things like that in the past. Moreover, I had seriously overdrawn my Emotional-Side Bank Account (ESBA) with Karen. My ESBA with our mutual boss, Len Fisk, however, was excellent. I decided it's "badge on the table time." You do this when you care so deeply about something that you will quit if they do not give you what they want. Either you, or your boss, symbolically pick up your badge at the end of the meeting. I cared deeply about a Hubble servicing mission success. I did not want, however, to lose my job.

Therefore, I began the shared interests inquiry: "What does Len want that I can want for him also?" Hmm. My first thought was "a successful Hubble servicing mission." He wants that, and I can want that too. What other shared interests are in play? He wants peace with Karen and the other directors. Yes, I can want that too. Then I thought more deeply, "Len wants never to testify about another Hubble failure." Wow, I thought, the testimony was bad for me, but it was much worse for him. He bore the brunt of the hostility. Then, the decisive factor came: "Len wants, in the event of a Hubble servicing failure, never to have to say he did less than everything he could to bring success." Thus, I, Charlie, accept full accountability including resignation if we fail. I can accept that. I am ready. It is time to go see Len.

Then I hesitated, since I am asking him to roll Karen. I should also ask, "What does Karen want that I can want for her also?" This was harder. The first thought that came to mind is that she wants power and control over me. Can I want that too? No way, I cannot want that. Can I want her to have ability to do her job without end runs from people like me? After a while, I could want that for her.

Can you now imagine the conversation after I placed my badge on the table? "Len, I am here because I want to hire Tim. I need to tell you the values that are in play. First, I want a successful repair mission more than a new car, and I really, really want a new car. I know you want a successful mission, too. Further, I want to ensure that you never have to testify about a Hubble failure again. Moreover, if you did, I want for both of us to say truthfully that you did everything we possibly could to ensure success. You never denied me any resource I requested. If the mission fails, I will name myself as responsible and resign from NASA. Finally, please tell Karen that I promise to never end-run her on personnel or travel matters again."

What do you think he said? Len said, "Charlie, you have your hire." I snatched my badge off the table and promptly departed. (I learned long ago that when you get what you want in a meeting, you stop talking and leave.)

If you are in pending conflict with anyone, try asking, "What do they most want that I can want for them also?" Again, one of my favorite expressions, "People do things for their reasons, not ours." When you address shared interests, your reasons and their reasons are the same.

An Application Summary for Shared Interests

Humans are naturally tribal with deep needs to feel we belong to groups. We bring our first loyalty to these groups. Therefore, many teams experience difficulties working across organizational boundaries. For NASA projects, this difficulty is most profound across the boundary of two NASA centers because there is no clear, mutually accepted hierarchy. The most vicious fights are often within families. The closer the two entities are to seeing the other as peers, the more difficult it is for one party to subordinate themselves to the other. Some years ago, I asked the great project manager Tom Young his most important rule for successful projects. He said, "For everything you care about, you need one neck to grab and one ass to kick." I agree and am concerned when I hear that two entities are going to do a project as partners.

I chose, however, a NASA-contractor boundary for the following example. Workshop participants make great progress in building bridges across organizational boundaries with the following shared interests exercise. Write the shared interests inquiry so everyone can read it: "What do they want that I can want for them also?"

This exercise is similar to the *story-lines* exercise. Again, I will use NASA and their contractor for the example. Begin with NASA asking, "What does our contractor want that we can want for them also?" Record the responses on a flip chart. After each response ask the contractor, "Is this something you want?" for confirmation. It is usually easy to generate a half-dozen or so. Then, do the same process with the contractor: "What does NASA want that we can want for them also?" Again, it should be easy to generate a half-dozen or so. As before, ask the NASA people, "Is this something you want?" When you are finished, have someone type the results and provide them to the participants.

Most important, use recurrent *Individual Development Assessments* and *Team Development Assessments*. These will bring your *Attention* and *Mindsets* to addressing shared interests. Moreover, reassessments track your progress and your team's progress, providing encouragement to continue.

CHAPTER 14

People Need to Feel Included by You

This chapter is about what people next most need from you after feeling appreciated: feeling included (Figure 14.1).

Personas and Authenticity

We routinely don masks and assume roles to get our needs met for feeling appreciated (loved) and feeling included by others. Psychologists call these "personas," which is Latin for masks.

Do you put on an appearance that is different from your fully authentic self when you are in each of these contexts?

- Attend a football game with your buddies?
- Don a military uniform?

FIGURE 14.1   Including, the Third of the Eight Behaviors

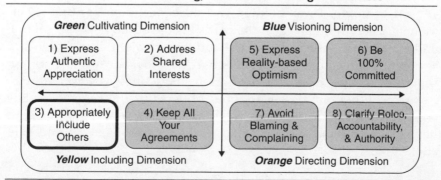

Green Cultivating Dimension		*Blue* Visioning Dimension	
1) Express Authentic Appreciation	2) Address Shared Interests	5) Express Reality-based Optimism	6) Be 100% Committed
3) Appropriately Include Others	4) Keep All Your Agreements	7) Avoid Blaming & Complaining	8) Clarify Roles, Accountability, & Authority
Yellow Including Dimension		*Orange* Directing Dimension	

- Answer questions in a University oral examination?
- When you make your first briefing to top management?

These brief excursions into persona are as useful as putting on a jacket to go outside in the winter. Personas, however, limit us when we (unconsciously) adopt habituated personas (from childhood) that:

- Are rooted in fear/pain avoidance.
- Prevent us from interacting authentically with others.

A Troubled University President

When I first moved to Boulder, I was surprised to see local news dominating the front page of the Boulder newspaper, the *Daily Camera*. The newspaper was pummeling the university president, Judith Albino, day after day. Even in Washington, I had never seen anything quite like it. After watching this for a few weeks, I saw her dilemma as a leadership problem. I photocopied the top newspaper stories and passed them out to my undergraduate students. We talked for a few classes about what advice we would give the president. Then my students came to my house on a Saturday afternoon. We used a "post-it" process to write a one-and-a-half-page letter that consolidated 20-plus people's opinions, which we all signed.

A few weeks later, one of my students spoke to Dr. Albino at a social function. He identified himself as a member of the leadership class that sent the letter. She said she had received the letter and thanked him. He then invited her to come to class and speak. My students knew they were empowered to make those kinds of commitments.

At the time, I was holding two misconceptions: 1) that a permanent position might be in the cards for me at the business school, and 2) that the president of the university might have some say about this. I wanted the president to have a good experience, so the student who made the invitation and I met with Dr. Albino. I explained that our class was about leadership, and we were totally committed to confidentiality. I asked that she speak candidly about her current difficulties and experiences. She thanked us and said she would.

She arrived at our classroom a few days later. I introduced her and then sat with my students in our amphitheatre-style classroom. Have you ever seen a person speaking as if they inserted a tape into their head and played it? That is exactly what she looked like. I began to worry. I had taught the class the BS sign we used in the Astrophysics Division. Whenever someone spoke BS, we would use a forefinger to lift our tie and hold it under our noses. People who were speaking BS knew they were speaking BS, and we all had a good laugh.

A workshop participant demonstrated another BS signal, which I like better. You place your hands beside your head and wiggle two fingers. It springs from the notion of ants pushing a piece of BS up a hill. Sometimes a piece of BS would escape and began rolling down the hill. They signaled the ants below by wiggling their antennae as if to say, "Look out, here comes the BS." What would I do if my students gave the president the BS signal? Would this be the end of my teaching career? I was becoming anxious.

I stood up, walked over to Dr. Albino, and said, "You know, there are some great leaders in this room. People will blast them at some future time. I have never seen anything like what the *Daily Camera* is saying about you day after day. Can you tell the students what this is like for you to open your front door and pick up the paper? It's safe here." I returned to my seat. She continued as before.

After a few minutes, I noticed students squirming in their seats. Fearing a mass eruption of the BS sign, I walked back over to her. I turned her toward me and said, "Dr. Albino, please tell the students what it's like to open your door every morning and look down at the *Camera*." I also took the risk of touching her shoulders as I spoke. She looked me in the eyes, and I said, "I promise you that it's safe here" and sat down again.

When she began speaking this time, we could actually see her mask drop. She now spoke to the class fully authentically. I had never heard such a persuasive and moving discourse. We were all spellbound. As the class ending time drew near, I reluctantly interrupted her. The mask popped back up and the "tape" resumed. I thanked her and she left.

This large undergraduate class ended just before lunch. A large table occupied the front center of the room. I learned early on to center myself behind the table before dismissing the class. If I were in front of either of the side doors, the students would sweep me into the hall. I positioned myself and said, "Class dismissed. See you on Wednesday." Nobody moved. Not knowing what to do, I sat back down. Still nobody spoke or moved. I went to the front of the room and said, "What do you want to do?" They answered, "We want to talk about what we just saw." We talked for another hour and stopped only because another class wanted the room. In the end, Dr. Albino transferred to Denver relinquishing her presidency. It is tragic that a fear-driven persona so limited this person.

Effective leaders choose when to wear a persona and when to bring their authentic selves to situations. Do you think I brought my full authentic self to the Congressional hearings? I did not. I put on my Mr. NASA Director persona. In Star Trek terminology, it was "shields up and phasors armed."

The Great Santini

This movie demonstrates the damage done by an inappropriate persona. Bull Meechum, a Marine aviator speaks to his children as though they were soldiers. He refers to them as hogs and says he is tired of them bellyaching about moving to the new town. He directs that bellyaching will end as of 1530 hours. Then he says, "Do I make myself clear?" The children answer, "Yes, sir."

Bull continues, "You are Marine kids and can chew nails while other kids are sucking cotton candy . . . I want you hogs to let this berg know you are here. I want these crackers to wake up and wonder what the hell blew into this town. Okay hogs, by nightfall I want this camp in inspection order. Do you read me loud and clear?"

The children answered, "Yes, sir." Bull, shouting now, "I said, did you read me loud and clear?" The children answered together, "Yes, sir." Then Bull spoke to Ben, his young son, "Outstanding. Sergeant, dismiss the troops." Ben (dejectedly) said, "Dismissed." His young daughter MaryAnn then said, "He does remind me of someone from the movies but it's not Rhett Butler." Karen said, "Who is it?" Then MaryAnn said, "Godzilla."

Workshop participants choose a persona they might actually use. I display some of the personas they have chosen in Figure 14.2. Personas usually correlate with one's innate personality, but not always. When people say they cannot name their persona, their

FIGURE 14.2   Some Sample Personas from Workshop Participants

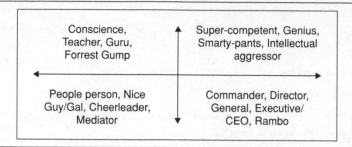

teammates can easily name a persona for them. Can you name one you use? My primary persona is Dr. Super-competent.

Interviewing Your Mask (Persona)

After everyone has chosen a persona, people pair up and interview each other's persona using the interview format below. To be clear, we are not interviewing real people. We are interviewing their personas. I now will demonstrate this process with my Dr. Super-competent persona being interviewed.

Interviewer: Please introduce me to your persona.

Dr. Super-competent: I'm Dr. Super-competent.

Interviewer: It's nice to meet you, Dr. Super-competent. Tell me about yourself. What are you most proud of?

Dr. Super-competent: I am so smart and clever. It's wonderful.

Interviewer: How do other people appear to you?

Dr. Super-competent: Actually, you all look kind of stupid. I need to see you that way so I can feel super-competent.

Interviewer: What is your leadership strength, Dr. Super-competent?

Dr. Super-competent: Oh, that's easy. I'm smarter than just about everyone else.

Interviewer: What is your leadership weakness, Dr. Super-competent?

Dr. Super-competent: I beg your pardon? I don't understand the question.

Interviewer: (chuckles) Well, I guess we'll move on. What are the benefits of this role at work?

Dr. Super-competent: I get to feel big and strong and smarter than anyone else.

Interviewer: What scares you the most?

Dr. Super-competent: (choking a bit) Being wrong.

Interviewer: Drop your persona and go back to your authentic self.

Charlie: This feels much better.

Interviewer: Can you see how this persona arose in childhood?

Charlie: Yes, I can. I spent a lot of my childhood with a grandfather who immigrated to America as a child. He went from sweeping the floor to CEO of an oil well supply company in Louisiana. He encouraged my intellectual abilities from the start.

Interviewer: Is there anything else you realize about yourself?

Charlie: Yes, that super-competent mask is really hard to hold up. I'm glad that I seldom need to wear it.

I believe that repressed scared-group emotions most frequently cause us to adopt personas unconsciously. These personas prevent us from authentic relationships with others.

What's Next-Most Important to People

What do you think is most important to people after feeling appreciated? People next-most want to feel included. (Note: "feel" appears again.) What is it like when your boss invites all your peers to an important meeting and not you? Intentional exclusion and unintentional exclusion both hurt. Business organizations routinely manage inclusion poorly. Sloppy management of group achievement awards is a classic example.

What insights does the 4-D System now provide? Notice in Figure 14.3 that "What people most want" and "Next-most want" are both on the emotional side. What are your habits about tending to the emotional side? How much attention have you given to your mindsets and behaviors regarding inclusion? For most of us, the answer is "not much."

FIGURE 14.3   The Emotional Side Is Most Important

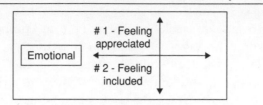

The Inclusion Mindset

Effective inclusion begins by adopting the mindset that inclusion matters, then paying attention to how you include others or fail to include others. In simple terms, inclusion is about how we delegate power and share information and rewards. More inclusion is not necessarily better; we are looking for thoughtful, appropriate inclusion. Here are our thoughts about appropriate inclusion.

First, Do No Harm

Avoid (thoughtless) omission of people from information, meetings, and awards. I put the word "thoughtless" in the sentence because if you want to make someone extremely uncomfortable, intentionally disinclude them. They will soon leave, while maximizing destruction on their way out.

This is a story about how thoughtless inclusion damages, even at a celebration. Some years ago, I worked with a proposal team managed by a retired executive the company brought back to lead the team. He had little use for the people who had followed the capture of the program for several prior years. He only included the new team he had assembled. Power struggles broke out everywhere as the excluded people acted out their discomfort.

After they submitted the proposal, and before they knew whether they won or lost, I interviewed the participants and prepared a presentation for the responsible management. When the managers saw comments like "it was like *Lord of the Flies*," they were aghast: "You can't show that to the workforce, it will depress them." "Where do you think I got it?" I responded. After some discussion, I presented a slightly moderated version to the team. Nobody was surprised.

Incredibly, the proposal won. I can only assume that the competition was very weak. The responsible VP charged the proposal manager to organize a celebration party. The company invited me to attend. When the VP recognized the contributors, she recognized the retiree's in-group, and totally ignored the capture team members. I watched one individual drop his face onto the table with a thud. I walked over to him. He cursed and said, "I will never work on a proposal for this blank-blank company again." Ironically, the celebration event had done more harm than good. The damage from thoughtless inclusion omissions can be profound.

A 4-D client wanted to award people who had worked on a project spanning more than six years. He understood the effect of exclusion even when it is unintentional. He placed a large photograph in the hall and invited everyone who had contributed to the program to sign it and pick up a T-shirt. To his surprise, scores of people he had never heard of had contributed to the project. They happily signed the photo and received their shirt. We now look at a powerful inclusion action, giving people a sense of feeling heard.

Listen Deeply

Philip Stanhope puts it this way: "Many a man would rather you heard his story than granted his request" (Stanhope and Welsh, 2008).

As a NASA director, I frequently had to make resource reallocations that moved money from one part of the organization to another. I worked hard to be as fair and objective as possible. I was therefore perplexed when a staff member on the losing end would continue to argue with me about what I had decided. It seemed clear to me that any rational person would have made the same choice. Then, I decided to perform an experiment. I invited the person on the losing end to give me their arguments beforehand. I listened deeply, giving all the time they needed to express themselves.

This information, which I largely already knew, seldom affected my decision. Yet, after these conversations, people willingly and cheerfully accepted adverse decisions. They had much greater need to feel heard than win the argument! I have come to believe that feeling heard is right up there with food and water in the scale of human needs. The following is broadly attributed to Dean Rusk. "The best way to persuade is with your ears—by listening to them."

Further, Maslow's needs hierarchy corroborates this view. The lowest level of this triangular configuration contains air, water, sleep, and food. The next level is only safety. Interestingly, the level above that is belonging. Maslow's notion is that you must satisfy your needs at each level before moving up to the next. This means that until people feel appreciated and included, they cannot move to higher-level tasks like problem solving or creativity.

Be Sensitive to Inclusion Manners

Try replacing negative expressions, like "I only have 15 minutes to talk with you," with positive ones, like "I have 15 minutes to talk with you." Pay attention to your body language. Do not talk to people over desks. When my boss, Len Fisk came to see me, he walked in, we closed the door, and we sat directly facing each other and talked. It seemed that he had absolutely nothing on his mind except talking with me. I felt included and appreciated. His deputy would stand in my doorway and talk *at* me. It is not the same.

Include Others by Sharing Something Personal

Sharing personal information builds trustworthiness because it demonstrates a willingness to be vulnerable. Make whatever personal item you want to share proportional to the depth of the relationship. For new relationships, keep it professional.

When I was consulting for TRW (now Northrop Grumman), my clients were often vice presidents. VP turnover was high. I frequently had to convince the new person that I created value. I knew the *story-lines* they were running about me because they shared them later. They were some variation on "consultants charge a lot of money to tell you what you already know."

When I met a new VP for the first time, I would say something like this: "I have worked in organizations since I was 18 years old, beginning as a co-op student. Now, for the first time in my life, I am working by myself at home. Your company is my organizational family. I have deep networks of close friends here. We have worked on programs together. I have an important personal connection to your company. Consulting for you is not just about the money I make. It is about my needs to belong to a community of people with similar experiences. Can you see how this fills the space with *Green story-lines*?

Make It Easy for Others to Include You

When I was at the University of Colorado, I was required to post office hours on my door. The university took this very seriously as it was required by state law. When a student showed up during these hours, I stopped whatever I was doing and gave them my undivided attention for as long as they wanted. If you are a boss or supervisor, try this. Post office hours on your door for walk-ins; you may learn a lot.

My close friend Tony Calio was administrator of the National Oceanic and Atmospheric Administration (NOAA). He told me this story about office hours. One of the fun aspects of that job was the ability to travel to interesting places in NOAA's airplanes and boats. Tony took such a trip during Congressional budget hearings. The chairperson walked into the hearing room and said, "Where's Calio?" His deputy apologized profusely explaining that urgent business had called Tony out of town. She banged her gavel saying he will pay for this in the NOAA budget and walked out. Tony quickly returned to town and tried to see her. Nothing worked. She would not see him. He was becoming increasingly anxious as time went on. Then he thought, "office hours."

Sure enough, she had one day per month set aside to see constituents. Tony went to her home office, signed in, and sat down to wait. After some considerable time they called his name. He walked in with a box of chocolates and a dozen roses. She laughed and gave him a big hug. All was okay from then on. Why not try posting office hours—you never know what might happen!

Finally, make it easy for others to include you by appreciating being included. It is as easy as saying, "Thank you for including me in this decision. I appreciate the opportunity to contribute."

Recovering a Troubled Project

The Compton Gamma Ray Observatory (CGRO) was the second of the four Great Observatories. CGRO was a most innovative program. We even had (informal) arrangements with the prime contractor to share savings resulting from their innovations.

Early in the program, I became aware of an emerging major problem. One innovation, a highly automated system for producing the drawings, was not working. The delay was threatening to move all the milestones out, triggering a large overrun. You may find this hard to believe, but there was a time when deficits in the federal budget caused U.S. presidents to cut programs. When the CGRO problem appeared, the Office of Management and Budget was looking for programs to cancel. If I surfaced a major CGRO overrun, I was sure the administration would cancel the project, ending not only gamma ray astronomy, but also stopping the entire Great Observatories program.

Although perhaps not broadly known, NASA historically spends about 90 percent of its budget on contracts. Therefore, it was customary to visit contractor plants when problems arose. The Astrophysics Division spent $750 million per year on contracts, mostly for complex space systems. It took me some time, but I finally realized that visiting contractors and talking about the technical difficulties was fascinating but near useless in actually fixing the problem. I then told the CGRO contractor that I would not visit until they were ready to present their recovery plan, and I wanted to visit soon. I gave them very specific direction about their recovery plan, including the possibility of deploying all of our reserves immediately. I went to their plant the following week to review their plan.

Their response was impressive. Although I did not know of the 4-D System then, their plan was very four dimensional. They began by showing me a recovery plan built in three-week segments (directing dimension). They would produce the drawings manually as they had previously. The new drawing release rate was fast enough that we could get back on schedule within nine weeks. We could absorb the additional costs with current reserves and almost preserve the master schedule. This would keep us under the radar screen of the people looking for programs to kill.

Now, how could our contractor motivate their technicians and engineers to put in the extreme effort that would be required? The contractor's program manager had spoken in depth to the CGRO team about core values. The stakes were high; both their professional reputations and those of their company were at stake (cultivating dimension). Everyone was motivated to fix the problem and save the program (and the contract).

CGRO was a generally well-designed and appropriately budgeted program, particularly for the work at the prime contractor plant. The contractor's program manager did another quick grass-roots cost estimate and promised his CGRO team that they would never have to endure anything like this again (visioning dimension).

The contractor's innovative action in the including dimension is the reason this story is here. They said to the recovery team, "We know that you are ready to do this. Your families, however, will suffer during this effort. If we are on schedule at each three-week milestone, the company will pay for you and your families to have dinner at a restaurant of your choice and give you that weekend off. Then, back to the grind on Monday. We hope that this small symbol that we care will be helpful."

We soon had CGRO back on schedule, and few ever knew of our deep trouble. I believe the four dimensionality of their response was central to the mission's survival.

Over-Inclusion—Too Many E-Mails?

Has excessive e-mail become a burden for you? A typical information worker who sits at a computer all day turns to his e-mail program more than 50 times and uses instant messaging 77 times, according to one measure by RescueTime, a company that analyzes computer habits. The company, which draws its data from 40,000 people who have tracking software on their computers, found that on average the worker also stops at 40 web sites over the course of the day (Richtel, 2008). In addition, the research firm Basex estimated the annual cost of unnecessary interruptions at work of $650 billion!

I suggest two simple strategies. Avoid the reply-all option when you can. Three out of every five e-mails generate a response. Whenever possible, put the entire message in the subject line. I have found that the longer an e-mail is the lower the probability of a response.

A Possible Team Meetings Agreement

John E. Tropman has researched meetings (see Korkki, 2008) finding that companies hold twice as many meetings as necessary. He names meetings "inept social forums," which managers may use to avoid work.

We urge teams to write meeting agreements like these and place them in plastic stands in their meeting rooms.

Every meeting has a meeting leader who:

- Sets the agenda, invites participants, and names intent as "information" or "decision" so people can determine if their attendance is required or not.
- Justifies meetings longer than 30 minutes (50 minutes should be the maximum duration of a meeting or a segment of a longer meeting; with so many back-to-back meetings, 60 minutes systematizes being late).
- Meetings start on time, with a defined grace period. Our company policy is $5 late fee for more than one minute late to our teleconferences. Because we are geographically distributed, they pay the fee by adding $5 to their next meal tip, providing an appreciation opportunity.
- Assures agreement on behavioral norms and meeting rules.
- Records and distributes minutes and action items appropriately.

Participants agree to:

- Arrive on time. (If late, quietly join the meeting, and process your broken agreement later using the process in the next chapter.)
- Support the designated meeting leader.

The Project Manager's "Truth Translation Table"

This is, of course, in here for some humor:

- "Essentially complete" means: *We are half done*.
- "We predict" means: *We hope to God*.
- "Risk is high but acceptable" means: *With 10 times the budget and 10 times the people, we stand a 50-50 chance*.
- "Potential showstopper" means: *The team has updated their resumes*.

- "Serious, but no insurmountable problems" means: *It will take a miracle.*

- "Task force to review" means: *25 people who are incompetent at their regular jobs will criticize the project.*

- "System is ready for delivery" means: *The money is all gone. We give up.*

An Application Summary for Including Others

The persona interview exercise works really well in workshop contexts. Again, I think it is too much of a stretch for most technical teams to conduct in their work context.

However, I suggest you gather your team and do the following exercise. Confirm that most members have read this chapter. Invite some conversation about insights people may have gained. Then, have each person write the over-inclusions (e.g., too many e-mails, insufficient meeting management discipline) and under-inclusions that limit team performance.

Have the team members speak what they have written and assign action items as appropriate. Of course, you can beneficially do this exercise by yourself.

Most important, use recurrent *Individual Development Assessments* and *Team Development Assessments*. These will bring your attention and mindsets to appropriately including others. Moreover, reassessments track your progress and your team's progress, providing encouragement to continue.

CHAPTER 15

Building Trustworthy Contexts

How important is your trustworthiness? John Whitney, director of the Deming Center for Quality Management (hardly a soft-skills enterprise), said mistrust wastes or compromises up to half of all daily business activities. Here is my favorite statement about trustworthiness: "We tend to judge ourselves by our intentions and others by their actions." It is cited in many books on leadership.

Your Agreements Management Habits

How about this quote broadly attributed to Ralph Waldo Emerson: "What you do speaks so loudly I cannot hear what you say?" How would you score your habits managing explicit agreements like these? (See Figure 15.1 for the fourth behavior.)

- Delivering work as promised;
- Meeting budget commitments;

FIGURE 15.1   Keeping Agreements, the Fourth of the Eight Behaviors

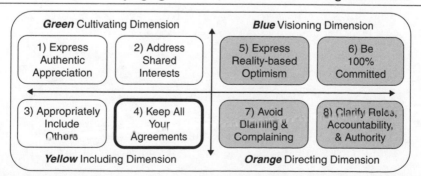

Green Cultivating Dimension		**Blue** Visioning Dimension	
1) Express Authentic Appreciation	2) Address Shared Interests	5) Express Reality-based Optimism	6) Be 100% Committed
3) Appropriately Include Others	4) Keep All Your Agreements	7) Avoid Blaming & Complaining	8) Clarify Roles, Accountability, & Authority
Yellow Including Dimension		**Orange** Directing Dimension	

- Meeting family commitments, like going home for dinner at the time you said; and
- Being responsible about what you ask others to agree to.

The last inquiry listed is especially important when there is a power differential, as in the case of a "government to contractor," or "contractor to subcontractor" interface. People frequently fail to think about *their* responsibility for what they ask others under their control to agree to. It is unfair to force agreements under duress and then beat people up when they cannot meet them.

How do you manage implicit agreements like showing up at meetings on time? Many have never thought of meetings as agreements. If you make this mindset shift, you will stop showing up late.

A mindset of commitment to keeping your agreements supports the state of integrity. Integrity means matching word to deeds. When you are out of integrity, you appear fuzzy to others, like the misprinted cartoons in the funny papers.

Costs of a Late-to-Meetings-Is-Okay Mindset

Many people habitually arrive late to meetings, oblivious to the impact they have on others. Here is our summary of the costs.

- You energize mad-group and sad-group emotions lowering the quality of feelings (mood) at the meeting:
  - Mad group: Irritated, annoyed, frustrated, and jealous;
  - Sad group: Alienated, rejected, and insulted.
- You energize negative *story-lines*:
  - About your motivations—they will have power and almost surely be wrong (95 percent of the time); and
  - About your lack of respect for others—they are the judges of this, not you.
- There are also productivity impacts:
  - Disorganization wastes people's time;
  - You create barriers to acceptance of your input, reducing your influence and thereby the worth of your contributions;

- You separate yourself from others, apparently deliberately; and
- You draw attention away from the working subject toward the perceived interpersonal affronts.

Is being late worth all this?

A manager in his second workshop came up to me and said, "That meeting thing did not work well at all." "Tell me," I said. "Well I went back to work after the last workshop. One minute after our scheduled weekly staff meeting, I locked the door. People were out there banging on the door. But," he continued, "here's the problem: The following week, I arrived at the staff meeting a minute late, and they locked me out." I said, "Sorry Fred, you missed the fundamental point. There is no agreement until everyone agrees."

Processing Broken Agreements

We all break agreements from time to time. Some of the reasons include:

- Lack of discipline;
- Poor planning; or
- Unexpected circumstances.

Suppose you and I had an agreement to meet at 3 PM. I left my office across town with plenty of time under normal circumstances to get to our meeting on time. An accident stopped traffic causing me to arrive 15 minutes late. Do I have a broken agreement? Yes, I do.

Here is the point. It does not matter what caused the agreement to be broken. A broken agreement is a broken agreement, period. How you handle it bears heavily on your trustworthiness. We urge people to use the following four-step process exactly as presented:

1. Tell the truth, as in "I broke my agreement with you;"
2. Describe the circumstances;
3. Tell how you will prevent this in the future; and
4. Lastly, express regret and apologize.

Why is apology last? It is because people all too easily use apology as deflection. Notice in the previous example, I could have simply called and renegotiated our meeting time, and avoided a broken engagement.

This is the point. If you commit to using this unpleasant process, you will become much more vigilant about entering and renegotiating agreements before you break them.

An Application Summary for Building Trustworthy Contexts

I suggest you gather your team and do the following exercise. Confirm that most members have read this chapter. Invite some conversation about insights people may have gained. Then, have each person write any *Red story-lines* about their keeping agreements habits of the past. For example, "So, I break agreements from time to time. What is the big deal? Other people break agreements too." Then, ask them to write a shift to a *Green story-line*, like "How I keep my agreements bears heavily on others' perception of my integrity."

Then invite team members to write some agreements they find especially difficult to keep.

Have the team members speak what they have written and assign action items as appropriate. Of course, you can beneficially do these exercises yourself.

Most important, use recurrent *Individual Development Assessments* and *Team Development Assessments*. These will bring your attention and mindsets to keeping all your agreements. Moreover, reassessments track your progress and your team's progress, providing encouragement to continue.

CHAPTER 16

Creating the Future You Want

Visioning What You Want

Optimistic, reality-grounded visions can create the impossible (Figure 16.1).
I believe you can easily name the source of these visions:

- Building a heavier-than-air flying machine from bicycle technology;
- "Make my little Newport store the best, most profitable variety store in Arkansas within five years;"
- "I have a dream that one day little black boys and black girls will be able to join hands with little white boys and white girls as sisters and brothers;"
- "Put a man on the moon and return him to Earth within the decade;"

FIGURE 16.1   Reality and Commitment, the Fifth and Sixth
of the Eight Behaviors

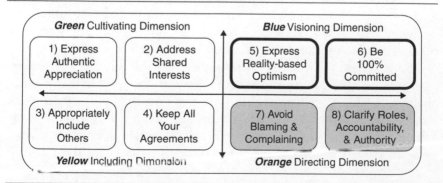

- "To democratize the automobile;" and
- "A New Physics in Our Lifetime." This is the vision I used to market the $8 billion Great Observatories program that I describe in detail later in this chapter. One of my colleagues recently said to me, "I don't see any new physics." I said, "Be patient, I am still alive."

Reality-Based Optimism (Hope)

The following is from Jerome Groopman, an oncologist (2003):

> Hope, unlike optimism, is rooted in unalloyed reality. Hope is the elevating feeling that we experience—when we see in the mind's eye—a path to a better future. Hope acknowledges the significant obstacles and deep pitfalls along the path. True hope has no room for delusion. Clear-eyed, hope gives us the courage to confront our circumstances and the capacity to surmount them. For all my patients, hope, true hope, has proved as important as any medication I might prescribe or any procedure I might perform.

We use the term "reality-based optimism" for what Groopman called "hope."

Reality and Truth as Platforms for Creativity

Facing the unalloyed reality is essential to creativity. Tom Friedman understands the necessity for reality (2008): "If there is anything I've learned as a reporter, it's that when you get away from 'the thing itself'—the core truth about a situation—you get into trouble. . . . So whether its cars, Kabul, or banks, we have to stop wishing for the worlds we want and start dealing with the things themselves."

When Andy Grove, the famous CEO of Intel, experienced diminishing margins in memory chip sales, he gathered his management team. They expressed the conviction that they could work more efficiently and reduce production costs faster than their Japanese competition. He was skeptical, suspecting that their investment in past decisions to build memory chips clouded their ability to perceive reality.

To create a new context, he asked a few of the people he most respected to pretend that the Intel board fired them all and brought in a new team. He then asked, "What would the new management do?" They decided to refocus Intel on microprocessors. What an interesting way to bring unalloyed reality into play.

Jim Collins (2001) writes, "Mediocre companies explain away brutal facts rather than confront them head on."

Using the Truth to Raise Hope

Will Schutz (1984) wrote the following: "Creating an atmosphere of truth is the one thing people seldom try—yet it leads to energy and aliveness, freedom to change, and increases productivity in every aspect of living."

I was working with a VP leading a proposal team competing for a multi-billion-dollar contract. The team's low morale concerned us all. We set up a 4-D *Team Development Assessment* with some special factors including a measurement of "P-win." P-win is the probability of winning. The team's P-win measured very low, about 0.2 or 20 percent. The team leader asked me what to do, as this would surely become a self-fulfilling prophecy.

I said, "Your problem is that you have been peddling unwarranted optimism. You need to move from optimism to reality-based optimism." Consider your morning pep talks. You tell them that the program is theirs to lose, that they are in first place, and if they just continue to work hard, victory is assured." He asked, "What's wrong with that?"

"The difficulty is that few believe these things, so all you cause is water-cooler conversations. You need to speak the unalloyed reality." I continued, "Tell them instead that this is really hard to win, they have not been given the resources they need, and are probably in second place. Then follow the reality with a statement that supports hope, a glad-group emotion. Tell them that top management is committed to this win—that's why you, a VP, are here and you are going to fight for what the team needs and will get it."

The manager delivered the reality-based, optimistic message and continued 4-D *Team Development Assessments* at three-week intervals. The team significantly improved, including monotonically raising P-win, and they won the contract!

The Great Observatories:
Problem Solving versus Creativity

Here is the difficulty with problem solving. Too many problems have mutually exclusive solutions. Learn to look for this characteristic and replace problem focus with creativity. Consider this story.

In the fall of 1982, NASA does what it always does when projects overrun. They get rid of the people who knew what they were doing, replace them with new people who do not know anything, and give the new people the money they would not give to the original managers.

When Hubble had its first $400 million overrun, the powers-that-be ran off my brilliant boss, Frank Martin, and made me director of the Astrophysics Division. I was just returning from 16 weeks at Harvard Business School, which qualified me, I suppose, as not knowing anything. I had just turned 38 years old.

Every few days (it seemed), a prominent scientist visited me telling me that I should do the Advanced X-Ray Astrophysics Facility (AXAF) instead of the Space Infrared Telescope Facility (SIRTF) and vice-versa. These were equivalent missions to Hubble measuring light at shorter (x-ray) and longer (infrared) wavelengths. The scientists posed the problem of which to do first believing that it would be a very long time before the later mission would be done, if ever. The argument might have been worth having if one mission supplanted the need for the other. However, either mission increased the necessity for the other. Can you see this as a problem with mutually exclusive solutions? I refused to enter the problem-solving path of deciding which would go first. I chose instead to find a creative solution to the dilemma.

Creativity starts with facing reality. First, although I had the power, in principle, to decide the sequence of the missions, I knew that no matter what I decided the battle would continue. The loser would mobilize their political/scientific constituents and come after me with a vengeance. More important, they would attack the chosen mission and make it more difficult to fund. The reality was that I needed to create a fresh, compelling strategy that would mobilize everybody behind both missions, including the two (Hubble and CGRO) already underway. Hubble's recurrent overruns kept the astrophysics program in constant peril, complicating matters.

Martin Harwit's book, *Cosmic Discovery* (1981), made the case that astronomical discoveries follow advances in measurement capabilities.

His book also listed the 10 biggest unsolved questions about the universe. Here are two of my favorites. What is the 90 percent of the matter in the universe that emits no known radiation? (Astronomers call this "dark matter.") How do quasars emit as much energy in one second as the sun does in 30,000 years?

I began to wonder whether measuring the extreme states of matter in the universe across all temperature regimes could sufficiently constrain theory to bring a new physics forward. Physics has had few fundamental advances since the middle of the last century. If we bundled Hubble, CGRO, AXAF, and SIRTF with ground-based radio astronomy, we could measure all the wavelengths of light that could travel through the universe. This was equivalent to measuring all temperature regimes in accordance with Planck's law.

This idea of an integrated program with the objective of being the first country to find the new physics was both appealing and technically defendable. Moreover, the requirement for contemporaneous measurements helped all four missions. We could fight descoping Hubble if visible and ultraviolet measurements were required to understand SIRTF's infrared data, and so on. My biggest problem was that many of the political people I had to convince lacked an understanding of physics or, for that matter, anything technical. Moreover, they ran *Red story-lines* that astrophysics was too hard to understand. I am speaking of the politicians and career civil servants throughout the government.

I thought that if we made the communications medium simple enough we could convince these people. So, I conceived of using a comic book to describe the program. Comic books should not scare anyone. Then, I asked my deputy to assemble 10 great astrophysicists to meet with me in a month. I said, "Tell them that NASA's director of astrophysics wants them to make a comic book." He said, "What if they won't come?" I said, "Tell them they can call me if they need to—otherwise I'll expect them to be there."

These people were like gods to me when I was a researcher. I began to get nervous about managing the meeting. I called Martin Harwit, whom I had never met, and asked him to run the meeting for me. With Martin worrying about the mechanics, I would have time to think.

Martin and I had dinner together the night before and immediately liked each other. We decided to put flip-chart papers on the floor with one of his unsolved mysteries of the universe questions at the top of each page. We would give the world-renowned astrophysicists crayons and ask them to sketch the object in question (for example, quasars) and draw each of the observatories measuring whatever it could to help understand the physics. In addition, of course, they needed to provide the detailed science arguments.

At the end of the day, Martin gathered the charts and worked with Valerie Neal to make a booklet with cartoon-like drawings. The question then was what to call the program. George Field, who had just wrapped up the National Academy of Sciences decadal survey of priorities for astronomy stopped by my office. I told him what we had done, and he said he wished the academy had thought of this idea. I said, "George, my only dilemma is what to call this program of observatories, it's so great." George said, "Why don't you call it the Great Observatories."

We had a name! Martin and Valerie finished the layout, and it was time to print. The question now was how many booklets I could have printed. No one seemed to know, so I ordered 50,000. Martin and I took them everywhere—to the administration, Capitol Hill, the NASA centers and school districts. The only thing we did not do is drop them from airplanes, although we considered it. Within a year, the "Great Observatories" was a household name, at least in political Washington, DC.

Today, all four have flown successfully with three still in orbit collecting fresh science every day! Creativity trumps problem solving. The key to this creative solution was acceptance of the real and unpleasant consequences of my making a sequencing decision.

In 2007, the American Astronautical Society (AAS) gave me their highest recognition, the Space Flight Award, for the Great Observatories program. I am very grateful to the AAS.

Project Overruns:
Problem Solving versus Creativity

People generally approach project cost overruns from a problem-solving perspective. By overrun we mean that a project has exhausted its financial resources and requires more money (and usually time) to complete. Project managers reach a point where there is no solution to the overrun except to ask for more money.

From the sponsor's perspective, providing this additional funding has an opportunity cost, and for government programs perhaps unpleasant hearings with Congress. Because few people understand the power of context, they make the attribution error of naming the project manager as the problem. They remove him or her and name a new project manager (PM).

Sponsors and new PMs frequently denigrate the remaining team members, compounding the project's difficulties. When we use *Team Development Assessments*, these teams benchmark in the bottom quintile. Moreover, they know that the resources are still insufficient and a similar cycle is likely coming.

You will see in Chapter 17, "Your Team Can't Afford Drama," that sponsors' blaming energy results from their own unacknowledged roles in creating the problem. They probably had a say in selecting/approving the PM they are now removing. We know the common root causes of project overruns—people have studied them for years. It is interesting that the root causes of NASA project overruns has much more to do with sponsors' actions than PMs'. Here are a few:

- Insufficient study/pre-approval study funding: There is a correlation with the amount of pre-approval study/analysis and overruns. Two factors are at play here. First, the better we understand a project early on, the easier it is to adjust requirements downward to meet cost targets. Moreover, the precision of any cost estimate is only as good as our understanding of the technical details. Second, you have a much better insight into the technology readiness. Sponsors set the amount of pre-approval funding, not the PMs.

- Tight budgeting: Sponsors are pushing price estimates and reserves downward and optimistic PMs are complying. Up-front funding seldom meets project needs efficiently—the nearest budget years are always the tightest. Finally, nobody has reserves for the unknown unknowns that frequently arise in difficult technical projects.

- Procurement processes: Winning industrial proposal teams know that they must bid the market price to compete regardless of what they believe the project will ultimately cost.

The managers of NASA's biggest projects frequently tell me they expect to be fired within two years or less no matter what they do. What a horrible context for the most important people in the workforce. I suspect the situation is similar in all industries with large, high-visibility projects.

The mindsets in play cause these actions on the project side:

- Projects meter bad news out carefully trying to avoid the "being fired" or "project cancellation" thresholds;
- Project performance trends ever downward in the increasingly stressful social context;
- As being fired nears, project managers care less and less about the project; and
- A sense of powerlessness sets in as project managers increasingly adopt the victim state (more about this in Chapter 17).

The mindsets in play cause these effects on the sponsor side:

- Trustworthiness breaks down as information is withheld;
- Sponsors increasingly adopt a hostile, blamer mindset that prevents them from seeing the situation objectively; and
- Sponsors also feel increasingly powerless.

The irony is that both parties see the solution in an action by the other that they cannot force. The sponsor wants the PM to stop the overruns, and the PM wants sufficient funding to do the work in a high-performance social context.

Creating the Project You Want

1. You must begin with truth-based, unalloyed reality. Embracing unalloyed reality is difficult to master and very human to avoid. Here are some reality-surfacing inquiries:

    a. Where are we? We officially passed the XYZ milestone but did not really meet all the requirements.

    b. How did we get here? We bamboozled the review board with PowerPoint slides. We also deceived our sponsor. It seemed better than risking cancellation.

    c. Why are there so many new technical requirements? As project manager, I did not push back hard enough on new requirements from the functional organization. (Aerospace organizations use matrix-management. They house technical staff in the functional organization and loan these people to project teams.) As sponsor, I shortchanged the study phase spending only two percent of estimated project cost before approving the project. As contractor, I justified bidding the market price by ignoring essential technology development costs.

2. Now, having faced reality, what do you want to create?

   a. I want to create a lean, efficient, motivated *Orange* team with the resources to do the job right, and not one cent more.

   b. I also want our team's members responsibly taking care of their families.

3. How will you make this happen?

   a. I use the material in *How NASA Builds Teams* to create a high-performance context. Firing project management will be a last resort, and only with well-identified cause.

      i. First, we measure the personality foundations, culture field, and coherence of the project paradigm. I take action in all three areas as required. (A three-day 4-D workshop could be useful.)

      ii. I launch full team assessments for all the organizations and individual assessments for all key personnel immediately.

      iii. Team leaders promptly debrief team members including assigning action items. Individuals who need improvement engage in coaching.

      iv. I schedule *4-D Team and Individual Development Reassessments* at appropriate intervals, in three months, for example.

      v. Before every difficult communication, I use the Context Shifting Worksheet (perhaps with a 4-D certified coach) so the sponsor can hear the truth about what they need to provide the project with to complete in the most efficient manner and ultimately succeed.

The recycling stops. The project completes within the revised budget, meets all the technical requirements, and performs flawlessly on orbit. The team and sponsor have a sense that they are capable and powerful, enjoying forthright communications.

Outcome Commitment

W. N. Murray, of the Scottish Himalayan Expedition, said the following (which he got from Goethe): "The moment one definitely commits oneself, providence moves too. All sorts of things occur . . . that would otherwise never have occurred. A whole stream of events issues . . . which no one could have dreamt . . ."

We call "definitely committing oneself" 100 percent commitment. This is the most magical notion in this book. It is about the connection between our level of commitment and our perceptions of reality.

You may be familiar with the *Red* convertible syndrome. Have you ever had it in your mind to buy a certain kind of car? You then see them all over the place. When my wife, Junko, first moved here from Japan, we stopped next to a metallic purple car. She said to me, "I have never seen a car with that color before. Are they common in America?" I said, "I guess not. I've never seen one either." We saw four more in the next 10 minutes.

This can be uncanny. On a trip to Europe, the train doors in the Denver airport broke the handle on Junko's "wheelie" suitcase. As we walked around DC during a stop on the way, 90 percent of the people we saw had wheelie bags in tow. Our concern about replacing her bag caused our perception to become hyper-vigilant for wheelie bags of all kinds.

Outcome Commitment and the Hubble Servicing Mission

People used to say to me, "Putting the Hubble servicing together must have been really hard for you." Actually, it was the easiest thing I have ever done. All the trauma and strife supported me in 100 percent commitment to fixing the telescope. My 100 percent commitment caused solutions to appear naturally and magically.

Scientists from the Hubble Space Telescope Science Institute visited me asking for $50,000 to study possible fixes. They left with the money 30 minutes later. Normally, anyone would have to participate in a competition for a $50,000 grant.

At that time, nobody wanted to hear about a repair mission. In fact, it was not even clear that one was possible. The congressional representative with control of NASA's budget told me directly they would provide no appropriated funds for a servicing mission. Therefore, I sat with my budget analyst and found $60 million in one hour. I would have quit NASA if anyone did the damage to my programs that we did. I called my staff together and told them what I had done to each of their programs. There were no complaints.

At that time, nobody wanted to be associated with the broken telescope. I made a list of the most highly qualified people in NASA to mount a servicing mission (before we knew that a technical fix was possible) and called each one. I said, "I am committed to mounting a space repair to fix Hubble, will you help?" Every person enthusiastically said yes.

I became convinced that the Hubble lead at a NASA center was insufficiently committed for a successful repair. The only person who could replace him was his center director who was on a two-week vacation on his sailboat. I went to my boss and said I could not wait for him to come back. We called the Coast Guard to find the boat and relay our order to come to NASA headquarters immediately. When he arrived, he was very angry. He turned to my boss and asked (with some expletives) why he was here. My boss pointed to me and said, "He's my man." I said to the center director, "It's like this. The person you have managing the Hubble servicing mission is unacceptable to me. Go place someone who is acceptable in that job and you can return to your boat." He stormed out. I had a new 100 percent committed Hubble servicing mission manager before the day ended. Then, I guess he went back to his boat.

A clever engineer at Ball Aerospace came up with a fix for the flawed mirror called "COSTAR." It appeared that the device would cost about $20 million. Usually buying something like this would take many months as the procurement process lumbered along. I went to the head of NASA procurement and said, "I want a letter contract to start building the COSTAR by tomorrow." He said this was impossible and asked what we would do when other companies complained. I said, "You send them to me. I'll take care of this." He looked into my eyes and saw the blaze of 100 percent commitment. The letter contract went to Ball and work began.

My Hubble servicing manager came to me and said, "Johnson is refusing to assign the mission specialists for the mission. They want to wait until we are closer to the flight. I am concerned about sufficient time for the astronauts to train for this very complex space operation." These astronauts, named in the dedication of this book, don space suits and work outdoors to repair the telescope. It is extremely hazardous work. Astronauts work and train at NASA's Johnson Space Center (JSC).

When I was at Harvard Business School, we talked about "first, get their attention" with a dramatic move. If people are not communicating, remove all the office doors over the weekend. If you are having trouble having folks attend staff meetings, call one for 4 AM. It was time to make a statement at JSC.

The NASA administrator had a marvelous business jet at his disposal, a Gulfstream III with call sign "NASA-1." Admiral Dick Truly was NASA administrator during the time of the Hubble crisis and did not use the plane often. My secretary and I figured out how I could use NASA-1 nearly anytime I wanted. I only had to fill the place (14 people) with senior executives. With my big program, I had no difficulty doing this. (I did not share this finding with my colleagues.) NASA-1 is not Air Force-1, but it is still cool to come and go at my leisure, and to climb like a rocket to 44,000-foot cruise altitudes. With call sign NASA-1, we never had an air traffic control delay.

I asked the JSC director Aaron Cohen to gather his senior staff and the astronaut candidates for a conversation about assignments for the Hubble servicing mission. Also, please have several cars meet NASA-1 at Ellington Air Force Base. Our pilot would radio an ETA in once we were airborne. I carefully chose the 14 most senior Hubble managers from headquarters and Goddard. I believe Aaron and his team were both shocked and honored at the management presence (and our transportation) and immediately grasped that we saw this as a very serious concern. Of course, we appreciated them, stated our intention to work together, held the vision of a mutually satisfying conclusion, and requested an early crew assignment. (A power struggle would have been disastrous.) JSC named the servicing mission astronauts soon thereafter.

Therefore, when you have a situation that requires the attention of powerful people, remember these examples and decide how committed you are. Conversely, if you notice that you are taking bold, crazy actions, you are probably already 100 percent committed.

Outcome Commitment and My Wife

Actually, when I was 100 percent committed to the Hubble servicing mission I did not name my actions as such. I had never heard of the concept. Years later, I enrolled in a somatic psychology certification course with Kate and Gay Hendricks. I mentioned to Gay that, after being divorced for 10 years, I thought it was time to remarry but could not find a suitable mate. He said, "Don't you know that it is easy to have anything you want?" I was dumbfounded. Gay continued, "Why don't you drive down to Colorado Springs and we will have lunch and talk about it."

A few weeks later, I drove from Boulder to have lunch with Gay. He explained, "The way to get what you want is to become 100 percent committed and you will then see how to get it." I thought about the Hubble servicing and realized that that is exactly what happened. Then, I thought about marriage and realized I actually was ambivalent about remarrying and that was why no suitable person had appeared.

I have been attracted to Japanese people for a long time. (The fact that I lived on Okinawa from age 8 to 13 might have something to do with this.) When I became director of astrophysics I used the shared interests work to establish broad, mutually beneficial cooperation with my Japanese counterparts as described earlier. After I retired from NASA, I became the U.S. chair of the Boulder-Yamagata, Japan, friendship society. I linked up with a group of Japanese "Cosmos Ladies" who stayed in my house when in Boulder, and I stayed in their houses when I traveled to Japan.

One day, I got it. I was ready to be 100 percent committed to remarrying, and I knew my wife-to-be was in Japan. I closed my business for three months and moved to Yamagata. Speaking little or no Japanese in a small town in Japan was turning out to be much more problematic than I thought. I had a three-month lease on a "mansion" (Japanese-English for an apartment) and could not easily move. Therefore, I traveled frequently to Tokyo and went on dates mostly arranged by my Harvard classmates. Taking care of employees, including finding them spouses, is part of a senior Japanese business executive's role. However, it soon became clear that romance develops 10 times slower in Japan than in the United States, and my plan would not work.

I left the mainland to visit Okinawa for a week. When I returned to my Tokyo hotel, a large pile of phone messages was waiting for me. My Cosmos Ladies friends had found my match, a lady named Junko, in Sapporo. Unfortunately, we could not find a time to meet before my planned departure, and I returned home.

Communicating through a third party, I invited Junko to visit me in Boulder—many now-married Cosmos Ladies had done this.

Moreover, if we were to marry, we would have to live in the United States, as I could not work in Japan. The dialogue went on for weeks then died out. One day, a paper rolled out of my fax machine in Japanese. I studied it and saw that it was a flight schedule with the cities' names handwritten in English. Junko was arriving in Denver this coming Saturday and spending a week with me in Boulder.

I went to the airport to meet a woman I had never spoken to, never seen a picture of, and knew little about. I stood with a sign with her name on it and waited. Frankly, I was astounded that she came. Later, she explained that New Years is, by far, the most important holiday of the year. Moreover, dreams during this time are very important. She said that she had New Years dreams that this was the year she would meet her destiny partner. She learned about me in late December of that year.

We spent the week together, and, knowing her as I do today, I did nearly everything wrong (such as taking her snowshoeing in the backcountry during a major storm). Nonetheless, we were both ready, 100 percent committed, and fell totally in love. We remain very happily married nearly 10 years later. I remain 100 percent committed to happy marriage with Junko and manage the context we live in. With the understanding that context trumps everything, I am careful to sustain a context that supports a happy marriage. We manage our money carefully, never impose unpleasant relatives on the other, and travel together for work and pleasure.

Which Outcomes Are You Committed to Achieving?

Check out this film clip in the movie *City Slickers* (1991). The scene is a conversation between Curly (Jack Palance) and Mitch (Billy Crystal). Curly addresses Mitch telling him, "None of you get it." He continues by asking Mitch if he knows what the secret of life is. When Mitch answers no, Curly says, "This." (Holding up his forefinger.)

Mitch: Your finger?

Curly: One thing, just one thing—you stick to that and everything else don't mean shit.

Mitch: That's great, but what's the one thing?

Curly: That's what you've got to figure out.

Now reflect on this from the play *Joan of Lorraine* (1946). I modified the dialogue a bit substituting "committed to" for "believe in."

> I know this now. Every man gives his life for what he [is committed to]. Every woman gives her life for what she [is committed to]. Sometimes people [are committed to] little or nothing, and so they give their lives to little or nothing. One life is all we have, and we live it as [we are committed to] living it and then it's gone. But to surrender whom you are and to live without [commitment] is more terrible than dying—even more terrible than dying young.

The Commitment Scale

We calibrate commitment with a percent scale. We call whatever-it-takes commitment "100 percent commitment." This state of being produces the magical shifts in perception revealing solutions that lesser levels of commitment will not. Figure 16.2 shows the emotions and *story-lines* for different levels of commitment.

A workshop participant said to me, "I feel I am 100 percent committed to this program. But, I don't see any 'magical' changes in my perceptions." On a guess I asked him, "What time do you go to work in the morning?" He said, "I get in about 7. I like to get a good start before too many people arrive." Then I asked, "What time do you go home at night?" He said, "Well, actually I don't like to leave much before the West Coast shuts down. I probably leave a little after 7 PM." I said, "You don't perceive anything odd about routinely working 12-hour days?" He answered, "No, seems reasonable to me." He is right. It is reasonable, if you are 100 percent committed.

FIGURE 16.2 The Commitment Calibration Scale

Commitment	Emotions	*Story-Lines*
~100%	Accessing the power of Glad, Mad, Sad, Scared, and Love-group emotions.	Hopeful (reality-based), *Story-Lines* about "Whatever it takes."
0%–95%	Low emotional intensity.	Optimistic versions about "I'll try"

Movie scripts provide good opportunities to observe 100 percent committed people. Look for these two characteristics:

1. Passionate expression of emotions, often mad-group, and
2. Reality-based optimism.

Apollo 13

Here is a scene with Apollo Flight Director Gene Kranz and his team-mates John Aaron and Jerry Bostick in the movie *Apollo 13* (1995). John reports the harsh reality that they have to turn off the radar, cabin heaters, instrument displays, and guidance computer. Jerry notes that without the guidance computer they will not know where the engine points if they have to do another burn. John brings them back to reality again, saying, "The more we talk down here, the more juice they waste up there."

Gene finally agrees and says, "I want you guys to find every engineer who designed every switch, every circuit, every transistor, and every light bulb that's out there. Then I want you to talk to the guys on the assembly line who actually built the thing. Find out how to squeeze every amp out of both of these God-damned machines. I want this mark all the way back to Earth with time to spare. We've never lost an American in space, and we're sure as hell not going to lose one on my watch. Failure is not an option."

This demonstrates 100 percent commitment with harsh reality (turn off everything) and passionate mad-group emotions.

Braveheart

In the movie *Braveheart* (1995), William Wallace (Mel Gibson) responds to a fellow Scot's contention that they will not fight the British troops because there are too many and they would die with the following reality-based optimism. Wallace says, "Aye, fight and you may die. Run and you will live, at least a while. And dying in your bed, many years from now, would you be willing to trade all of your days, from this to that, for one chance, just one chance, to come back here and tell our enemies that they may take our lives, but they'll never take our freedom?"

Notice that he did not say, "Don't worry, we will win, and you will live." Again, this is 100 percent commitment with harsh reality (fight and you may die) and passionate mad-group emotions.

Miracle

In the movie *Miracle* (2004) about the U.S. hockey team's improbable Olympic gold medal in 1980, Herb Brooks motivates his young American team with the following: "I am sick of hearing how good the Soviets are. If we played them 10 times, we would lose nine. But not tonight. Tonight is your night. Tonight we skate with them. Tonight, we shut them down because we can. Tonight is your night. So, go take it."

He expresses 100 percent commitment and harsh reality (If we played them 10 times we would lose nine) and passionate mad-group emotions.

These are three great films about 100 percent outcome commitment. If you aren't familiar with them, go see them.

My (Charlie's) Commitments

Right now, these are my commitments:

- *Mindsets*: 100 percent committed to living in gratitude, abundance, and service. (Other peoples' responses in our workshops include follow my bliss, uplift others, stewardship, open mind, finding God before he finds me, good laughs every day, see grace in small things, generosity of spirit, expressing my creativity, conscious choices, giving back, vibrant health, 4-D living, no regrets, joy and harmony with my mate.)
- *Work*: 100 percent committed to broadly fielding the most effective team and individual development processes in the world.
- *Family*: 90–100 percent committed to serving my wife, children, and granddaughters, depending on whom we are speaking about.
- *Life*: 100 percent committed to a meaningful life, expressing my creativity, and having fun. About 70 percent committed to health excellence.

I ask workshop participants how they perceive me. Do they see the passion and 100 percent commitment to them during the workshop? They answer in the affirmative.

Then, I say, "Can you look at me and tell that I am only 70 percent committed to health excellence?" (I have been about 20 pounds overweight for years.) "Here is my trouble, I am an oenophile," I say, pause briefly. "I live in a constant tug-of-war between fine wine and health."

What Are Your Commitments?

Take a few minutes to begin your personal inquiry. I recommend using a 3×5 card as in Figure 16.3 so you can keep this handy.

If you complete this inquiry, you will discover your current commitments and the depth of your commitments in percentage points. Your results might surprise you. In our workshops, people write for about 10 minutes then speak their commitments to the group. This exercise moves everyone deeply as participants express significant emotional experiences. I have heard participants say, "I see that I am not sufficiently committed to this project, so when I get back to work I will transfer to another job. I owe this to the rest of you." I have watched people stand up with tears streaming down their faces saying, "I have been neglecting my wife and children all these years. I will change that now." I have heard, "I never thought about the purpose of my life. I will start working with the charities I deeply care about but never did anything with." My favorite is a woman who said, "I am 100 percent committed to my children and about 50 percent committed to my husband. He's an adult and can take care of himself."

When you decide you are 100 percent committed, notice where your attention goes and the mindsets you are holding. For example, when you are 100 percent committed to losing weight, healthy salads appear more delicious than pasta dishes. If this is not your perception, simply tell yourself the truth that you are not 100 committed to diet and revise your number downward. It might help to write down the forces pulling you in each direction and see if you can see how to strengthen the one you want and lessen the countering force.

FIGURE 16.3   What Are Your Commitments?

Write your commitments on a 3×5 card including %:

Mindsets: ___ % to _____

_____

Work Outcomes: ____ % to _____

_____

Family Outcomes: ____ % to _____

_____

Life Outcomes: ____ % to _____

_____

The Mindset of a Purposeful Life

I greatly admire Katharine Graham. After her husband's suicide following prolonged mental illness, she took over managing the *Washington Post*. This broadly cited statement from her about life moves me every time I read it: "To love what you do and feel that it matters—how could anything be more fun?" That is the life I am committed to having.

I wrote earlier about my life vision. This work is in the important-but-not-urgent category—until you are on one of life's cusps, some kind of career or life juncture, then this work becomes both important and urgent.

Writing a life vision that connects you to the purposes that give your life meaning is an exciting adventure. When I was working on mine, I looked through some old files. I found a Strong Interest Inventory from my high school days. This instrument compares your values with those of people in various occupations. Physics was not on the list, but chemistry was. My rating was very low. My high ratings were in medicine and teaching. This explained why I had obtained a PhD in physics and left research soon after. I began planning my move from NASA to academia.

You May Have Less Time Than You Think

A clerk in Boeing's retirement department noticed that people who retired at 65 received, on the average, only 18 monthly checks. This surprising finding led to a longitudinal study with the following average results for Boeing:

- People who retired at 55 lived for 30 more years;
- People who retired at 60 lived for 15 more years; and
- People who retired at 65 lived for 1.5 more years.

I later learned that Martin Marietta in Denver (now Lockheed-Martin) performed a similar broad study with a similar finding. They found that their people who retired at 65 only survived 17 months. Workshop participants have reported that Lockheed-Martin prominently displays a graphic describing the above data in the Denver employment office.

People respond to this information in interesting ways. Some discount it saying, "Yes, but that doesn't apply to me because . . ." Others have told me later that they saw the chart when they were under 60 years old and retired immediately.

Occasionally someone will say, "I am already over 65. What should I do?" I respond, "Whatever you do, don't retire. It's too dangerous!"

Carpe Diem

I hope the information above creates a sense of urgency. This is the notion of *carpe diem*, as expressed in the following scene from the movie *Dead Poets Society* (1989). Prep school teacher John Keating takes his class to look at old photographs of prior students. Then he reads from Robert Herrick: "Gather ye rosebuds while ye may, Old Time is still a-flying. And this same flower that smiles to-day, To-morrow will be dying."

He discusses the meaning of the poem, and continues:

> We are food for worms, lads. Because, believe it or not, each and every one of us in this room is one day going to stop breathing, grow cold, and die. I'd like you to step forward over here. Peruse some of the faces from the past. You've walked past them many times, but I don't think you really looked at them. They're not that different from you, are they? Full of hormones, just like you. Invincible, just like you feel. The world is their oyster. They believe they are destined for great things, just like many of you. Their eyes are full of hope, just like you. Did they wait until it was too late to make from their lives even one iota of what they were capable? Because, you see gentlemen, these boys are now fertilizing daffodils. If you listen real close, you can hear them whisper their legacy to you. Go on. Lean in. Listen. Your hear it? (whispering) Carpe, Carpe diem—Seize the day, boys, make your lives extraordinary.

Marketing, Selling, and President Reagan

This story is here to illustrate how crazy appears perfectly normal to 100 percent committed people. I like to say that I spent 16 intense weeks at the Harvard Business School and only learned one thing, but it was worth it. I learned the difference between marketing and selling.

Selling is trying to push a customer to buy what you want to sell. Marketing is finding out what a customer wants and providing it.

I worked to customize marketing for the third Great Observatory, the Advanced X-Ray Astrophysics Facility (AXAF), my greatest challenge in moving the program forward.

- The *Orange* NASA administrator wanted something to use the Space Shuttle; AXAF was Shuttle launched and serviced;
- The *Blue* science community wanted premiere science; AXAF promised great discoveries; and
- The *Orange* Congress wanted cost certainty; we had a good story for AXAF's cost control.

After years of effect, I finally got AXAF into the president's budget. AXAF had even escaped the usual "Thanksgiving massacre," which is the Office of Management and Budget's (OMB) changes to the agency's budget as they prepare for Congress. Strangely, they call this the "mark-up" when all I saw them do is "mark-down." Then in December, my boss, Len Fisk, walked into my office and said, "Charlie, I have bad news. OMB has removed AXAF from the budget. The economy is below projections and last-minute cuts have been made." He went on, "The administrator has decided not to reclama." "Reclama" is budget jargon for appealing a cut. Ultimately, reclamas required personal meetings with the president in an attempt to roll the OMB director. I felt the wind knocked out of me.

With Len's permission, I went to see NASA administrator Jim Fletcher. Jim told me that he was not inclined to reclama. "I'm sorry," he said, "but there are higher-priority problems in the NASA budget." This was Jim's second time as administrator. During the period in-between, he chaired a board that I worked with. I treated him with the respect that an ex-administrator deserved. Most people did not. We built a nice friendship.

Now, as second-time administrator, Jim called me from time to time to get a "sanity check" or just chat about the NASA workforce. He thus agreed to listen to me about the importance of AXAF. (I actually probably begged and pleaded for help.) My recollection of what happened next is hazy, but suddenly word came from the administrator's office to prepare a presentation. We would meet with President Reagan in five days!

"What will I do? I wondered." I have slides to sell AXAF on science, shuttle use, and cost certainty. Nevertheless, I doubted that the
president would override his OMB director and put this multi-billion-
dollar program in the budget for any of these reasons. My friend
Riccardo Giacconi had lunch with President Reagan and broached
the subject of x-rays. Reagan interrupted him saying, "I know all
about that. In London when you squint through the fog, you are seeing x-rays from the sun." X-rays do not penetrate Earth's atmosphere.
We could forget about science as an argument. Moreover, the dollars involved were insignificant in the scale of the federal programs.
Finally, AXAF was in a very long list of canceled programs.

I thought, "Selling vs. marketing. Selling vs. marketing. Hmm?
What does the president really care about?" I cleared my calendar
and called Trish Pengra, my wonderful support contractor. We sat all
day staring at my computer repeating, "Selling vs. marketing. What
does the president really care about?"

Then we got it. The "Evil Empire" was the President's deal. More
than anything, President Reagan cared about besting the Soviets. At
the time, I co-chaired the first working group on Soviet-American
cooperation in space science (astronomy) with my counterpart,
Rashid Sunyaev. Rashid had given me a picture of the MIR space station with an x-ray instrument, the Kvant module, attached. Bingo!

We learned that presidents do not strain their eyes looking into
projected view-graph images. Presidential briefings require 2-foot by
4-foot foam-boards. Trish found a contractor, and we made a set of
five. The first four were the usual AXAF marketing materials about
the science, the technology, and the cost control. The final image had
two semi-transparent flags. The Soviet flag was on the left with MIR
in the background. The American flag was on the right with AXAF in
the background. The heading said, "To whom will the future of space
astronomy belong." We had the winning story. How would we get
it to OMB?

NASA thoroughly reviews anything that goes outside, much less
to the OMB or potentially to the president. I called Len's administrative assistant and said, "I made some charts for OMB. Does anybody
want to see them?" To my delight and amazement, she said, "No." I
then called the administrator's assistant asking the same question and
received the same answer.

At that moment, I had a choice. I could call these people
back and explain the full import of what I was doing, which would

trigger a deep review. Management would surely not permit me to send my last chart as it would trump other NASA priorities. That is what anyone who was less than 100 percent committed would see as the proper course of action.

Being 100 percent committed, we addressed a label to the director of OMB and wrote "AXAF Reclama Materials" on the wrapper. We sent the foam boards without a cover letter. Trish called a courier to deliver the package directly to the OMB director's office. I am still amazed that we managed to send this briefing directly to OMB with no review by anybody, but we did. We were now two days away from the scheduled meeting with the president.

I received a call from Len Fisk the next day. He said, "Charlie, I don't know what happened, but Administrator Fletcher just called and AXAF is back in the budget!" I offered no explanation other than, "That's really good news. Thank you for calling" and hung up as quickly as I could.

I recently had a participant in a 4-D workshop who worked in OMB during that time. He told me that the chart became famous for its audacity. When the OMB director saw it, he immediately restored AXAF's funding.

Perhaps the most interesting aspect of this adventure was that I never thought much about the enormous risk I was taking. If management learned of what I had done, the punishment would have been severe. When one is 100 percent committed, his or her mind does not go to fear.

An Application Summary for Creating What You Want

I believe that this is the most profound section in the book. (What opinion did you expect from a *Blue*?) If you have not done the exercise on what you are committed to with assigned percentages, please do so now. You may be able to make the changes you want purely intellectually, but I doubt it. Major life change is more likely when accompanied by a Significant Emotional Experience (SEE) such as that described in the workshops above. My best thought, lacking this emotional catharsis, is to keep at it. Make a periodic inventory of what you are committed to habitually, bringing your attention to what matters most, shifting your mindsets and gradually your behaviors.

Decide what you want to create, a high-performance project team, for example. You must fully acknowledge difficult truths and realities as discussed above. Vision what you want, and when you are sufficiently committed the path will appear.

Most important, use recurrent *Individual Development Assessments* and *Team Development Assessments*. These will bring your attention and mindsets to expressing reality-based optimism and outcome commitment. Moreover, reassessments track your progress and your team's progress, providing encouragement.

CHAPTER 17

Your Team Can't Afford Drama

Mounting the Stage—Performing Your Melodrama

Now, here is the bad news. You can master everything in *How NASA Builds Teams* described so far and find yourself unable to take action unless you are in the mindset of response-ability. What takes us out of this state? We lose our capacity to respond by entering one of the four drama states: rescuer, blamer, victim, and rationalizer. Boy George is broadly cited for, "If you have to be in a soap opera, try not to get the worst role."

Dr. Steve Karpman pioneered this work with his "Drama Triangle" (1968). The fourth state, the rationalizer, came from placing the 4-D System on drama. (As in previous chapters, note in Figure 17.1 that we continue tracking progress assessed behavior and assessed behavior as we go.)

FIGURE 17.1   No Blaming or Complaining, the Seventh of the Eight Behaviors

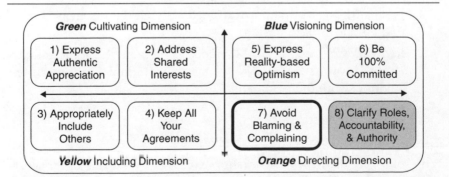

Green Cultivating Dimension		*Blue* Visioning Dimension	
1) Express Authentic Appreciation	2) Address Shared Interests	5) Express Reality-based Optimism	6) Be 100% Committed
3) Appropriately Include Others	4) Keep All Your Agreements	7) Avoid Blaming & Complaining	8) Clarify Roles, Accountability, & Authority
Yellow Including Dimension		*Orange* Directing Dimension	

FIGURE 17.2   Icons for the Four Drama States

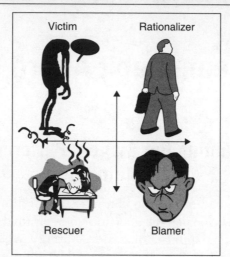

Ineffective Emotional Management → Drama States

Figure 17.2 shows the icons for the four drama states.

Victim: Sad-group feelings launch the victim's "Nothing I can do" *story-lines*. Victims then need others to join our "ain't it awful" complainer clubs.

Blamer: Ironically, scared-group feelings about being blamed launch the blamer's "It's your fault" *story-lines*. Anger covers up blamer's uncomfortable feelings.

Rescuer: Love-group approval needs launch the rescuer's "I need to do it" *story-lines*.

Rationalizer: Uncomfortable feelings launch the rationalizer's "It does not matter" *story-lines*, as they attempt to repress their emotions with their thoughts.

Let's Complain

The following describes a workshop exercise. I (and our other workshop presenters) invite participants to write complaints on Post-It notes. I suggest they write about a person (or persons) using a noun and a verb, as in "My boss doesn't listen to me." If they never complain, write down the complaints of someone they know.

As they complete the Post-Its, place them on flip charts and read them aloud. This exercise is an interesting blend of deadly seriousness and lighthearted fun. One team leader wanted to take the charts back to her office and post them outside. When people came in, she said to them, "If you have a complaint, find it on the chart—I've heard them all."

Although complaining is the victim's special signature, I demonstrate all four drama states with one of the participant's complaints. For example, consider, "My boss doesn't listen to me."

- *Victim:* "My boss doesn't listen to me, and there is nothing I can do about it."
- *Rescuer:* "My boss doesn't listen to me. It's okay; I'll do what I can without his guidance."
- *Blamer:* "My boss doesn't listen to me—the inconsiderate SOB makes me really mad."
- *Rationalizer:* "My boss doesn't listen to me, and it really doesn't matter. This doesn't bother me."

Who Is Responsible for the Complaints?

When the complaint rate slows (we quickly get about 50 from a 24-participant workshop), I show this quote from M. Scott Peck (1978, 2003): "Whenever we seek to avoid responsibility for our own behavior, we do so by attempting to give that responsibility to some other individual or organization or entity. We then give our power to that entity, be it 'fate,' 'society,' the government, or our boss."

I then ask participants to let this exercise play out if they have read about it, or seen it before. I place a $20 bill on the projector table. Then I ask repeatedly, "Who's responsible for this $20 bill being here?" Participants typically respond with the following: "You because you put it there"; "The U.S. government because they printed the money"; and the like.

When the dialogue stalls, I ask, "When does responsibility begin?" After a while, I say, "When you take it." Then, if nothing happens I cycle between "When does responsibility begin?" and "When you take it." Finally, someone will pick up the $20 and offer it back to me. I then say, "Response-ability has its rewards" and tell them to keep the money.

Now, I ask the group about what occurs when nobody takes responsibility, which is, of course, nothing. Then, ask the group about what happens when everybody takes responsibility, which is, again, nothing. No action occurs until individuals decide to become response-able.

Now I refer to their complaints and ask, "Who's response-able for these complaints?" The room becomes very quiet. "When does action occur to resolve them? You resolve your complaints when each of you takes personal responsibility for them. Once you assume response-ability for your complaints, you have two choices 1) Turn your complaint into a request, or 2) Forget about it."

I then select a Post-It from the flip chart and read it: "Headquarters information technology people are incompetent." I then ask, "So now, what do you want to do? Can you think of a constructive request? How about having your boss ask headquarters to review their information technology office? Of course, he must frame the request four dimensionally or you could engage in a power struggle. (Do you remember Charlie's two rules about power struggles? 1) Avoid power struggles and 2) Never power struggle when you do not have the power. Who has the power here? Headquarters has the power.")

Then continue, "If you cannot think of a request you can make, drop this complaint. Stop yourself from obsessing about it. Ask your colleagues to help you by refusing your invitations to join your "ain't it awful" clubs. This enables you to direct your energy to do what your job requires and you will feel good."

Turning Complaints into 4-D Requests

I used to perform this exercise in workshops. More recently, I just relate the following story. I walked through the room asking each person to give me some specific amount of money. If the participants were civil servants, I asked for a dollar. It they were in industry, I asked for $5. (I found that not all civil servants had $5 in their wallets.) Most people gave their money to me.

I collected their money and placed it in some conspicuous place, perhaps on the wall with a stickpin. I then proceeded with the workshop ignoring the money. After a while, someone asked, "What about our money?" I let the conversation flail around for a while, and then asked, "Do you want it back?" They answered, "Yes!"

I told them that I would give their money back to them if they did two things:

1. Told me why they gave me their money; and
2. Took the proper action to get me to return their money.

They muddled around on point 1 with words like "Because we trust you." I responded, "Oh, you were sitting there and had this sudden experience of trust that caused you to open your wallets and give me money?" After a while, they understood. They gave me the money because *I asked for it*.

With this insight, they soon grasped point number 2 and asked for their money. The understanding that people generally like to give others what they want is potent. I find that asking for what I want brings bountiful results whether it is an extra effort on someone's part or a hotel room upgrade or whatever.

This is how you should deal with your complaints. Turn them into requests or drop them. This is a simple and effective defense against the victim state. Is there a particularly effective way to ask for what you want? Yes, of course. Make your request four dimensionally as shown in Figure 17.3.

Recall Skip's statement: *"When dimensions are omitted, people under stress will fill them with their most toxic emotions and most pathological story-lines."* Take care not to omit a dimension.

Why does making requests work? It is because the social psychological force "reciprocity" is in play. We grant wishes because returns are implied. People who understand how our minds work have many tricks to market to us. Understanding that concessions demand concessions

FIGURE 17.3   4-D Analysis of Request Making

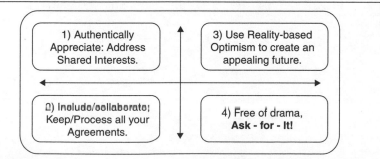

they ask us for something large first. For example, a Boy Scout may ask us to buy tickets to a concert for $10. They know that after we decline, we are much more likely to buy a $3 candy bar.

Here is another trick. If you first ask, "How are you?" most people answer "good." With them now invested in a glad-group emotion, you have doubled your chance of success.

Make 4-D requests as a matter of habit. You will be amazed at what you receive! There is one caveat. Never ask for something they cannot give you. This will only frustrate (mad-group) both you and them.

Try this 4-D request. As you walk up to a hotel desk clerk, notice something about them you can authentically appreciate. Recall that people respond best to something they appreciate about themselves. "Wow, you have a wonderful smile. You have surely uplifted me." (This all has to be fully authentic.) Next, try including: "This is one of my favorite hotels. It's so nice to be here." Now, use visioning, "I am leading a workshop here this week, and I would really enjoy a room upgrade." Now, ask for it: "A suite would be really great if you can swing it." Our suites are marvelous.

The Victim Mindset

What initiates the victim mindset? Our understanding comes once again from the interplay between the two components of mindset: emotions and thoughts, as seen in Figure 17.4. Inadequately processed sad-group feelings of helplessness start the process. Helplessness *story-lines* follow, as in "It's being done to me. There's nothing I can do." The sad emotion deepens.

FIGURE 17.4   The Victim's Emotion—*Story-Line* Interplay

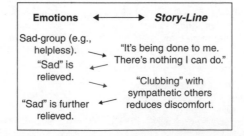

The victim now reduces their sad-group discomfort by forming "clubs" with sympathetic others. Once the club meetings are over, however, the feelings and *story-lines* may return. These clubs enhance and spread the victim mindset. Teams that decide to be response-able do not support victim clubs. Habituated victims need clubs, so they move into other organizations that support victim clubs.

What are the benefits of this pattern? The primary benefit is that all need for action vanishes. The victim traded the ability to respond, response-ability, for the temporary comfort of a helplessness *story-line*.

Escaping the Victim Mindset

The escape strategy is simple: Slow down, then notice and name your feelings by group. Then, notice and name your *Red* power-robbing *story-lines*.

A senior business executive complained, "I am so sick of these onerous reporting requirements out of New York." I said, "You are complaining. Let's turn your complaint into a request." We outlined a 4-D letter in four steps:

1. Cultivating Dimension: "We really appreciate your efforts to efficiently manage the company."
2. Including Dimension: "Will you work with us to find a more efficient process?"
3. Visioning Dimension: "This should increase profitability significantly. (The firm was an LLC. The partners share the profits among each other.)
4. Ask for it: "Could we meet with you next week and begin to work on this?

I prepared a letter using the above outline and asked her to sign it. She said, "It's no use. They will never change." I called her attention to her power-robbing *Red story-line* and said, "How about this *Green story-line*? If we don't send it we'll never know." "Okay," she said and signed the letter. Their response was constructive, and a better reporting system emerged. The 4-D communication avoided a power struggle that would have surely ensued given the mad-group feelings just below the surface.

A senior executive complained that she could not get the administrative support staff for travel that she thought she needed and deserved. Her boss told her that he had not had that kind of support when he had a job like hers. Therefore, she could not have support either. We prepared a 4-D request. At the last minute she said, "I just can't ask for things for myself." We shifted her power-robbing *Red story-line* to *Green*: "This support is in the best interest of my program." She conducted the 4-D conversation and received the support staff.

A director for a major division at a NASA center told me, "Every time I meet with my center director, he asks me to stop whining." I asked about the *story-lines* he ran during these meetings. He told me, "My division is not high priority and I probably won't get what I want." I told him that he had habituated *Red* victim *story-lines* and recommended coaching.

Coaching people out of victim has been successful from the start. Just after we successfully launched our web-based *Individual Development Assessment* tool, a colleague asked if he could use it. He was unsuccessfully coaching a client at a trucking company. The company president hired him to coach Mary. The president told the coach, "Please see if you can help Mary. She has been on the 'VP bench' for two years now. I want to promote her, but something is bothering me that I can't put my finger on."

We ran Mary's *Individual Development Assessment* for the coach. The results returned with bottom-quintile benchmarking in the *avoids complaining* behavior. Neither Mary nor the coach had been aware of this habit. They both went to work on this behavior, and the habit was broken in a month. The president approached Mary and said to her, "Mary, I don't know what's different, but you sure have changed. I am ready to make you VP." She said, "I have stopped complaining and being a victim."

Discovering and Exiting Victim

Some years ago, I was dating a woman who expected me to pay for our meals in restaurants. At first, I did not mind, as my financial resources were greater than hers and I have my life practice of living in abundance. However, as time went on I found myself resenting that she never even offered. I had trained myself to notice when I felt lousy. I checked, and there I was—feeling lousy. I then asked myself,

"What emotion-group am I now experiencing and which drama state does this suggest?" I was having a mad-group experience of low grade anger suggesting I was caught in blamer. It was absolutely clear that she was the source of the problem. The difficulty clearly had nothing to do with me or my behaviors. Although this is classic blamer, I could not see any limitations in my perceptions.

Fortunately, I had another course of action. I inquired about the *story-line* that was producing my anger. I discovered (quite easily) that I was running something like, "This is not that expensive. She should offer to pay more often, even if I insist on paying anyway." I wondered why I had not just asked her to pick up the tab. I came up with some version of "I don't want to spoil the pleasant mood." I immediately recognized that *story-line* was nonsense and that I had begun my journey into drama with victim. I was running the victim's complaining *story-lines*!

I bypassed the temptation to undertake self-psychoanalysis of why this happened as we were sitting in a restaurant in an otherwise pleasant moment. I immediately moved to my two simple choices to escape the victim state. I could either (1) Drop the complaint because there really is nothing I could do, or (2) turn the complaint into a request. Clearly this was a category 2 opportunity. I turned off my internal dialogue and simply said, "Would you mind paying for dinner tonight?" She smiled and said, "Of course not," and picked up the bill. To exit victim, just turn complaints into requests.

Although this situation did not require a 4-D request, many do, so use the 4-D process when the complexity or stakes so warrant. The essence, as I believe you know by now, is to speak to each dimension in the following sequences: *Authentically* appreciate person or situation; *Include* by offering to work together toward a solution; *Create* with an optimistic mindset grounded in any unpleasant reality; then, Free from drama, ask for what you want.

The Blamer—Victim/Rescuer Dance

Habituated blamers need to find habituated victims or rescuers to support their abusive behaviors. Fully authentic people do not participate in relationships with habituated blamers for very long. This is because people in long term relationships with blamers must adopt victim or rescuer personas. Fortunately, many refuse to do so.

Blamer-victim and blamer-rescuer relationships are "dances" in that each person moves within their prescribed roles as surely as choreographed dancers. Neither party is fully aware of the "dance" because the state they are in alters their perceptions. Regardless of the reality of the situation, blamers inappropriately see others as the cause of the difficulty. Likewise, the victims and rescuers readily accept the blame inappropriately heaped upon them. This might be difficult for you to imagine, but this human condition is sufficiently common that it recurs not just in real life, but in movies.

For example, a scene in the movie *Joe Versus the Volcano* (1990) illustrates the blamer-victim dance beautifully. Mr. Waturi, Joe's boss, approaches Joe angrily and accosts him about the fact that his secretary said there are only 12 catalogues left. He attacks Joe with "Listen, Joe, what's this Jean tells me about the catalogs?" Joe tells him that there are only 12 left. Mr. Waturi demonstrates blamer by asking Joe how he let them get down to 12. Joe responds by telling Waturi that he had informed him of the situation 3 weeks ago and again 2 weeks ago.

The blamer responds with the only recourse left. "Did you tell me last week?" Victim Joe sheepishly answers no. Waturi then shoots back with "Why not?" Joe, backed into a victim's corner tells Waturi that he did not know why he did not tell him and says he thought Waturi knew.

What do you imagine happens next? A Mr. Waturi absent blamer drama might stop there, and even apologize. However, a person caught fully in blamer state cannot. He unconsciously feels the onset of an intolerable emotion and fear. So he "acts out" (as opposed to internalizing) the self-anger by attacking Joe. He uses his anger to cover up his uncomfortable scared-group emotions.

Mr. Waturi: Not good enough, Joe, NOT NEARLY GOOD ENOUGH . . .

Joe: You put the orders in to the printer, Mr. Waturi, not me. That's how you want it.

Mr. Waturi: You are not competent to put the orders into the printer. That's a very technical job.

Joe's response to this is inaudible, and of course feeble.

Deeply habituated blamers and victims/rescuers need each other. If Joe left this job (which he actually did for other reasons) Mr. Waturi would find another victim habituated person to replace him. Joe would similarly find employment with a blamer, although finding someone as irrationally toxic as Mr. Waturi might be difficult.

The Blamer-Victim/Rescuer
Dance in the Workplace

Scenes like those described are more common in the workplace than you imagine. They require a power differential as in a supervisor-to-subordinate relationship, contractor-to-subcontractor relationship (outsourcing), or government-to-contractor relationship.

When I worked at NASA I saw supervisors (usually male) and their secretaries (usually female) in the blamer-rescuer dance. Blamer NASA Headquarters program managers "danced" with the victim field center (e.g., Goddard Space Flight Center) project mangers. However, it was not until I became a consultant for the aerospace industry that I saw government project managers abuse their contractors with profound rage. Further, I watched an industry contractor abuse their teammate (subcontractor) with so much hostility that the recipient dismissed the entire team for the remainder of the day. Everybody went home as they were unable to function.

An interesting aspect of these events is that it requires *both* participants to assume their roles as blamers and victims/rescuers. If the victims and rescuers refuse to accept the blamer's behaviors, blamers stop and look elsewhere for their "dance" partner. This chapter provides multiple strategies to detect and exit drama states if you are prone to them.

Self-detection of Drama States

There is an incredibly simple way to detect whether you are caught in a drama state. It is a very simple form of emotional intelligence. Ask yourself, "How am I feeling?" If your answer is great, you are almost certainly not in a drama state. If your answer is lousy, you are probably caught in victim, hero/rescuer, rationalizer or blamer.

You can gain more insights if you can name the emotional group you are experiencing:

- Mad-group suggests you are using anger to cover-up your scared-group fear of being blamed that takes you into blamer.
- Sad-group suggests the victims' and rescuers' feelings of helplessness.
- Scared-group, especially anxiety suggests the rationalizers' feelings of general discomfort.

Let's briefly return to dialogue from *Joe Versus the Volcano*.

Mr. Waturi: And what's this about a doctor's appointment? You're always going to the doctor.

Joe: I don't feel good.

Mr. Waturi: So what? You think I feel good. Nobody feels good! After childhood, it's a fact of life. I feel rotten. So what! I don't let it bother me. I don't let it interfere with my job. And, Joe, I want those catalogs.

Joe: Then please order them.

Mr. Waturi: Watch yourself, Joe.

This is great dialogue, isn't it?

The Life-habituated Victim

I do, however, know people who (most often *Green* badge personalities) who plunge themselves into victim at the slightest provocation.

There is yet another wonderful victim scene in *Joe Versus the Volcano*. Joe and Patricia (Tom Hanks and Meg Ryan) leap into a volcano expecting to die. (There is a longer story behind all this. You have to see the movie to find about it.) At that instant, the volcano erupts, propelling them far into the ocean. The dialogue begins as they surface. Joe begins by noticing that they jumped in and the volcano, rather than roasting them to death, blew them out. Patricia is incredulous, noting the impossibility of what apparently transpired. Joe names the event a miracle from Konawa, the name of the volcano's island. We now enter a recurrent dialogue pattern with Patricia, making an optimistic, cheerful statement, followed by Joe going into victim.

Cycle 1: Patricia notes cheerfully that they are alive in the ocean instead of dead in the volcano with "Yeah, we really made out!" Joe is unable to bask in the happy moment and returns to his victim state with yeah, well, yeah, but! Patricia expresses concern and asks him "But what?" Joe says he hates to bring the subject up, but they are a million miles from no place and are going to drown. At this point they are both treading water and watched the island Konawa sink into the water. Patricia comes back with "No we're not. We're going to be all right.

I don't know how, but we're going to be alright." Then four huge travel trunks surface. In the next scene, the four large trunks are tied into a large raft with Joe, Patricia, and a lamp on top.

Cycle 2: Patricia, with a big smile and hug, notes the romantic venue and says "Like, who gets a honeymoon like this?" Joe cannot tolerate the happy moment and says "well, yeah, yeah but!" Patricia, as expected, looks perplexed and asks, "Now, what's the matter?" Joe tells her that he still has a problem. When Patricia asks about Joe's trouble, he tells her he has a brain cloud. Patricia is incredulous. Joe responds that perhaps he should have gotten a second opinion. Patricia cannot believe that Joe did not get a second opinion about something called a brain cloud and asks him whether he is a hypochondriac. Joe says that he was, but is not anymore. (Recall, feeling lousy indicates a drama state is in play.)

As the dialogue continues, we learn that a Doctor Ellison, who made the diagnosis, is totally owned by Patricia's father. They both quickly realize the entire event—their travel to the island, their jumping into the volcano, Joe's near term fatal "brain cloud"—was fiction from a complex lie to manipulate them. Let's look at the dialogue.

Joe: You mean I don't have a brain cloud?

Patricia: Brain cloud. Brain. . . You'd think they could think of something better than a brain cloud!

Joe: My whole life, I've been a victim. I've been a (cough) dupe. A pawn (coughs)—my throat—closing up. (Distressed)

Patricia: Oh, no! Look Joe, your whole life is ahead of you.

Joe: Well, yeah, I guess that's true.

Patricia: (cheerfully) I, I mean that's good news.

Joe: Well, yeah, I suppose it is.

Patricia: I mean it's GREAT!

Joe: Yeah, that's good. I'm relieved. That's great. I'm saved. But, still . . .

Patricia: What is it now?

Joe: We're on a raft, with no land in sight. I don't know.

Patricia: It's always going to be something with you, isn't it, Joe?

I love the ending, *"It's always going to be something with you, isn't it, Joe?"* This is the habituated victim writ large.

Is This the Hill You Want to Die On

People have been pondering anger management since Aristotle. From his *Nicomachean Ethics* (1999), "Anyone can become angry— that is easy. But to become angry with the right person, to the right degree, at the right time, for the right purpose, and in the right way—this is not easy."

Redford Williams, MD (1989) performed a fascinating experiment. When he was in medical school, he gave his fellow students a test to measure their tendency to be hostile. He then followed their lives watching who died when. Here is what he found: "Those with high scores on a test of hostility . . . were seven times as likely to have died by the age of fifty as those with low hostility scores. Being prone to anger was a stronger predictor of dying young than smoking, high blood pressure, and high cholesterol."

I become hostile all too easily. When I feel hostility rising I energize the *Green story-line*, "Is this the hill I want to die on?"

The Blamer Mindset

Figure 17.5 outlines the blamer process. Notice that like drama states in general, it begins with an emotion in the upper left of the figure. Ironically, I believe the primary reason we become blamers that we fear others blaming us! A scared-group emotion arises when we are afraid others will blame us, initiating the blamer mindset.

Next, as seen on the right side of the figure, uncomfortable scared-group emotion energizes an "It's your fault" *story-line* that brings a mad-group emotion into play as seen on the left side of the figure.

FIGURE 17.5   The Blamer's Emotion—*Story-Line* Interplay

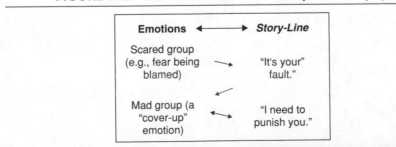

Psychologists call mad-group emotions "cover-up" emotions because they are so strong and are used to suppress other emotions. Our anger covers up our underlying fear and we no longer experience it. This relief has a huge price. These mad-group emotions are deadly for us and make massive emotional-side bank account withdrawals.

Blamers now are fully convinced that another person is the culprit and run the *story-line* in the lower right of the figure, "I need to punish you."

Escaping the Blamer Mindset

The blamer state also distorts our perception. In this state, our assignment of blame is both unambiguous and wrong. Thus, we cannot learn what caused the problem. We have focused all our energy on blaming the apparent offending person. Bring your team together, download the workshop slides, and do this exercise together.

Instruct your teammates to place their hands in the blamer configuration—index finger out, the other fingers curled in—and practice the "blamer state." Have everyone say "It's your fault!" loudly while vigorously shaking his or her fingers at a nearby person. Inevitably, energy soars as adrenalin surges. Note that three of five fingers point back at the blamer and this is appropriate.

The underlying dynamic that fuels the blamer state is fascinating. Psychologists name the blamer state as self-anger projected outward. What are we so angry about? We are angry with ourselves for our role in creating the difficulty.

Now have your teammates place their fingers in the curiosity configuration, all fingers and thumb aligned together. Next, have each make the curiosity noise, "hmm," directing their fingers toward themselves. Then have each ask, "I wonder what my role is in creating this difficulty?" Incredible as it may seem, this is an effective way to exit the blamer state.

The Find-Your-Role Two-Step

If the method above does not work, you need a whole body process to escape the blamer mindset called the Find-Your-Role Two-Step. Outline two areas on the floor. Name one the blamer/aggressor area, and the other the curiosity space. You enter the curiosity space when you are wondering about your role in creating the difficulty. You may require another person to help you dance.

I have a black belt in blamer. Here is a demonstration from my own experience I perform in workshops. I begin standing between the two areas. "While I was at NASA, my boss hired a new budget manager for the entire office. Boy this guy was a jerk." (Workshop participants motion me over to the blamer space where I continue raving for a while.) Then, I make the curiosity move with my hand and say, "You know I disliked this guy before I even knew him. I wonder if I'm projecting some old stuff on him." (Participants move me over into the wondering space.) The process continues back and forth for several cycles until I finally acknowledge my role and decide to heal this important relationship. You cannot afford the habit of blamer—it will kill you.

The Hero/Rescuer Mindset

Have you felt chronically overworked? This is the common condition of the hero/rescuer, driven by approval needs. Like the victim, they believe that the problem is out there. The interesting factor in the dynamic is that they take on work they should not because in the moment of the request, they want to please the requestor. In this mindset, the task looks appealing. Their desire to please temporarily overrides their judgment.

I believe that the rescuer process goes something like this. Confronted with a task, a love-group (for example, yearning for approval or deeper relationship) emotion supports a *Red story-line* like, "I want to please this person, so I will take on this task." In this moment they surely do. Soon thereafter, they realize that they are once more overcommitted and overworked. They often then become angry with the person who gave them the work, moving into the blamer state. In this place, they cannot see their role in creating their troubling situation. Rescuers can pair up with blamers and dance together just as Joe (victim) and Mr. Waturi (blamer) did in the movie.

Escaping the Hero/Rescuer Mindset

How can one escape the hero/rescuer mindset? When the boss shows up with new work, slow down and buy a little time. Otherwise, your approval needs may take you to "yes" much too quickly. If you are able, name and notice your emotions. Then process the request four dimensionally:

1. Begin in the *Green* cultivating dimension by appreciating your boss, or situation he or she is in, as in "I understand that you are in a really difficult situation, and I am motivated to help as best I can." Then address your shared interests, "I want to find a solution that works for both of us."

2. Now, in the *Yellow*, including dimension, express authentic willingness to collaborate, as in "I am committed to work with you on this until we create a solution." Keep all your agreements: "However we solve this, I will make sure I protect our trustworthiness with our customer."

3. Then, vision in the *Blue* dimension with reality-based optimism, as in "The truth is that I habitually agree to more than I can possibly do well and this doesn't serve either of us. By managing what I agree to, I can deliver the high quality your deserve. Give me a little time so I can develop some creative solution."

4. Finally, in the *Orange* directing dimensions, make sure you are free of drama, then, ask for what you want as in, "I have a friend who understands my job and is excellent. Could we hire her part-time to get us over this bump in the road?"

The Rationalizer Mindset

As mentioned earlier, Karpman's papers in the 1960s identified three drama states. I wondered whether the 4-D System would reveal a fourth and it did.

Blue personalities are especially likely to be rationalizers, as we easily live in our heads. Here is how the rationalizer state works. You experience an uncomfortable emotion. You probably know the source of the discomfort and can perhaps name the emotion's group. This is a giant step if you can. Describing the emotion in matter-of-fact language tends to remove the emotion's power.

Rationalizers, however, attempt to mitigate their discomfort with the *story-line* "It doesn't matter," when it actually does. This is ineffective because we are trying to use thoughts from a small part of our body, our baby-blanket-sized cerebral cortex, to overwhelm our

emotions, a whole-body phenomenon. This is why the relief is temporary and rationalizers have to recycle, repeatedly.

A Rationalizer Example

In our early years, a company hired us for four or five workshops per
year, working gradually downward into their organization. Each year,
we competed with other much larger firms for the following year's
business. The HR staff used the "smiley sheets"—the rating forms at
the end of each workshop to estimate effectiveness. Our recent ratings were above 8 out of a possible 10. Our competitors were scoring
about five or six. While we enjoy good smiley-sheet ratings, they are
not currently a measure of our effectiveness. The behavioral changes
measured in recurrent Individual Development Assessments are far
more important. We did not have assessments in those early days.

At the time, I was cross-country skiing regularly with my friend
Jack. I believed that Jack would really benefit from the workshop, so
I requested that the company admit him to one of my workshops.
The company was at first reluctant because he was not sufficiently
high in the management. I persisted with the argument that "there
are always open seats because of last-minute cancellations." Jack
joined the next class.

After the class ended, I read the smiley-sheets: 8, 9, 10, 10, 8, 9,
2. Two! Who gave me a score of two? We have never received such
an evaluation. I looked at the name and nearly fell over. The rating
was from my friend Jack. I said to myself, "It doesn't really matter.
When averaged over 23 other scores it will have little effect. I don't
care about this."

I gathered the sheets up and gave them to our customer, the
HR director. As I drove home, I felt an uncomfortable pressure in my
chest. What is this anxious feeling about, I asked? Then I remembered
Jack's score and spoke again to myself, "It doesn't really matter." I felt
better—for about 30 seconds. The process repeated a few more times.
This is classic rationalizer behavior—attempting to reduce uncomfortable emotions with mental activity, *story-lines* in this case.

This was maddening. I went home and called Doug, the HR
director, who was still in his office. He quickly said, "Oh, don't worry
about that. Once I saw who wrote it, I threw it into the trash." My
relief was immediate.

Listen for *Red* "it doesn't really matter" *story-lines* when it does. Slow down, experience your feelings, and see what you can do to deal more directly with the stressor.

Truth-Withholding Incites Melodrama

Melodrama is drama, such as a play, characterized by exaggerated emotions, stereotypical characters, and interpersonal conflicts. Do you want this in your workplace? Of course, you do not! Check out the drama section of wherever you rent movies. Notice how frequently withheld truths fuel the drama. If we all stopped truth withholding, the drama section of the video stores might disappear. My friend Kate Hendricks believes there is a withheld truth in every psychologist's (and psychiatrist's) family of origin.

Truth-Withholding *Story-Lines*

Watch for *Red* truth-withholding *story-lines* like "I would tell them, but I don't want to upset them." More likely, you do not want to deal with the emotional fallout. Change to a *Green story-line*: "I have a truth that needs expression to avoid inciting drama I cannot afford." Now, express your truth four dimensionally:

- *Green*: Appreciate person or situation, and address shared interests;
- *Yellow*: Include, and process any broken agreements;
- *Blue*: Vision a realistic and optimistic outcome; and,
- *Orange*: Make your request.

I had supervisors working for me who complained all year about a certain subordinate. Then, the annual performance evaluation documents came to me for approval with the person rated excellent. This is classic truth withholding. What emotional fallout did they fear? The anger of their subordinates, I suppose. Of course, I would forcefully insist that they redo these, telling the truth in the paperwork and to the subordinate. Who does this truth withholding most disservice? Mostly, it disservices the employee who fails to receive the feedback they need to hear and act upon.

Many program/project managers run the *story-line* "If I tell them the truth about the schedule, they will just slack off." After a while, people catch on and drama sets in. In the limiting case, the schedules lose all meaning. Shift to the *Green story-line* that honest and open discussion of the schedule will support creative adaptations.

I was presenting slides in a workshop when a participant suddenly cried out, "What's that?" She stood up and pointed to "NASA has decided to bring work 'X' in-house" on a flip chart. A subgroup conducting an exercise casually made the notation. It soon became apparent that all the NASA participants were aware of the change, as was the contractor's management. The contractor's management, however, had decided to withhold this unpleasant truth from their staff. If anyone ever needed proof of the way withheld truth incites melodrama, here it was. Workshop participants expressed every emotion group, except the "glad" and "love" groups for nearly an hour.

Think about the drama that surrounded the withheld truths of Watergate and Monica. Suppose Nixon had said, "I apparently encouraged some improprieties. I will get to the bottom of this and report back." Would the tapes have ever surfaced? Suppose Bill Clinton had said, "While I have been guilty of some transgressions, these are personal matters between me and the involved parties which I will address privately." Would the House have impeached him? It is not the crime; the drama in the cover-up keeps interest high.

Dakota Tribal Wisdom

The response-ability section is a bit heavy, so I lighten things up with the following humor. When Indians discover they are riding a dead horse they take the response-able action and dismount. However, we often try other strategies, like the following:

- Use a stronger whip.
- Appoint a committee to study the horse.
- Visit other organizations to see how they ride dead horses.
- Revisit the performance requirements for horses.
- Request additional funding to increase the horse's performance.
- Hire contractors to ride the dead horse.
- Promote the dead horse to a supervisory position.

An Application Summary for Drama Your Team Cannot Afford

This chapter has, I believe, adequate information for you to take drama-reducing action. However, if you tend toward drama, I recommend that you enlist your teammates/colleagues to help you. Educate them about the information in this chapter, and ask for their support in detecting and exiting drama states.

Of course, you can also help others avoid drama states. Of course, you need to ask them whether they want your feedback before you give it. If they do not want it, no good will come from your good intentions except to annoy (mad-group) them.

If your team makes a concerted effort to eliminate drama, people who are addicted to these states will gradually leave. Victims need people to join their complainer clubs. Rescuers and victims need insensitive blamers and the like to dance with them. Likewise, blamers need victims and rescuers who will tolerate their abuse.

People habituated to drama states have difficulty noticing and naming their drama. Try paying attention to how you are feeling. If you are feeling good, you are probably not in a drama state. If you feel lousy, you are probably in victim, rescuer, rationalizer, or blamer.

Most important, use recurrent *Individual Development Assessments* and *Team Development Assessments*. These will bring your attention and mindsets to resisting blaming and complaining. Moreover, reassessments track your progress, and your team's progress, providing encouragement.

CHAPTER 18.

Don't Put Good People in Bad Places

Team members need to clarify and communicate what others can expect of them. We call these expectations "RAAs" for Roles, Accountability, and Authority. Our definitions of the roles, accountability, and authority are as follows (see also Figure 18.1):

- Roles are the functions of a person in their work context.
- Accountability is the results individuals must deliver.
- Authority is the power granted to individuals, generally through delegation.

FIGURE 18.1   RAAs, the Eighth of the Eight Behaviors

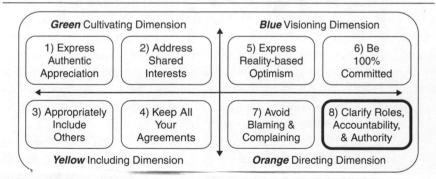

Green Cultivating Dimension		**Blue** Visioning Dimension	
1) Express Authentic Appreciation	2) Address Shared Interests	5) Express Reality-based Optimism	6) Be 100% Committed
3) Appropriately Include Others	4) Keep All Your Agreements	7) Avoid Blaming & Complaining	8) Clarify Roles, Accountability, & Authority
Yellow Including Dimension		**Orange** Directing Dimension	

RAAs in 4-D Assessments

Initially, we added the RAA measurement to our assessments to cross-strap with a similar tool assessing project processes. It seemed wise to have one social context measurement in the process assessment and one pure logical-side measurement in the social context assessment.

I was then surprised to see very low RAA scores in what I believed were well-organized flight projects. We also saw that unclear RAAs created contexts that lowered all the other behaviors. Therefore, although we dropped the process assessment tool (another great idea of mine unblemished by success), we retained the RAA measurement.

When people are unclear about the organization's expectations of them and others, everything is harder. When you do not know, for example, whom to appreciate for what, effective appreciation is problematic. It had become clear that RAAs were important social context indicators. Therefore, we continue to measure RAAs as they powerfully influence team context.

Accountability

Think about these three items roles, accountability: and authority. Which of the three has the most power? I suggest accountability. Individual assumption of accountability is essentially the same as the mindset of response-ability in the previous chapter.

Consider these examples from the 2006 NFL football season. When the Indianapolis Colts were losing games because their defense was weak, quarterback Peyton Manning said, "Well, I just have to make sure I put at least 35 points on the board." Compare this with Terrell Owens, who said after a loss that involved his mistakes, "I never got in the flow because they did not throw to me often enough in the early part of the game." These people are both highly talented. How important are their habitual mindsets in their ultimate performance? Whom would you want on your team?

What do good football players do when they fumble the ball? Do they stand around looking for who to blame, or go for the ball, ignoring physical peril? Good players assume accountability for the effect of the fumble on the game, ignoring assignment of blame.

A very senior NASA headquarters manager asked my opinion about his accountability for a worker's death at Kennedy Space

Center (KSC). I referred him to the football analogy. He was account-able, in my view, for being certain that the KSC director was competent putting the right people and safety processes in place. This would be analogous to a football team having able, well-practiced players with good plays. If the senior manager did his job before the accident, he should not dwell on accountability for the event itself.

Now, just as in the football analogy, he should accept accountability for the effects of the accident (fumble) going forward. He should mitigate the impact of the accident on the deceased's family, on KSC, and on the broader agency. Then, he should accept accountability for ensuring that such accidents do not recur.

RAAs—Basic Requirements

What are the two basic requirements for adequate RAAs?

1. Individuals draft their RAAs, and supervisors approve them. Common documentation methods include performance evaluation plans and organization charts. One project that had difficulty communicating RAAs put these descriptions on people's office doors.

2. RAAs must be tested and optimized in processes. Imagine a football team that never tested their playbook in scrimmages? I recommend the following methodology for any troublesome process, especially when they are recurrent. Use a projector to display an Excel spreadsheet with the players involved in the process in the room. Write their names across the top of the spreadsheet. Record each step in the process chronologically working down the page with each person's role entered. This works really well, highlighting and resolving confusion systematically.

Processes with Owners

Every team/organization has processes. Otherwise, they could not perform work. Unfortunately, they often do not document or optimize their processes. Top management frequently initiates grand, expensive optimization programs like Deming's statistical process control, TQM, and more recently, Six Sigma. However, "because people do things for their reasons, not ours" (that is, management's reasons), the desired efficiencies are seldom realized. There is a better way.

When NASA's Jet Propulsion Laboratory experienced back-to-back Mars mission failures, they developed 44 flight project practices for project management. These include systems engineering, risk management, gate products, requirements management, and the like. They assigned each process to a process owner with expertise in that area. The owners maintained and updated their assigned processes as part of their regular job. Management imposed the processes across JPL projects. The owners had PowerPoint charts that they used to train others in applying the processes.

Our small company, 4-D Systems, has about 40 processes with named owners. These include guidelines for implementing *Team Development Assessments*, workshop roles, and debriefing team development reports. I own many of them and constantly update our processes as we experiment and learn. All our processes and standard briefings are on the staff web site. When our people do work, they download and use the current briefing or process.

Do Not Put Good People in Bad Places

Teams that score in the bottom quintile in *Team Development Assessments* are particularly interesting. They are difficult to work with and experience inconsistent improvement with our normal processes of assessments, workshops, coaching, and reassessments.

I wondered whether these teams had been magnets for low-ranking individuals. We investigated this by running correlation analysis between bottom-quintile team scores and the assessment scores of the individuals' on the team. Perhaps surprisingly, they are weakly correlated with a correlation coefficient, r, of <0.3. Therefore, if the individual team members are not suppressing the team score, the cause must be context.

The Seven Deadly Sins of Teams

Early Christianity identified the following seven deadly sins: lust, gluttony, greed, sloth, wrath, envy, and pride. As we worked with approximately 100 bottom-quintile teams over the past five years, we found that one or more of the seven deadly management short-falls described on the next page were present in all of them. When a team has a bottom-quintile score, we go through the list with the team's leaders. Team leaders readily identify the specific shortfalls. If they knew the shortfalls were present, why did they not address them? We heard various versions of "we are too busy" to "the sun was in my eyes." In any case, the leaders usually took prompt action with the shortfalls' impact on the team was apparent in their *Team Development Assessment*.

These are the seven deadly sins of bottom-quintile teams. If your team's overall benchmark is in the bottom quintile, one or more of these sins is in play:

1. Ineffective team leadership: This is first in the list because it is the most potent. A low score in your team leader's *Individual Development Assessment* provides the easiest diagnostic for this sin. In many, but not all, cases, the leaders knew they were ineffective and were grateful to us for helping them develop or see that they should change jobs.

2. Task undoable because of inadequate resources: A VP asked me to work with a team with an ineffective leader. We performed an *Individual Development Assessment*, and the project team leader benchmarked near the top quintile—he was not the problem. We followed with a *Team Development Assessment* that benchmarked the project team in the bottom quintile. During the team debrief, I learned that when the company submitted the proposal for the very complex instrument, the prior VP arbitrarily cut the already low bid price in half! The customer hammered the project team relentlessly, angry about the overruns. We do not workshop such teams. To do so is like training a marathon runner with a thorn in his or her foot. You have to remove the thorn first. In this example, the company has to tell the customer the truth about the resources required and either lose the program or receive sufficient resources to do the job right.

   I referenced work by David Bearden of the Aerospace Corporation in Chapter 6. He shows clear evidence that underfunding (and inadequate schedule) is a root cause of mission failure. Inadequate resources bite twice. First, you cannot do the work right. Second, you have a flawed social context causing low performance. Actually, I believe insufficient funds caused Hubble's mirror manufacturing flaw; then, the continued broken context caused the cover up of the subsequent test data.

3. Flawed procurement implementation: All too frequently, inexperienced people take shortcuts with procurement. This results in having the wrong contractors, doing the wrong work, with the wrong incentives. This happens in NASA when a project has money they are afraid they will lose unless they spend it quickly.

4. Team affected by a larger broken context: Examples of this include a company's top management relentlessly nagging staff to increase sales when suitable bid opportunities are virtually nonexistent. Imminent layoffs also break team contexts.

5. Team engaged in a power struggle with another organization: Power struggles are common across organizational interfaces. As I said earlier, we humans are tribal at our core. When the power struggle has a power imbalance, as in a government-contractor interface, the weaker party will resort to guerilla tactics—the contractor withholds information that will result in criticism. Problems are not effectively addressed.

6. Team members temperamentally unsuited to required work: I gave an example earlier where a team of *Blue*, visioning leaders, who were so effective in the formulation phase, lacked the closure mindset required for the *Orange*, implementation phase. This factor is most damaging when another *sin* is pushing everyone to be one dimensional.

7. Flawed organizational structure: I believe that technical managers often place more emphasis on organization charts than is warranted. However, clear and unambiguous lines of authority are essential.

An Application Summary for Don't Put Good People in Bad Places

This chapter is straightforward to implement. Here are the four basic steps:

1. Maintain clear and current organization charts.
2. Ensure that you and everyone have RAAs and that everyone who needs to understands them.

3. Flow RAAs in important processes to clarify and optimize them.

4. Use the seven deadly sins as a team health checklist.

Most important, use recurrent *Individual Development Assessments* and *Team Development Assessments*. These will bring your attention and mindsets to clarifying roles, accountability and authority. Moreover, reassessments track your progress and your team's progress, providing encouragement.

Finally, we urge NASA team members to fill out the following form when RAAs benchmark low.

ROLES, ACCOUNTABILITY, AND (DELEGATED) AUTHORITY

This is as basic as clarifying what others (particularly your supervisor) can expect from you. There is no way you can be sure of being successful without this mutual understanding. You are to fill this paper out and bring it to your workshop if one is scheduled. If you can get your supervisor's approval, that would be great. If not, you can get approval later.

Write your name here: _____

Write your supervisor's name here: _____

• Describe your Role, your functions in your team context.

_____

_____

(For example, I am the Project Manager, providing leadership across the team.)

• Describe your Accountability, the results others expect you to deliver.

_____

_____

(For example, I lead the project, meeting Level I technical requirements, budgets, and schedules.)

• Describe your delegated Authority, the power granted to you by others.

_____

_____

(For example, I direct the project's workforce within the Level I envelope, and applicable institutional requirements.)

My authority is sufficient (check one) Yes _____ No _____

• I own and maintain the following processes:

_____

_____

(For example, "Project monthly reporting process." "Project systems engineering error trees.")

• I use and comply with the following processes:

_____

_____

(For example, "Flight Project Practices" (NASA Jet Propulsion Laboratory), "The Golden Rules" (NASA Goddard Space Flight Center)

Supervisor's Approval: _____ Date: _____

Hubble's Legacy

The Hubble mirror flaw has become a distant memory. Heroic astronauts have since visited Hubble four times to correct for the flawed mirror, replace aging components, and install new, advanced instrumentation. Hubble is now in its 18th year of productive scientific research. More than 3,500 technical publications have reported Hubble results, according to Hubblesite.org, making it one of the most profoundly successful scientific instruments in history. Science results frequently grace the front pages of newspapers all around the world. The telescope has exceeded all our expectations!

It is my earnest belief that, in the final analysis, the Hubble mirror flaw was a good thing for me. I doubt that I would have been motivated to develop the 4-D System any other way. If the 4-D System prevents future space accidents, particularly those that take lives, the flaw was a net good for us all.

I was having lunch in Australia with the human resources director for NASA's Canberra Tracking Station. She said to me, "Your work is wonderful. However, do you know that you are asking people to behave in unnatural ways? I, for example, love the violence in American football." This is exactly the point. Most would agree that our social evolution has not kept pace with technological progress.

It seems to me that humanity is at a crossroads. Pick your favorite risk: the environment, nuclear attack, avian flu, mass starvation, and so on. We have a choice. We can choose to manage social contexts, and therefore our behaviors, or not. The technology is here in this book and our web assets. All we need now is willingness. I developed the 4-D System to make technical teams more productive and better places to work. My dream is that success in the workplace will take these powerful processes around the world.

Charlie Pellerin
Boulder, Colorado

REFERENCES

Apollo 13. Ron Howard (Director), Universal Pictures; Imagine Entertainment, 1995.

Aristotle, and Terence Irwin. *Nicomachean Ethics*. Indianapolis, IN: Hackett Publishing Company, 1999.

Bearden, David. *The Reliability of Cost Estimates During Early Conceptual Design*. El Segundo, CA: Aerospace Corporation, 2007.

Bennis, Warren. *Why Leaders Can't Lead: The Unconscious Conspiracy*. AMACOM, 1976.

Blakeslee, Sandra. "What Other People Say May Change What You See." *New York Times*, June 28, 2005.

Braveheart. Mel Gibson (Director), Icon Entertainment International; Ladd Company; Twentieth Century Fox, 1995.

Chesterfield, Philip Dormer Stanhope, Earl of, and Welsh, Charles (Ed.). *A Selection from the Letters Of Lord Chesterfield: To His Son and His Godson, 1742 to 1772 (1904)*. Whitefish, MT: Kessinger Publishing, 2008.

City Slickers. Ron Underwood (Director), Castle Rock Entertainment; Columbia Pictures Corporation, 1991.

Clark, Kenneth E., and Miriam B. Clark. *Measures of Leadership*. West Orange, NJ: Leadership Library of America, Inc., 1990.

Coffman, Curt, and Jim Harter. "A Hard Look at Soft Numbers." Dallas, TX: Nielson Group, 1999.

Collins, Jim. *Good to Great*. New York, NY: Collins Business, 2001.

Dead Poets Society. Peter Weir (Director), Touchstone Pictures; Silver Screen Partners IV, 1989.

Farrell, Warren. *The Myth of Male Power*. New York, NY: Berkley Trade, 1994.

Fisher, Roger, William L. Ury, and Bruce M. Patton. *Getting to Yes*. New York, NY: Penguin, 1991.

Friedman, Tom. "Cars, Kabul and Banks." *New York Times*, December 13, 2008.

Gardner, Howard. *Leading Minds: An Anatomy of Leadership*. New York, NY: Basic Books, 1995.

Gilbert, Daniel. *Stumbling on Happiness*. Essex, England: Vintage, 2005.

Gittell, Jody Hoffer. *The Southwest Airlines Way*. New York, NY: McGraw-Hill, 2003.

Gladwell, Malcolm. *Outliers*. New York, NY: Hachette, 2008.

Gladwell, Malcolm. *Blink*. New York, NY: Back Bay Books, 2005.

Gladwell, Malcolm. *The Tipping Point*. New York, NY: Back Bay Books, 2002.

Goleman, Dan. 1998. "What Makes a Leader?" Harvard Business Review, Reprint R0401H, reprinted in 2004, pp. 1–11.

Goleman, Dan. *Emotional Intelligence*. New York, NY: Bantam., 1995.

Groopman, Jerome. *The Anatomy of Hope*. New York, NY: Random House, 2003.

Harwit, Martin. *Cosmic Discovery*. New York, NY: Basic Books, 1981.

Johnson, Stephen. "Success, Failure, and NASA Culture." *ASK Magazine*, Fall 2008.

Joan of Lorraine. (stage play) Maxwell Anderson, 1946.

Joe Versus the Volcano. John Patrick Shanley (Director), Warner Bros. Pictures; Amblin Entertainment, 1990.

Karpman, Steve. 1968. "Fairy Tales and Script Drama Analysis." *Transactional Analysis Bulletin*, 7(26): 39–43.

Kelling, George L., and James Q. Wilson. "Broken Windows." *The Atlantic*, March 1982.

Klein, Gary. *Sources of Power: How People Make Decisions*. Boston, MA: MIT Press, 1999.

Korkki, Phyllis. "Another Meeting? Say It Isn't So" *New York Times*, July 20, 2008.

Kouzes, James, and Barry Posner. *The Leadership Challenge* (4th ed.). New York, NY: Jossey-Bass, 2008.

Levitt, Steven D., and Stephen J. Dubner. *Freakonomics*. New York, NY: Harper Collins, 2006.

Milliken-Davies, Mary. "An Exploration of Flawed First-line Supervision." PhD diss., University of Tulsa, 1992.

Milliken-Davies, Mary. *Measures of Leadership*. West Orange, NJ: Leadership Library of America, Inc., 1990.

Miracle. Gavin O'Connor (Director), Pop Pop Productions; Mayhem Pictures; Walt Disney Pictures, 2004.

Niebuhr, Reinhold. *Moral Man and Immoral Society*. Kessinger Publishing, LLC, Whitefish, MT, 2006.

NOAA N-PRIME Mishap Investigation Final report, September 13, 2004.

Ornish, Dean. *Love and Survival: The Scientific Basis for the Healing Power of Intimacy*. New York, NY: Harper Collins, 1998.

Peck, M. Scott. *The Road Less Traveled*. Austin, TX: Touchstone,, 1978, 2003.

Richtel, Matt. "Lost in E-Mail, Tech Firms Face Self-Made Beast," *New York Times*, June 14, 2008.

Ruiz, Miguel. *The Four Agreements: A Practical Guide to Personal Freedom, A Toltec Wisdom Book*, San Rafael, CA: Amber-Allen Publishing, 2001.

Safire, William. *Before the Fall*. Garden City, NY: Doubleday, 1975.

Schutz, Will. *The Truth Option*. Berkeley, CA: Ten Speed Press, 1984.

Semler, Ricardo. *Maverick: The Success Story Behind the World's Most Unusual Workplace.* New York, NY: Grand Central Publishing, 1995.

Simons, D. J. *Surprising Studies of Visual Awareness.* DVD. 2003.

Stolovitch, Harold D. and Erica Keeps. *Training Ain't Performance.* ASTD Press, 2004.

The Amazing Howard Hughes. William A. Graham (Director), Los Angeles, CA, Roger Gimbel Productions, 1977.

The Speeches of Dwight Eisenhower. MPI Home Video, Orland Park, IL, Documentary filmed on site, 1988.

Truman, Karol. *Feelings Buried Alive Never Die.* Brigham City, UT: Brigham Distributing, 1991.

Twain, Mark. "The Lowest Animal" in *Letters from the Earth.* New York, NY: Harper & Row, 1962.

U.S. Chamber of Commerce. 1986. *The Balanced Program.* Washington, DC, Chamber of Commerce of the United States.

Vaughan, Diane. *The Challenger Launch Decision: Risky Technology, Culture, and Deviance at NASA.* Chicago, IL: University of Chicago Press, 1996.

Vedantam, Shankar. "Science Confirms: You Really Can't Buy Happiness." *Washington Post,* July 3, 2006.

Williams, Redford. *The Trusting Heart.* New York, NY: Crown Publishing, 1989.